CHANGING PATTERNS OF HUMAN EXISTENCE
Assumptions, Beliefs, and
Coping with the Stress of Change

CHANGING PATTERNS OF HUMAN EXISTENCE

Assumptions, Beliefs, and Coping with the Stress of Change

By

LOUIS E. LAGRAND, PH.D.

Potsdam College
of the
State University of New York

With a Foreword by

Therese A. Rando, PH.D.
Therese A. Rando, Associates, Ltd.
Warwick, Rhode Island

CHARLES C THOMAS • PUBLISHER
Springfield • Illinois • U.S.A.

Published and Distributed Throughout the World by

CHARLES C THOMAS • PUBLISHER
2600 South First Street
Springfield, Illinois 62794-9265

© *1988 by* CHARLES C THOMAS • PUBLISHER
ISBN 0-398-05464-9
Library of Congress Catalog Card Number: 88-1496

With THOMAS BOOKS *careful attention is given to all details of manufacturing*
and design. It is the Publisher's desire to present books that are satisfactory as to their
physical qualities and artistic possibilities and appropriate for their particular use.
THOMAS BOOKS *will be true to those laws of quality that assure a good name*
and good will.

Printed in the United States of America
SC-R-3

Library of Congress Cataloging-in-Publication Data

LaGrand, Louis E.
    Changing patterns of human existence : coping with the stress of
change / by Louis E. LaGrand : with a foreword by Therese A. Rando.
      p.   cm.
    Bibliography: p.
    Includes index.
    ISBN 0-398-05464-9
    1. Grief.   2. Attitude change.   3. Death-Psychological aspects.
4. Separation (Psychology)   I. Title.
BF575.G7L34   1988
152.4—dc19   88–1496
                                        CIP

FOREWORD

When it comes to dealing with separation and loss, human beings have only two options: We can choose to survive them or not. We do not choose whether or not we experience these events, for they are inevitable and unavoidable aspects of living. If we do decide to survive separation and loss, we have the additional choice of how we will survive, that is, how we *cope* and to what extent.

The word "coping" is quite popular today in social science and mental health. It has an emphasis on attempting to respond constructively to stress, as opposed to that previously implied in the word "defense," which had been misinterpreted as being bad or unhealthy, and had come to mean an evasive denial or avoidance response that allowed one to "run away." In fact, defense mechanisms are adaptive when used appropriately, and the inability to use appropriate defense mechanisms when confronted with stress and threat has long been a hallmark of emotional illness. Because of the confusion, "defense" or "defense mechanism" has been supplanted by the more positive "coping" or "coping mechanism" —terms which more accurately describe their purpose. They connote actively contending with stress and moving to deal with it, as opposed to running away or stonewalling.

Webster's Ninth New Collegiate Dictionary (1987) defines cope as "to deal with and attempt to overcome problems and difficulties." A more specific psychological definition has been offered by Lazarus and Folkman (1984) in which coping is viewed as "constantly changing cognitive and behavioral efforts to manage specific external and/or internal demands that are appraised as taxing or exceeding the resources of the person" (p. 141). Here we can see that coping is (1) process-oriented, (2) distinct from automated adaptive behavior, (3) not to be confounded with outcome since the efforts to manage are what counts regardless of their effectiveness, and (4) that there is an avoidance of equating coping with mastery, and that "managing" can include minimizing, avoiding, tolerating, and

v

accepting the stressful conditions, as well as attempts to master the environment.

Both definitions and their implications focus on active attempts to contend with a stressful situation and/or environment. This brings up a crucial and typically overlooked aspect of grief and mourning following major loss—the fact that active, and not solely passive, *coping* responses are *absolutely necessary* in order to fully adjust and recover from loss.

In the field of grief and bereavement, clinical literature and research has focused primarily on the description of responses that occur subsequent to loss. However, these usually are reactions which the mourner experiences as feelings occasioned by the loss, for instance, sadness, anger, guilt, depression, confusion, and so forth. In general, mourners and their caregivers *do* pay attention to these. However, the feeling of emotions is only part of the necessary mourning process, and for too many there is a breakdown in their further accommodation to the loss. They do not engage in the active processes of mourning in which there is demanded more than mere reaction, but active work to accept the fact of death in the external world and to effect the corresponding changes in the inner world (A. Freud, 1960). In essence, their mourning is not complete because they focus on the reaction to the loss, but not the ongoing coping with it.

Proper grief work following the death of a loved one or the loss of a significant relationship entails, therefore, not merely the passive experience of emotions and other consequences of the assault of loss, but actively working to do things and undertake specific courses of action and thinking in order to adjust to the loss, integrate and resolve the grief, and prepare for the future. It means that the coping, as noted in the aforementioned definitions, must consist of process-oriented, not automated, cognitive and behavioral attempts to manage the situation of the loved one's absence. The ultimate goal of grief and mourning, therefore, is to take the mourner beyond the reactions to separation and loss and through the active work of adaptation to them. Coping in mourning includes such specific, action-oriented processes as: readjusting to the new world without the loved one; changing emotional attachment and investment in the deceased; developing a healthy new relationship with the deceased; finding ways to appropriately hold on to the loved one; developing a new personal identity; and reinvesting emotional energy (Rando, 1988).

Too many mourners fail to take these additional steps past the passive experiences of reacting to their loss. True, they have indeed worked on the initial phases of resolving their grief and mourning. For example, they have acknowledged their anger, articulated their uncertainty, and cried about their sadness. Yet, the processing of emotion is necessary, but not sufficient, to bring the recovery they seek. According to the definitions of coping, they have not "coped" per se, only reacted. They have not done what is necessary to go beyond taking what comes. They have not managed the new situation. The problem with their mourning is that these individuals simply have not finished with it. They either may stay victimized by their passive experience of reactions to their bereavement or they may work through the emotions but go no further. In either case, they fail to go on to create the new world and new self that necessarily must be developed to accommodate the fact that their loved one is gone—precisely what must be done to ultimately cope with the loss successfully.

To Dr. LaGrand's credit, he has recognized the critical requirement of actively working to respond to loss, of going past feelings to do something about reshaping self and world to allow the loss to be healthily integrated into life. His book is devoted to identifying and examining those particular coping techniques and strategies that enable mourners to contend most effectively with the stress of loss, grief, and their ensuing demands for change. Without minimizing the natural pain of loss and separation, Dr. LaGrand's book is based on the premise that human beings can, and indeed *do*, have the power to survive major loss, and through appropriate coping strategies can reduce the stress of the change it brings. He delineates dozens of these coping strategies, making this book a most thorough and practical resource. Via careful explanation of how our assumptions, beliefs, and expectations determine how we feel and behave, he illustrates the indispensability of developing proper cognitive—behavioral stances that delimit excessive pain and promote healing, and help the individual escape the unnecessary suffering caused by faulty cognitions, absent emotional resources, and ineffective social support. Integrating psychosocial, physical, and spiritual components, Dr. LaGrand offers effective coping techniques and life-affirming perspectives to deal with dying and death, and to insure survival after the immense blows rendered to self-esteem by any major loss. His material is relevant and immediately useful, and he specifically identifies the tools of coping he has synthesized from thousands of young adults and others with whom he has worked.

However, Dr. LaGrand does not stop there. He goes beyond the explanation of what can be done to cope with a loss that has already occurred, and offers valuable instruction and specific information about what is necessary in order to be appropriately prepared in advance for death and other major losses. In this regard, _he provides precious instruction in primary prevention._ In advance, as well as after the fact, he believes that while mourners cannot be kept from suffering, they can be kept from suffering for the wrong reasons.

Finally, through noting that the breakup of a love relationship is a stimulus for a "death reaction," Dr. LaGrand implicitly recognizes the often overlooked issue of symbolic (psychosocial) losses giving rise to grief reactions and a demand for mourning. These types of losses, no less than a loss through death, require the proper attitudes, beliefs, and psycho social resources in order to be coped with successfully. Again, he identifies the specific coping techniques that are therapeutic to promote healing.

Through this helpful book, richly illustrated with the words of the college students he teaches and the dying who have shared their most intimate thoughts, feelings, and experiences, Dr. LaGrand provides a major resource to all who are determined to face the vicissitudes of life in the most healthy manner possible. He outlines the beliefs, perspectives, and psychosocial factors which facilitate adaptation to major loss, serve as antidotes to its ensuing feelings of victimization and depression, and promote optional recovery. It is an important contribution to our field.

THERESE A. RANDO, PH.D.

REFERENCES

Lazarus, R.S. & Folkman, S. _Stress, appraisal and coping._ New York: Springer Publishing Company, 1984.

Rando, T.A. _Grieving: How to go on living when someone you love dies._ Lexington, MA: Lexington Books, 1988.

Freud, A. Discussion of Dr. John Bowlby's paper. In _The psychoanalytic study of the child_ (Vol. 15), New York: International Universities Press, 1960.

ACKNOWLEDGMENTS

As one grows and develops there are many people and experiences which shape the nature of one's journey through life. I have been fortunate to have a wife and family who have possessed exceptional patience and understanding in view of my professional endeavors. To them I express my continued love and gratitude.

On a professional level I am very much indebted to Monsignor Bernard Kellogg, a man of great wit and wisdom, who has taught me much about the care of the dying. Much of that learning is the basis for Chapter 5, Beliefs About The Dying: Establishing Relationships.

A special thanks goes to William C. Knott, an outstanding writer, who spent many hours in editing and making suggestions for the final copy.

And last but certainly not least I express my gratitude to all of the special people in the Young Adult Study and The Hospice of Potsdam-Canton for sharing with me their thoughts, hopes and concerns.

INTRODUCTION

RECOLLECTIONS

It has often been said that everyone has two events in common: birth and death. Unfortunately, there is a third series of life events which are integral factors in the changing patterns of human existence, events which everyone have in common: the ending of interpersonal relationships. Beginning with infancy through old age many temporary and permanent changes in relationships occur.

The Conditions

The infant struggles with being left with the babysitter and the temporary parting from the security of the mother; the young child makes a painful separation on going to school for the first time, shedding the secure environment of the home for the new surroundings of the classroom.

The young adult leaving for college or taking a new job away from home confronts separation from family and friends while at the same time having to adjust to the new demands of education or the work place. Older adults are forced to find new work when their skills are replaced by automation or the computer. An assault on self-esteem occurs when the cold efficiency of machines replaces human input at a fraction of the previous cost.

Unfortunately, the elderly meet a multiplicity of relationship changes: moving from home to an apartment or an apartment to nursing home, distancing themselves from married children who settle new families away from their birthplaces. The deaths of spouses, friends and family members bring stresses associated with adapting to an environment without the deceased. This readjustment and the formation of new routines and relationships with the world is called *grief work*. Everyone is subject to the work of grief.

These and hundreds of other interruptions in the expected continuity of relationships form the basis for emotional turmoil, physical discomfort, and difficulties in meeting new challenges. This is the result of transitions that are inescapable in human growth and development.

Can We Reduce the Stress of Change?

Yes. But only if we revise our perceptions of it. Relationship losses, either temporary or permanent, not only are constant factors in lifespan change but are among the most demanding on the individual and require an array of coping strategies to reduce the intensity of stress. Strikingly, relationship loss calls into question the needs and abilities of individuals to deal with recovery. Specifically, how people manage loneliness, fear, the acceptance of their plight, and the new world to be faced without the presence of their loved ones depends on *how they decide to view their dilemmas.*

Not surprisingly, these same losses are reasons for those close to the primary griever to wonder how they may help a child cope with the death of a parent or with divorce. In addition, they may also question how they may support a friend whose loved one is slowly dying or how to meet the needs of those who are terminally ill. Learning to find comfort as both a griever or caregiver is a task most are ill-prepared to assume.

The Purpose

My purpose in writing this book is to explain the indisputable role which assumptions and beliefs play in coping with any major loss, how default assumptions and self-defeating notions complicate the grieving process, and how we can adopt a more positive belief system. For our beliefs about how people are supposed to cope with loss have a powerful influence on whether we express emotions in public or private, grieve for specific periods of time, choose to follow or forgo funeral ritual, and eventually find peace of mind.

Our major focus will be on dying, death and the breakup of love relationships. Undoubtedly, changes in lifestyles and coping with the traumatic separations of life are always preceded by profound changes in how and what we think.

The Problem

Half-truths, misconceptions, and totally false information lie at the heart of many of the crises of life, causing the process of adapting to complicate recovery. The resulting fear, loneliness, and sense of hopelessness accentuates the pain of loss. Although pain is inescapable—the price of love—excessive trauma can surely be lessened. Therefore, because this is a book about coping, it will be useful to the griever and caregiver alike, to the student of thanatology and to anyone adapting to the problems created by unrealistic expectations or who is helping others in these transitions. The presentation of material is a blend of both the theoretical and practical.

Not infrequently, separations and other loss events force us to revise and drastically change our assumptions and beliefs about life, death, and the meaning of existence; this occurs with both griever and caregiver. Failure to comply results in extended grieving and emotional pain. We will be better able to bridge our major crises if we learn how to let go of erroneous premises and assumptions formed early in life.

The Sources

Children are commonly recognized as great teachers due to their simplicity, trust, and perceptive awareness. I am convinced that young adults are equally effective teachers about the lessons to be learned from separation. The materials presented in the pages to follow are based on my experience with many grievers, hospice patients, and the study of thousands of young adults in a large research effort. The Young Adult Study involved nearly 4000 people between the ages of 17 and 24 over a nine year period. This resulted in over 50,000 observations on how they perceive the process of change and separation. They teach us much about how altering assumptions and beliefs help manage transition. I shall draw heavily on their examples. Interestingly, much of what they say is applicable to all other age groups.

The obvious question at this point is: Why equate the breakup of love relationships with that sense of loss which occurs after death? The answer is that the breakup of love relationships are powerful rehearsals for our confrontation with the deaths of loved ones; they are "small" deaths. The two events possess striking similarities: highly questionable assumptions about "why me?" the involvement of significant others who influence the griever's self-esteem, intense emotional reactions, a strong physical response, changes in usual behavior, and the need to reconstruct our personal world. Survivors are forced to adjust to life without the loved one. Furthermore, there is an abundance of anecdotal evidence to suggest that some breakups cause an intense grief response which parallels that experienced when a death occurs. The readjustment is always accompanied by the formation of new attitudes or beliefs which facilitate reintegration into the mainstream of life or regression into hopelessness and bare existence.

As we begin this journey of community it is necessary to consider a universal truth: *All relationships end in separation.* This truth, this unalterable fact, is not well understood. It poses many questions. Will we confront the reality of this truth? Are we willing to challenge the societal norms of silence and concealment which surrounds it? Can we view it as a means to enrich our lives? To stop living in the future? To enhance our relationships with others? To exchange quality for quantity? In the pages to follow, the reader will have ample opportunity to find answers to these questions.

CONTENTS

CHANGING PATTERNS OF HUMAN EXISTENCE

Assumptions, Beliefs, and Coping with the Stress of Change

Chapter One

THE POWER OF ASSUMPTIONS AND BELIEFS

We not only believe what we see, to some extent, we see what we believe. *The implications about our beliefs are frightening.*

Richard Gregory in *The Intelligent Eye*

The greatest discovery in our generation is that human beings, by changing the inner attitude of their minds, can change the outer aspects of their lives.

William James

Inherent in any system of belief is a self-fulfilling prophecy: what is expected is observed, and what is observed confirms the expectations.

Kenneth Pelletier in *Mind as Healer Mind as Slayer*

In beginning this discussion I recognize I am treading on fragile terrain; the subject is complex and therefore my analysis must be tentative and open to revision. Nevertheless, there is much to be learned about the assumptions and beliefs of those who are good copers as well as those who are not successful in meeting life-long loss experiences. The implications are wide ranging for counseling, education, parenting, and strengthening competence and resourcefulness in the face of transition. Experience and common sense tell us that the study of coping with various separations is inseparable from the study of beliefs and assumptions which fuel individual responses.

It is useful to understand from the outset that many authors who have written about the experience of bereavement bring attention to the potential of the experience to lead to personal growth and maturity[1-4]. These changes are always accompanied by profound alterations in perspective about the meaning of life, death, and the relationship between the two.

Since beliefs are so personal and held with a strength bordering on fanaticism, we should consider how they help us adapt to change. Governed by our assumptions and beliefs, we are often imprisoned by them. Beliefs

3

supply powerful motivation for human behavior. Although we usually associate beliefs with philosophical or religious doctrine, in reality, they and the assumptions they are based upon are what is behind whatever courses of action we take. If we are to cope, we must change our basic assumptions. There is ample evidence to show that how we cope is determined by how we think[5-8].

SOME DEFINITIONS

Beliefs are the convictions we hold about people and the world around us. They are convictions based on parental influence, the media, and, most significantly, personal experience. Beliefs may be inherently true or patently false, depending on the quality or source of information. They are not always logical. As Lazarus[9] points out in "The Costs and Benefits of Denial," many of our beliefs have been passed down to us from our families and often go unchallenged for a lifetime. Our beliefs are not always clear to us. Nevertheless, the tendency is to cling to them tenaciously.

Assumptions, on the other hand, are ideas and concepts we take for granted. We assume the world is round because that is what has been taught for years. We assume many questionable ideas about death, dying, and the breakup of love relationships which results in unwanted physical and emotional repercussions.

FAULTY ASSUMPTIONS

We assume that dying people are different, that somehow they are tainted—that they no longer possess the same basic needs as you and I. Therefore we isolate them. Unfortunately, we also assume that the breakup of love relationships is so common that they are easily managed by all parties involved, that grief is not a part of this separation, and that recovery is immediate and permanent. These are examples of negative or default assumptions[10].

Everyone must confront numerous faulty assumptions throughout life. It is notable that many of these assumptions are carried over from childhood. Psychiatrist Roger Gould[11] observes that there are four major false assumptions which combine to fuel the illusion of absolute safety:

1. We will always belong to our parents and believe in their world.

2. Our parents will always be there to help when we are unable to accomplish a task on our own.
3. Life is quite simple and therefore easily controllable.
4. There is no real death or evil in the world (pp. 39–40).

As one grows into adulthood these assumptions are recognized as being false but Gould contends that in the unconscious "they retain hidden control of our adult experience until significant events reveal them as emotional as well as intellectual fallacies." Obviously, a number of these significant revealing events have to do with major separations in life.

During those traumatic times assumptions and beliefs about life and death are scrutinized in an often intense, emotion-laden way. Not infrequently, the result is a positive change in outlook, but only at the price of temporary feelings of vulnerability and loss of control. Others refuse to give up their intellectual fallacies. Eventually, everyone has to abandon the omnipotent thoughts of childhood for more adult belief systems even though the former provided a needed sense of security.

Faulty assumptions often dominate our thinking and in doing so dangerously distort reality. Consequently, we are hardly aware of the fact that our reactions to life events are frequently based on misconceptions and complete falsehoods. Consider these common faulty assumptions associated with separation.

1. I shouldn't feel this way; there's something wrong with me.
2. This happened because of my previous behavior. This is a punishment. I'm getting what I deserve.
3. I'll never get over this; it will never end.
4. This is unfair; it shouldn't happen to me. I've always tried to do what is right.
5. I'll never fall in love again. I'll never trust completely again.
6. I can't help the way I feel. That's the way I am.

This kind of thinking not only hinders our ability to adjust to loss, but also portends difficulty for the future. Psychologists Ellis and Harper[12] suggest that negative emotion is sustained by this type of thinking and stems from the way people talk to themselves (self-talk) about their problems.

In general, negative emotions, such as feelings of depression, anxiety, anger, and guilt are intensified and sustained by such self-propagandizing sentences as 'This is awful!' 'I can't stand that!' and positive emotions, such as love, joy, and elations, are intensified and sustained by sentences such as 'This is fine!' or 'I like that!' Because this is so, human emotions can often be radically controlled or changed by determining precisely the kind of sentences lying behind them and then by changing these sentences (p. 50).

In other words, emotion is created by our perception of an event and therefore can be managed by altering the way we interpret it. For the most part, faulty assumptions are the result of early conditioning and the inability to consider alternate assumptions. What makes them so devastating to coping with separations is that they are believed as gospel without consideration or study; they have become a part of our subconscious mental life.

The results of these negative assumptions and belief systems are perpetual stress and the inability to deal with the many losses which are part of everyone's life. Indeed, it has been well established that psychological forces play a role in most diseases[13-14]. The cognitive forces contributing to disease invariably are the stepchildren of faulty assumptions and beliefs. The psychosomatic component in the etiology of disease is a strong link to the role of thoughts in physical feelings and resultant behavior—an ancient idea which recently has been given more and more credence. There are numerous examples of the effect of negative beliefs on human behavior at every age level.

THE ORIGINS OF BELIEFS

Like all beliefs, beliefs about death and other losses begin in infancy. Children often fall victim to the spurious death messages received from watching hours of television each day. For example, twin messages are constantly beamed to the unsuspecting: what should cause death doesn't, and grieving is a short one to two-hour event, quickly managed and forgotten.

Many mystery or crime serials show cars flipping over and skidding on their roof tops only to find the occupants gingerly exiting and running away. Others depict law enforcement officers crashing through plate glass windows or jumping from second story windows to catch criminals and always emerging unharmed. When death occurs, sitcoms present survivors in most unrealistic postures—seldom crying and often pursuing those responsible for the death with little or no grief shown.

What are the likely outcomes of such learning over time? The obvious and often lethal results are the imitation of what has been viewed. Children assume they are capable of similar feats. Seeing is believing is only partly true, however. Youths jump off roofs as a superhero would, even try to fly like Superman. Some even attempt armed robbery.

When grief models of television fame are copied, children suppress feelings, or conversely, are totally overwhelmed at the emotions felt when a loved one dies. Their idea of the world, created by their television fantasies, is far from what is realistically experienced. Aggression and various forms of violence in some children have been traced to their long hours of unmonitored television viewing. Many of these same behavior patterns remain with them throughout life to complicate the grief process. However, it is possible to correct erroneous beliefs and in doing so "we can damp down or alter excessive, inappropriate emotional reactions"[7].

I said previously that "seeing is believing" is only partly true. This is because beliefs about the world come through the senses and we often are not aware of the illusions of reality that spring from what we see in the environment, particularly in television and the movies. Consequently, so much of what is learned and seen is not real or to put it another way, defies the physical laws of the universe. As Gregory[15] states:

> It has sometimes been thought that behavior is controlled by information immediately available to the eyes and other senses. But sensory information is so incomplete—is it adequate to guide us among surrounding objects? Does it convey all we need to know about an object in order to behave to it appropriately? At once we see the difficulty—the continuous problem the brain has to solve. Given the slenderest clues to the nature of surrounding objects we identify them and act not so much according to what is directly sensed, *but to what is believed* (p. 11).

Our eyes do *not* always see reality any more than our central nervous system can tell the difference between the causes of stress or distress. The hand is quicker than the eye, and it is on this principle that so much television violence is centered. The unsuspecting child is often made a believer of the unbelievable. So too are adults. For example, most adults and children believe that the sun rises and sets; of course, this is not true. As the earth rotates, the sun is relatively stationary and only appears to be setting.

As the child grows into adulthood some of the early lessons from the media become integral parts of their belief systems. The world is an aggressive place to live, stereotypes of what are good guys and bad guys, and fear of big cities or ghetto areas become sources for how we conduct our lives. What this evolves into is a very scary fact of existence: *we see*

what we expect to see. The introduction of coherence into such an established framework is not easy to initiate. Strong, powerful expectations
negate the actual existence of a particular object, symbol, or experience
as it unfolds. This happens in many ways. A common example I have
used for years when illustrating this concept is the following:

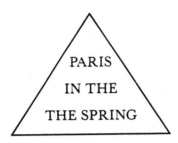

PARIS

IN THE

THE SPRING

This statement, commonly heard, has been established in our thinking,
it has become automatic, an expected string of words. Did you see the
second "the"? Perhaps you should reread the words in the triangle again.
Most people do not expect to see the double "the." By not including the
second "the," they are often victims of misreading because they expected
what was learned long ago, that the statement contains one "the."

Let us now take this same concept and apply it to an experience with a
dying person. The family member who has been "protected" from the
reality of death, who believes that death is synonymous with evil, horror,
and to be feared will perceive the dying person much differently from
one who has been reared in an environment in which death is an
accepted consequence of life. Not infrequently, the former will be preoccupied with the aura or symbolism of death focusing on the disease and
its tragic meaning, while the latter will direct energies and concerns to
the needs of the person and the importance of giving positive support.

Behavior around dying people is always an outgrowth of the attitudes
and beliefs about the meaning of death. Many of these attitudes and
beliefs lie deep in the unconscious, carefully buried to keep people from
experiencing the discomfort or terror associated with them. Such fear is
essentially of our own making, heavily influenced by parental and media
suggestion. However, when we are forced to confront the fact, and come
face to face with the inevitable, what has been suppressed for years comes
roaring to the surface of conscious awareness. This irrational fear of
death constricts and immobilizes caregivers, adding immeasureably to
the stress levels of family members.

At this time the opportunity and readiness for altering assumptions may present itself. Beliefs about life and death commonly are revised during times of great upheaval. Whether individuals are ready to deal with such reevaluation depends in large part on their role within the family, the type of relationships enjoyed with significant others, the quality of communication (particularly honesty) which exists, the ability to cope with stress, and the intensity of fear that has been generated by past experiences and the present crisis.

CHANGING EXPERIENCES TO ALTER ASSUMPTIONS AND BELIEFS

Assumptions and beliefs are just like habits, deeply ingrained in the psyche. Changing any habit takes time, planned repetition, and consistent application. Thoughts and assumptions are changed when we realize that anyone can alter their programming. That is what makes us so unique as humans. The capacity to adapt — if truly desired — is absolutely unlimited. Maltz[16] expressed it as follows:

> Within you right now is the power to do things you never dreamed possible. This power becomes available to you just as soon as you can change your beliefs. Just as quickly as you can dehypnotize yourself from the ideas of 'I can't,' 'I'm not worthy,' 'I don't deserve it' and other self-limiting ideas (p. 55).

How, then, do we tap into a belief system consistent with the commonness of loss, the continuous sequence of separations which must be borne, and of the ways in which such life-changes are accommodated? We need to broaden our perspective about other ways of looking at life and death.

This is accomplished best through acquiring experiential knowledge. This knowledge is that acquired through actual experience rather than from second-hand learning. It is devoid of the theoretical. As Borkman[17] states: "Experiential knowledge is truth learned from personal experience with a phenomenon rather than truth acquired by discursive reasoning, observations, or reflection on information provided by others" (p. 446). In my opinion, in the quest to alter beliefs, there is no substitute for experiential knowledge.

In a nutshell this implies that beliefs are altered as experience is altered. This phenomenon occurs on different levels throughout life. Take, for example, the change in our sense of security as we grow older. As teenagers we would think nothing of driving to a destination seventy or eighty miles away, even through a snow storm. But fifty years later, coupled with much experience and the witnessing of accidents occurring under such conditions, our beliefs change about the wisdom of such a journey. The main point here is to understand that knowledge alone about the dangers of such a trip is not enough; experience brings new meaning to knowledge.

Belief without experience leaves us as a partial believer, not fully convinced. So too with beliefs about separation; it is imperative that people gain knowledge about its nature as well as to learn from experience. Self-instruction is the principle medium for using individual coping potential[18]. Accordingly, we must take responsibility for developing the ability to prevail by ridding ourselves of the misperceptions and half-truths of the past.

Placing oneself in the company of others who have experienced major life-changes and survived is one way of learning from experience. How did they adapt? How did their identities change? What resources did they tap? Who were part of their support systems? These and other questions can surface and be discussed. Being around those who are good copers is a lesson in living; they have much to offer and their wisdom is invaluable; they are vessels of experiential knowledge.

Another problem in attempting to change our experiences is the pain associated with reliving the past. We tend not to dwell on past hurts. It often brings back feelings of rejection, abandonment, guilt and loneliness. The inability to make this ruthless self-analysis makes it impossible for us to learn from our history, from our false assumptions about fate, from the place of hope in survival, and from the failure to utilize the inherent courage that *every one* of us possesses in the face of catastrophe.

In particular, it is essential to examine beliefs about the following.

1. ourselves
2. separation, particularly death and love relationships
3. the people who provide support
4. how best to cope

First, how we feel about ourselves, the degree of self-esteem we possess at a particular time, our confidence level, and past successes and failures are fertile grounds for developing the capacity to revise beliefs and assumptions. Of significance in this regard is the understanding that there is nothing degrading about changing erroneous assumptions and beliefs for more functional ones. This process is not in any way an admission of weakness. The prime condition on which most people take new directions is an awareness of new information sufficient to change viewpoints. Altering erroneous beliefs is life-affirming; the process allows a range of choice and a degree of flexibility necessary to meet the constancy of change. The more individuals are willing to evaluate and revise their thoughts about themselves and their solutions to life's problems, the more likely are they to become successful copers.

Second, beliefs about death, dying, the importance of love relationships, and the responsibilities to others also portend how individuals deal with stress producing circumstances and how they meet future confrontations. We will examine these beliefs throughout the book. What is oftentimes forgotten in this regard is that there are many ways to perceive these topics which will enhance the nature of our coping styles. For stress (distress) depends on how we perceive and interpret an event[19].

Thirdly, beliefs about support people strongly influence the coping response. Are people accepted as assisting out of a sense of duty or true caring? Do they allow grievers to maintain a sense of dignity and control? Or, are they dominating the helping relationship by manipulating the responses of survivors? Are caregivers seen as trusting? Effective caregivers view those in need as having the capacity to find solutions and deal with their problems. Effective helpers view other people as able, friendly, worthy, dependable, internally motivated, and helpful[20]. Simply, their perception of others is highly positive.

Finally, as I have written earlier, the discussion of convictions about the way to deal with separations will open up avenues of rich insight into healthy ways to overcome problems and increase the number of coping options at one's disposal. How people perceive separation becomes the pivotal factor in dealing with traumatic change. All too frequently, survivors tend not to utilize some of the most practical means of dealing with loss experiences.

Crying for example, is a powerful means to dissipate pent up feelings, relieve anxiety, express outrage, and communicate sorrow. *Crying is coping;* but many individuals falsely believe it is a negative reaction, showing weakness and loss of control. The belief that crying is utter weakness is folly. It deprives grievers of an important coping mechanism, as well as a means of stress release and communication of hurt. Crying is a healthy release for the body and mind[21].

KNOWING AND BELIEVING

There are many people who possess great amounts of knowledge, who are expert at organizing information and disseminating it. Interestingly, it is equally true that many of these same people do *not* truly believe much of what they are saying. They may *know* something is true for others but do not *believe* it is so for themselves. This is a paradox which befalls everyone at various times. Everyone has had experiences where actions did not match beliefs. Many individuals say they know the importance of human rights for all, but allow discrimination to exist. Many others say they know that having a 55 mph speed limit for automobiles is prudent but constantly drive above that limit. Most individuals acknowledge that everyone dies yet they live as though they were immortal. It is one thing to know; it is quite another to truly believe and put those beliefs into practice. In essence, some people do not practice what they preach because they are not truly convinced of its application to their lives: they have not *personally* experienced the need for it.

Consider the dramatic difference in the relationship between effort and results. We teach our children that in order to achieve a particular goal, obtain good grades, win a prize, or be promoted in a job it takes strong effort. Nothing worthwhile is achieved without hard work; that is the American way. We all hear this and learn it very early in life, but many do not *believe* it.

It takes a long time to see the relationship between physical and emotional commitment to a goal and meeting that goal with all its rewards. Some individuals never believe it and refuse to give the effort needed in any endeavor. Or they substitute a belief system which features the concept that "I can get something for nothing." The difference between knowing and believing is that the former does not move one toward action the way strong convictions do.

What convinces people to become strong believers and alter assumptions? There are many answers to this query. Germane to our discussion are the following: (1) pain, (2) thwarting of expectations, (3) the experience of separation, and (4) significant support persons.

Pain is a great teacher as it points out sharply the contrasts in life. It has long been acknowledged that during painful moments we often become convinced of certain realities: how important being healthy really is, the joy of freedom from fear, and the necessity of changing our lifestyle. The nervously ill person is especially suggestible to the directions of others[22]. This occurs because pain is an intense personal experience which causes us to be open to anything which will relieve agony. All too frequently however, individuals fail to realize that "the mind is the safest and most powerful pain reliever"[23]. How it is reprogrammed will lead to the reduction of *any* pain.

Of equal significance is the willingness to revise our thoughts about life and death when expectations are not met. People expect their home towns to remain the same after being away for several months, or their parents to be able to sustain a torrid pace all of their lives. Old friends are expected to act as they did during high school or college days. They are often shocked to discover the sometimes subtle and other times not so subtle changes have occurred over time. These thwarted expectations are frequently the basis for sharp turns in their analysis of life and the impact of the years.

The storm of separations that befall us destroy some of our most cherished beliefs. We are dumbfounded when someone who we thought cared abandons us; the pain of rejection is unbearable and we often vow never to become vulnerable again. Death in western society continually forces individuals to view life differently, follow new paths, or take up the pursuits of fallen loved ones. Perhaps more than any other human event the death of a loved one, or the approach of our own death causes near seismic changes in our beliefs. Grief, in short, demands that we relearn the world, ourselves, and other people[24].

SOCIAL SUPPORT

During the days of adapting to major loss experience, those who provide support are often sources of new beliefs about the meaning of friendship, love, loss, and how to utilize strengths in the face of hardship. Next to personal resources, this social support is the single most potent force in recovering from relationship losses. A deep, abiding trust in others during such times allows us to be open to the new, to reluctantly give up the old.

Social interaction is a common source of belief formation throughout life. From birth, our view of the world and people in it evolve from three major sources: (1) parents, (2) the media, particularly television, and (3) experience. Parent-child relationships result in beliefs which often last a lifetime. Sometimes what is learned from parents proves to be anxiety producing throughout life. While we will take a more in-depth look at television and its influence on thought formation later, suffice it to say that many negative as well as positive messages are received from the set.

But, the most formative experience of all comes from personal experience. The most dramatic illustration of this occurs when one witnesses the last breath of a loved one. One who has never had the experience of being with a dying family member lacks the insight this experience can impart.

Many negative beliefs and misperceptions about separations are products of second hand information passed down by others and then filled in with details based on fantasies about what may have happened. Such distortions about death, loss, and people in need which are permeated with fear and tension are often the cause of great stress and may well be a potent contributor to feelings of depression and anxiety[25].

Events experienced with others usually determines what is believed about those events and what is ultimately believed about people in general. If success is experienced in relationships, that is, if relationships are trusting, positive, and rewarding, we begin to build confidence, assurance, and faith in the inherent goodness of people.

Conversely, when relationships feature disrespect, rejections, and conflict early in life, we develop images about adults and their motives which are untrustworthy and self-serving. Such beliefs and understandings about people will affect the quality of interaction with them and the expectations assumed about their behavior. It may eventuate into the need to control all relationships with others at *all* times, even into the death vigil. The person will see only what he wants or expects to see. It may take years to change our beliefs about people from hurtful to helpful when such an imprint is made early enough and continues long enough.

Positive personal experiences can also result in very dramatic changes in beliefs, often in a surprisingly short time. Talk to someone who has witnessed a paranormal event while grieving the loss of a loved one in which the individual believes the deceased was heard, seen or touched. For many, these paranormal experiences are interpreted as a message that the deceased is truly in another existence, a supernatural world; the survivor's grieving is frequently diminished[26]. Many people have reported near death experiences that involved self-visualizing events in which they report separating from their physical bodies and finding themselves in unearthly surroundings. Later, on returning to their physical bodies and regaining consciousness, they suggest that the experience is actually pleasant, that words are inadequate to describe what they witnessed, and astonishingly, they now have absolutely no fear of death[27].

Events such as these are the basis for enormous turnabouts in behavior and beliefs.

FACILITATING CHANGES IN ASSUMPTIONS AND BELIEFS

Every person possesses the capacity to meet any hardship and challenge. The external environment does not dictate how we should respond to an event, for what is internal, what we choose to see and do, is the pivotal factor in altering convictions.

Forming new patterns of behavior is an inherent part of being human. This is an innate capability; it does not have to be procured, it has only to be activated. It follows that outer conditions are in effect the way we visualize them from within. This is why two people can read an article or see a movie and come away with two different viewpoints about what was expressed. In *Seeing with the Mind's Eye,* the Samuels'[28] tell us:

> In essence, what people visualize is what they get. Likewise, what they have is the result of what they have previously visualized. And that is why we think that a way of choosing which life areas and which visualizations to concentrate on is important (p. 313).

In most cases, if self-change is to occur, it must be recognized that the biggest obstacle is the self. Individuals condition themselves to accept continuity without change. They expect their internal and external environments to remain the same: no aging, no loss, no change in relationships, no death. Those expectations are at the root of our inability to cope when dealing with the many turning points in life. There is a predisposition to ignore the truth of experience, when in fact every person has the power within to change that which befalls them from without.

When the hearts and minds of people change so does the environment in which they live. Christianity flourished underground in the catacombs and eventually changed the face of the world by first changing the convictions people lived by. Old beliefs melt away in a community of caring and mutual aid. Creating similar communities of mutual assistance, such as a hospice or a widow-to-widow program, are strategies which have proved most fruitful in ridding people of dysfunctional beliefs concerning death and dying.

INNER RESOURCES

The first step in the process of developing different ways to view the self, the world, and life's problems is to refuse to accept the conditioning of the past which dictates passive resignation to present circumstances. There is no more useless chatter than blaming our parents, friends, life, fate, or boss for what has occurred in the past; that is history. What is important at this stage is the here and now and what to do with it, not to recite (and reinforce) feelings of being victimized. This is a negative form of unconscious autosuggestion.

Therefore, we begin by developing an awareness of what can be done by ourselves for ourselves. Social scientists have for years emphasized that most people use less than 10% of their resources; that there is a vast untapped potential which lies in each of us waiting to be brought forth by a commitment to a cause.

To illustrate: biofeedback and autosuggestion (self-suggestion) are two important tools, among others, which utilize some of the potential lying dormant in each individual. Biofeedback is the process of using internal biological signals to voluntarily alter those same responses as desired. Thus, physiological changes in the body can be initiated by changes in our emotional climate. We can lower blood pressure, pulse rate, reduce muscle tension, change skin temperature, and even affect brain-wave patterns. The possibilities for controlling internal conditions are astounding and largely unused by the general public. The mind can control the course of disease[29].

Autosuggestion or self-suggestion is essentially talking to the self, that is, suggesting a specific idea, circumstance, or feeling to the unconscious mind which is repeatedly visualized in a relaxed manner.* The process has long been known to liberate tension and anxiety while releasing energy reserves which can be used in positive pursuits. The technique has cured numerous psychosomatic illnesses, employing the "education of the imagination."

Since it is unscientific and simple to use, this may be why its decline in popularity has occurred within the past generation. Nevertheless, the idea that the imagination can exert control of the central nervous system has much to offer in the way of utilizing inherent resources. *There is no greater unused resource than the unconscious mind.* For the central nervous

---

*For our purposes the terms subconscious and unconscious will be used interchangeably denoting that part of the self in which processes occur outside of conscious awareness.

system reacts on what it receives from the brain and what one thinks is true[16]. The pivotal force is what one chooses to think, whether right or wrong. These experiences can awaken in anyone a realization that there is much that can be done to change inward conditions. But the realization of this vast potential to cope with adversity should come early in life when fears and frustrations form visions of existence filled with images of helplessness and hopelessness. A thorough analysis of the use of autosuggestion is found in Chapter 7.

INDIVIDUAL POTENTIAL TO INFLUENCE AND BE INFLUENCED

It is unfortunate but true that dealing with any physical or mental phenomena on a subjective level is frowned upon by those wedded to the purely scientific approach. Nonetheless, quantum mechanics, the brain-child of a number of physicists, has made a shambles of some long-held laws of the universe. Most astonishing is the conclusion that what people observe in life depends solely on what *they choose* to observe. Particle physicist Alan Wolf[30] in *Taking the Quantum Leap* states:

> Even describing the true order of the universe is difficult because it involves something more than the physical world. It involves us, our minds, and our thoughts.... The gradual recognition that what we think may physically influence what we observe has led to a revolution in thought and philosophy, not to mention physics.

What Wolf is saying is that *individuals create reality* and their realities differ immensely. There are alternate realities other than the one our five senses indicate and millions of people live by them[31]. In truth, there are as many realities as there are believers. Reality is subjective. How we organize reality reflects our coping style. That revelation is not new. It has long been a part of recorded history, although consistently discarded by generation after generation as lacking in scientific proof. Having buried one of the most powerful individual resources for problem solving in the soil of scientific objectivity many people face their dilemmas by searching for answers from without when, in the words of Pogo, "We have met the enemy and he is us." The Newtonian view of objectivity in perceiving the universe does not hold true, for the very act of perceiving alters what we view. It follows that we do not have to be bound by a reality imposed by past experience.

This has enormous implications for what we believe, how those beliefs are formed, how they change, and what can be done to facilitate this change. Beliefs often change as a result of random or chance occurrences, especially when they involve separations, illnesses, or other traumatic events. These changes in belief are very consistent with exposure to contradictory or complementary sides of an event. In a word, there is paradox, uncertainty in a world which we have been taught is consistently orderly.

Because separations and other loss experiences force everyone to adapt they also frequently bring new understanding and a different view of the world and the self. This is one of the many paradoxes of life; negative happenings bring positive results. Cancer victims often report that their cancer has changed their lives—for the better. The famous actress, Jill Ireland, contracted breast cancer. She had a radical mastectomy and six months of intensive chemotherapy. She was devastated with the fears and thoughts of not surviving. But two years later she wrote: "In a strange way the illness was a gift. It strengthened my marriage and my family. If someone said I could replay 1984—no cancer, no chemotherapy—I'd say I'd like to go through it again, considering where I am now"[32].

There are complimentary and antagonistic sides to all life events. (A belief we would do well to consider.) As physicist Wolf[30] says:

> The discovery of the Principle of Complementarily marked a change in our thinking. It taught us that our everyday senses were not to be trusted to give a total view of reality. There was always a hidden, complementary side to everything we experienced (p. 139).

In effect, education about the self which would bring the most promising rewards in coping with massive change is the understanding of the role of the unconscious mind in the scheme of life. It is a storehouse of solutions to the problems of living. At the turn of the century William James offered: "The subconscious self is nowadays a well-accredited psychological entity. . . . Apart from all religious considerations there is actually and literally more life in our total soul than we are at any time aware of"[33]. Carl Jung put it this way: "The unconscious mind of man sees correctly even when conscious reason is blind and impotent. . . . The unconscious of man can reach God knows where. There we are going to make discoveries"[34].

One of the constructive thoughts that must be indelibly impressed in the conscious and unconscious minds is that our reaction to what happens on the outside, in the external environment, is the result of our internal environment. External factors by themselves may cause turmoil, but it is always *how one reacts* to these factors which is the key to coping with them.

Therefore, with hard work, it is clear that any separation can be managed. This does not mean that we will free ourselves from emotional pain; nothing can do that. There is always emptiness and pain when deep emotional attachments are severed. The implication is only that most of us can manage the painful transitions and *prevent* excessive suffering.

This is accomplished best when we choose to deal with the new environment, utilize support systems, and be committed to the task of accommodating separations and all life-changes as part of life, not apart from it.

THE UNTAPPED MIRACLE WITHIN

To many people, the words *unconscious mind* carries with them a mysterious quality; it is thought to be a subject of discussion only for psychologists and psychiatrists who are trained to understand its secrets. Yet the unconscious is the inner mind, accepted by many scientists as existing, although not fully understood. Each person possesses two distinct selves which influence each other. From ancient times to the present the unconscious was considered to play a major role in disease processes. If we become more aware of the potential of the unconscious to assist in problem solving, we will have developed a strong ally in the process of changing dysfunctional beliefs.

What does conventional wisdom tell us about the unconscious? Consider the following:

1. It literally interprets the information it receives. This means whether what we believe is true or false will be processed by the unconscious and result in behavior which could help or hinder reaching specific goals.
2. The unconscious controls the physical self, organs, glands, and physiology. Therefore, it highly influences our physical well-being.
3. The unconscious is always aware, always functioning 24 hours a day, even when under anesthesia. This is why some surgeons will never discuss how an operation is proceeding, if the patient is not doing well.
4. Our neurotic, psychotic, and psychosomatic disorders originate primarily in the unconscious.
5. The unconscious is the treasure-house of all memories. *Everything* experienced is stored there. This means repressed memories as well.
6. Beliefs held in the unconscious heavily influence how we cope with loss.

7. Perceptions of loss events (how they appear to us) are a function of beliefs held in the unconscious.
8. Thinking *habits* are indelibly etched in the subconscious. Therefore, if we are persistently negative in thinking it will be reflected ultimately in hapless, pessimistic behavior.
9. The impact of constant suggestions on the unconscious can lead to changes in belief and behavior.
10. The vast majority of mental activity takes place below the level of conscious awareness and one can tap into that level.

Most individuals are not aware of the unlimited power the unconscious mind has over their behavior. It is difficult to comprehend that the unconscious is creative, can solve problems, affect health, and change inner conditions. Indeed, the dramatic positive reversals in our lives originate in the unconscious not at the sensory level which all of us are overconcerned with.

AUTOSUGGESTION (SELF-SUGGESTION) AND THE UNCONSCIOUS MIND

Throughout history self-suggestion has played a leading role in utilizing the resources of the unconscious mind. The earliest written accounts of many of these principles are attributed to the Greek physician, Hippocrates, although some have been used since the dawn of history. Through self-suggestion, sustained and motivated by the desire to cope with the conditions of life, the most traumatic experiences have been mastered.

Everyone is subject to the power of suggestion in their lives. This is illustrated through learning in any subject matter or the development of physical skills. Mental practice, which involves repetitively visualizing the exact way we should perform a skill, imprints a pattern in the unconscious which assists in the formation and execution of that skill. Obviously, some people are more subject to suggestion than others, but it can be worked on through several approaches to culminate in new patterns of behavior and ways to deal with massive change.

The impact of suggestion is often immediate. If told by significant others that we do not look good in a particular piece of clothing or if our hairstyle is not appropriate, the tendency is to soon make changes. The Lady Di hairstyle has been adopted by many women as very desirable. Some suggestions are quite detrimental, as in the instance when someone tells us that we do not look well and ask if we are feeling ill. If two or three people do the same thing, as sometimes occurs in a joking way, the individual who is feeling well may take these suggestions literally and begin to feel sick.

The unconscious can be a gentle tyrant if it is not consciously managed. The power of suggestion which results in strong negative beliefs is illustrated in the development of our relationships with others. Notice that when a dislike is established for someone, regardless of the cause, an individual is likely to believe the worst about that person, whenever negative comments are made. Conversely, misdeeds are quickly overlooked in loved ones or at least not given full weight or consideration. But when others are not favored, the inclination is to believe any negative comments about them. In a critical vein, many suggestions occur at the unconscious level where they are acted upon without conscious volition.

Beliefs are the products of perceptions and reinforced suggestion. Everyone has the ability to decide which suggestions they will believe. Therefore, the ideas we inculcate into our belief structures and allow to become a part of our unconscious will change our lives dramatically. If warts can be ordered off the skin by hypnotic suggestion then everyone possesses a force than can shape their defenses to combat anything that life has to offer. Lewis Thomas[35] in *The Medusa and the Snail* writes:

> Some intelligence or other knows how to get rid of warts, and this is a disquieting thought. . . . And they can be made to go away by something that can only be called thinking, or something like thinking. . . . If my unconscious can figure out how to manipulate the mechanisms needed for getting around that virus, and for destroying all the various cells in the correct order for tissue rejection, then all I have to say is that my unconscious is a lot further along than I am (pp. 79, 81).

What Lewis and a host of other scientists are saying is that there is an intelligence within each person which far transcends "normal" expectations; it is further along than the conscious mind and this needs to be recognized and systematically put to use.

No one has ever seen the wind, electricity or a fundamental particle, but that does not mean they are non-existent. Neither has anyone seen the unconscious; but it too exists and is the source of the vast majority of our mental life.

Most of us do not understand the immense power of the unconscious to accomplish the impossible. We have not systematically tried to use it in creative ways. If you are an intractably negative skeptic this may sound rather Pollyannaish to your scientific mind. In an age of science it is hard to believe that an unseen internal force can change radically the world and our view of it. But this has been a reality to those who possess the *courage to believe* and have boldly tried the process of harnessing this internal energy.

As Wolf[30] says, "reality depends upon our choices of what and how we choose to observe. These choices in turn depend upon our minds or, more specifically, the content of our thoughts. And our thoughts, in turn, depend upon our expectations, our desire for continuity" (p. 128).

If we adopt Wolf's notion, and apply it to the quest to deal with life's problems, the conclusion is there are forces other than the five senses which provide unlimited power to cope with adversity. In the evolution of consciousness expectations play major roles in the process of adaptation. But even more important is the power of the unconscious mind to influence the management of change.

The motivation to believe and faith in beliefs lay the groundwork for changing the scope and dimension of any human problem. The success of clients who choose one of the many therapeutic modalities available through professional therapists hinges on modifying beliefs about expectations, images, and values over time[36]. While professional counselors and therapists are often catalysts in the process of altering thoughts, images, and beliefs, in the final· analysis each person controls when and how it will take place. Others may provide information about loss and recovery but the individual decides when to be open and accepting of new viewpoints. We will return to this theme later.

In the next chapter we focus on long held beliefs about death. In particular, the emphasis is on examining the assumptions upon which these ingrained beliefs are based and the introduction of alternate assumptions which leads to a reduction in anxiety. But let us close here by emphasizing that *each person is the most influential power for coping with separation. We can change the world around us. Each of us is powerful if we believe and use our hidden resources.* Everyone carries within him or her the means to cope with the most devastating changes imaginable.

REFERENCES

1. Cassem, N. Bereavement as indispensable for growth. In Schoenberg, B. Gerber, I. Weiner, A. *et al* (Eds.). *Bereavement: Its psychosocial perspective.* New York: Columbia University Press, 1975, p. 9–17.
2. Shneidman, E. *Voices of death.* New York: Harper & Row, 1980.

3. Downey, A. Living, loving and losing: Implications for health and well-being. *Health Values,* 1983, 7¹, 7–14.

4. Bertman, S. Bearing the unbearable: From loss, the gain. *Health Values,* 1983, 7¹, 24–24.

5. Abramson, L., Seligman, M. & Teasdale, J. Learned helplessness in humans: Critique and reformulation. *Journal of Abnormal Psychology,* 1978, 87, 49–74.

6. Bandura, A. *Social learning theory.* Englewood Cliffs, NJ: Prentice-Hall, 1977.

7. Beck, A. *Cognitive therapy and the emotional disorders.* New York: International Universities Press, 1976.

8. Burns, D. *Feeling good.* New York: New American Library, 1980.

9. Lazarus, R. The costs and benefits of denial. In J. Spinetta & P. Deasy-Spinetta (Eds.). *Living with childhood cancer.* St. Louis: C. V. Mosby, 1981.

10. Hofstadter, D. Metamagical themas. *Scientific American,* 1982, 247, 18–36.

11. Gould, R. *Transformations.* New York: Simon & Schuster, 1978.

12. Ellis, A. & Harper, R. *A guide to rational living.* North Hollywood, CA: Wilshire Books, 1961.

13. Totman, R. *Social causes of disease.* New York: Pantheon Books, 1979.

14. LeShan, L. *You can fight for your life.* New York: M. Evans, 1977.

15. Gregory, R. *The intelligent eye.* New York: McGraw-Hill, 1971.

16. Maltz, M. *Psycho-cybernetics.* New York: Human Sciences Press, 1984.

17. Borkman, Thomasina. Experiential Knowledge: A New Concept for the Analysis of Self-Help Groups, *Social Service Review,* 50, 3, 1976, p. 446.

18. Weisman, A. *The coping capacity.* New York: Human Sciences Press, 1984.

19. Selye, H. Stress: The basis of illness. In E. Goldwag (Ed.). *Inner balance: The power of holistic healing.* Englewood Cliffs, NJ: Prentice-Hall, 1979.

20. Combs, A., Avila, D. & Purkey, W. *Helping relationships.* Boston: Allyn & Bacon, 1971.

21. Raphael, B. *The anatomy of bereavement.* New York: Basic Books, 1983.

22. Weeks, C. *Hope and help for your nerves.* New York: Bantam, 1978.

23. Bressler, D. *Free yourself from pain.* New York: Simon & Schuster, 1979.

24. Attig, T. Relearning the world: A guided fantasy. *Newsletter of the Association for Death Education and Counseling,* 1986, 10,⁶, 7.

25. Beck, A. & Young, J. College blues. *Psychology Today.* September, 1978, pp. 80–92.

26. LaGrand, L. *Coping with separation and loss as a young adult.* Springfield, IL: Charles C Thomas, 1986.

27. Ring, Kenneth. *Heading toward omega.* New York: William Morrow, 1985.

28. Samuels, M. & Samuels, N. *Seeing with the mind's eye.* New York: Random House, 1975.

29. Simonton, O., Simonton, S. & Creighton, J. *Getting well again.* New York: Bantam, 1980.

30. Wolf, A. *Taking the quantum leap.* San Francisco: Harper & Row, 1981, p. 6.

31. LeShan, L. *Alternate realities.* New York: M. Evans, 1976.

32. Sperling, D. & Schreiberg S. "After Breast Cancer, A New Outlook on Life," *USA Today,* January 6, 1987, p. 20.

33. James, W. *The varieties of religious experience.* New York: Modern Library, 1936.

34. Evans, R. *Conversations with Carl Jung.* Princeton: Van Nostrand, 1964.
35. Thomas, L. *The medusa and the snail.* New York: Viking, 1979.
36. Frank, J. *Persuasion and healing: A Comparative study of psychotherapy.* New York: Schocken, 1961.

Chapter Two

DEATH: STIMULUS AND TEACHER

We all have to die! It is so unfortunate that it does not give us two weeks notice.

John, a College senior

No man knows whether death may not turn out to be the greatest of blessings for a human being; and yet people fear it as if they knew for certain that it is the greatest of evils.

Socrates

It is impossible that anything so natural, so necessary, and so universal as death, should ever have been designed by providence as an evil to mankind.

Johnathan Swift

The title of this chapter is a fundamental belief for enriching life and is held by many people, particularly those who work in hospices, are counselors, or teach courses in thanatology. Clearly, death carries social, psychological, and behavioral implications. We shall soon explore how it holds sway over how we live. However, the predominate view of death is wholly unrealistic at best, carved in the minds of individuals by a society set up to ignore its relationship to life.

To break through the societal norms which reinforce a myopic view of death—for the purpose of living *with* it and *coping* with it—it is essential to become aware of cultural factors which influence death attitudes and beliefs. More than that, this chapter suggests that death can be a source of wisdom to enhance the quality of life and that individuals can break the conspiracy of silence which gives death unbridled power to confuse and complicate the grief process. To accomplish this goal and understand why the grief-stricken respond as they do, we will explore the social environment and institutionalized settings through which their response evolves. From this social milieu, images of death and loss are formed. Obviously, these images affect behavior and feelings[1]. More importantly, the resulting beliefs and attitudes formed are expressed in

25

behavior as a support person or mourner and in the reconstruction of life after loss.

FACING DEATH

The fear of death appears to be prevalent among most people. Where does this fear originate? There seem to be two basic views: the first is the psychoanalytic view that death fears are an innate part of human nature, that we go to great lengths to repress fear, and that on the subconscious level we are terrified by the prospect of personal death[2]. On the other hand, there is much evidence to suggest that death fears are closely related to social structure and the way one is nurtured. The Chinese and Japanese have little or no fear of death in comparison to people in western cultures. The fear of death is met by the traditional Japanese through a belief that in all life transitions, dignity and control should prevail because life is a journey, and meaning is attached to every stage of that journey[3].

There is little doubt that our beliefs about life are closely tied to the fear of death. We learn to live in terror as if our death were imminent. The Japanese learn that death is a part of life to be met like any other emotional trauma, and therefore do not live in terror of its occurrence. Accordingly, it is important to destroy the negative image that death victimizes. The belief that we are victims implies hopelessness, and such a perception deepens anger, depression and fear of the future. *Fear always narrows our perception of a subject or event,* eliminating important considerations in coping.

A CRITICAL BELIEF

The most critical belief of all for changing perceptions about death is that the mind is capable of making a 360 degree turnabout. We can reprogram our thinking. Emerson said: "Fear always springs from ignorance." Believing that we can learn to include death as a stimulus and teacher instead of a fearful unknown is fundamental to coping with change. We must convince ourselves that the mind influences every phase of our existence. That is the beginning of dealing with any of life's problems. In short, what we put into our minds—or allow society to put into our minds—is what we get back. As the hacker says, garbage in, garbage out.

Assuming that anyone can alter their views about death, let us examine the topic and suggest less fearful ways of integrating it into life. If we are to make changes, it is best to first understand the origin of our difficulties with death.

PERSONAL DEATH AWARENESS

Despite the reams of materials on death that are flooding the marketplace and the many new courses and workshops available in both the private and public sectors, it is foolish to assume that society has achieved some kind of milestone in the development of personal death awareness. The public's distorted perception of death is always with us. Each succeeding generation must grapple with the same problems that have resulted from common cultural conditioning.

There are two subjects for which everyone needs preparation, but for which they receive little education: parenting and dealing with loss, especially death. These topics are not mutually exclusive. Most parents acknowledge their lack of training in how to confront the many problems which arise in family life and in the rearing of their children. Parents admit how inadequate they have felt in numerous instances when hard and fast decisions had to be made.

And when it comes to realistic death awareness, parents shy away from the topic. Nevertheless, they are far less willing to admit to any lack of insight on their part into a subject with such far-reaching implications. This resistance occurs because some parents believe death is a taboo subject, not to be discussed openly, while other parents resist the reawakening of painful feelings and emotions. Dealing with the death of a loved one is often overwhelming to the point where parents cannot cope with their children's questions and reactions. Fathers, especially victims of the "little-boys-don't-cry-syndrome," are unable or unwilling to confront their feelings and model authentic behavior to assist children in a healthy grief process. Even before death occurs in the family, parental fears and uneasiness limits open discussion. We normally tend to sidestep topics which cause us to struggle for answers to penetrating questions. It is too difficult to say to a child, "I don't know." Yet, when and what children are told, combined with parental expectations for response, seem to significantly influence the child's reaction to loss[4].

I suggest that there are two types of awareness: one is an intellectual, shallow type consisting of factual data; the other is a deep profound awareness of the intimate, emotional meaning of relating to a universal unknown. The former is easy to reach and fleeting in impact. The latter, such as that concerning death, is a source of strong motivation for change and increased understanding of life. Confronting death means that we must confront our repertoire of avoidance techniques, recognizing those which are incompatible with developing a more realistic model. If we choose to challenge cultural images we need not fear death. This task, this journey against the tide of deception, is arduous, but rewarding. As psychiatrist Robert J. Lifton[5] reminds us: "We must open ourselves to the full impact of death in order to rediscover and reinterpret the movement and sequence of life" (p. 52).

CHANGING OUR ATTITUDES TOWARD DEATH

Attitudes toward death are formed basically by the range of experiences we have had with it. Death is similar to the tip of an iceberg—only the misleading tip. This is a critical distinction to consider. This tip is like a screen, preventing us from acquiring a more complete view of reality and denying to us the belief that there are other dimensions to death, dimensions which exist below the distorted version that society permits us to see.

As Edwin Shneidman[6] has observed: "America's current attitude toward death is deeply ambivalent: awe of death and attraction to death; risking death and loving life; wanting happiness and behaving in self-destructive ways; regarding death as taboo and insisting on a new permissiveness to talk about it; an obsession with the Bomb and a deep concern with spiritual rebirth" (p. 70). That discussions regarding death can and do generate such polarities in thinking supports the charge that society restricts our discussions to superficialities because more profound thinking would tap into buried fears and unleash a torrent of emotion by getting to the deeper issues underlying ambivalence.

We can gain control of our fear of death by changing our personal view of it. This is a duty of spiritual emancipation which each must perform in order to forge realistic assumptions about life's problems. Since solutions are not easy to come by, *they hinge on altering well-established patterns of behavior, challenging long-held beliefs, confronting the meaning of death,* and strengthening our ability to deal with stress. We can do this by looking at the ambivalent attitudes which lie at the heart of death anxiety in western culture. We can safely conclude that such a commitment will strip away the superficial relationships society presently fosters regarding death.

DEATH AS A SOURCE OF PROFOUND APPRECIATION OF LIFE

Could there be a source of untapped information which sheds new light on interpersonal relationships, emotions, the behavior of friends under duress, and on our lifestyles? Yes, such information is available, but it lies hidden in a sea of pretense, distortion, and facade. We encourage the continuance of this outmoded thinking by our willingness to allow the negative connotations of the word "death" to flourish, just as we have done with words like "cancer" and "old age." To have cancer or be aged is to be somehow irreversibly tainted, to be stamped with a set of undesirable characteristics and behaviors.

Our association with the word "death" carries the same blight, preventing death from becoming one of the richest resources available for developing individual potential. Death sends us messages about the quality of life, messages too often ignored. As Herman Feifel[7] has reminded us: "Man can completely understand himself only by integrating the death concept into his life" (p. 123).

A truism forgotten in the crush of twentieth century productivity and achievement is the fact that expected and unexpected losses, especially death, shape the character and skills by which survivors live. Renewed moral strength is a by-product of adversity and the willingness to use death as part of a life-long *growth* process. Before World War I, illness and death were familiar partners; contemporary life, however, regards them with indifference, if at all.

Actually, the central issue in the study of death becomes one of analyzing the quality of our lives in reference to our awareness of our mortality. The study of death defines the meaning of existence and can assist personal struggle. As Rollo May[8] observes:

> The confronting of death gives the most positive reality to life itself. It makes the individual existence real, absolute, and concrete. Death is the one fact of my life which is not relative but absolute, and my awareness of this gives my existence and what I do each hour an absolute quality (p. 49).

This unequivocal fact is manifested in putting our pencil down to take a walk in the spring, going on that vacation we've put off, and watching a beautiful sunset. If we are young, it means realizing that maybe we'll only have twenty summers left to go surfing or water ski. Not fifty. Not one hundred or two hundred. There are limits. It means we'll stop postponing, we'll exhalt life, profoundly appreciate it. We'll say, "I love you," more often before it's too late. We will live in the NOW. We will thrill at the colorful foliage of fall. We will recognize, that despite our intellectual gymnastics, life is short.

EMBRACING THE UNKNOWN

The unknown is a major source of anxiety for most. The unexplained, the unfamiliar, that which is concealed, is frightening. If we neither know what to expect, nor realize the cause and effect relationships involved, it is like stepping into an unlighted room. Yet, every step we take through life is filled with an assortment of unfamiliar and unexplored experiences.

Nonetheless, if we can uncover some of the myths, find possible explanations for feeling ill-at-ease, we can begin to cope with the emotions which surface. Like Hardt[9], Simpson[10] and Leviton[11] I maintain that attitudes toward death are learned—a process of socialization that can be altered.

This is not to imply that the study of death necessarily results in becoming more accepting of it. Not at all; the mystique of death acceptance is elusive. There is one certainty: Many fears are overcome when the beliefs and assumptions they are based upon are faced directly, when we penetrate their illogical veil. False beliefs—Bowlby[4] refers to them as cognitive biases—formed early in life are at the core of most fears, and death is no exception. Gradual exposure to the elements of fear, will reverse the distorting trend. We encourage fear when shallow, inauthentic experience is substituted for actual confrontation, and false prophets tell us what to feel and how quickly to forget. Simultaneously, we are both victims and the primary source of societally fostered deception. Kavanaugh[12] rightly suggests that in overcoming deception the task is more than a mere intellectual experience.

> It became clear to me that an honest and humane approach to death can begin only when we allow ourselves to get in touch with our viceral *feelings*. Otherwise, any stance we adopt toward death will be no more than another form of blocking and avoiding honest confrontation. It is

not the dying or the dead we fear as much as the unknown and untested *feelings* they evoke within ourselves.

Honest recognition of our latent feelings about human mortality enables us to be free enough to make some choices. Only when we know our feelings can we respect our unique reactions.

No books or conferences, no movies or discussions, will be effective, ultimately, in helping us master the art of peace and graciousness near death, until we permit our feelings to be honestly and fully felt, and admit it is all right to feel as we do. Until than, newly acquired skills will be no more than fresh evasions (pp. 23, 25, 26).

There are few topics which create internal conflict more than death. It is death that has always provided the framework in which lack of control, misunderstanding and feelings of helplessness are highlighted by a lack of systematic awareness and communication *before* it occurs. It forces new relationships on survivors. They must live without the help, companionship and love of the deceased. They must find new meaning in a context which at first appears meaningless. Frequently, closer ties develop among survivors, but sometimes tensions develop because guilt, anger and despair are confronted at an intensity never dreamed possible. Suddenly, skills must be acquired to cope with additional duties and responsibilities which have been thrust upon us. Re-evaluation of beliefs and goals occurs. New fears are encountered.

Death now becomes the reason for assessing values and reordering priorities. The emotions it generates in survivors bring new understanding, but it also brings new questions about the self. Many examples abound, when coming to grips with the fact of mortality has caused people to change careers, and others to alter their lifestyles dramatically. Death often forces us to place a high priority on people within our daily lives whom we had previously taken for granted. Survivors frequently become less oriented toward the future and live more fully in the present.

We cannot escape shock, numbness, and emotional pain when a loved one dies — but we can use death as a stimulus instead of a source of depression. Learning to manage our lives when they are influenced by death, to maintain contact with life when death seems to have taken everything away, is within our reach. How? An honest, long-term confrontation with death is the answer; putting death back into life, by replacing antiquated societal beliefs with realistic views of the ongoing universality of loss. I am not suggesting a morbid preoccupation with death. Nor is this to imply that everyone can instantly and completely be honest and realistic in all circumstances concerning death. Most of us have to address social pressures, fathom cultural influences and false expectations which have created the need to suppress feelings. However, as M. Scott Peck[13] in his inspiring book *The Road Less Traveled* suggests: "...if we are unwilling to fully face the fearsome presence of death on our left shoulder, we deprive ourselves of its counsel and cannot possibly live or love with clarity. When we shy away from death, the ever-changing nature of things, we inevitably shy away from life." (p. 134).

Death As An Expected Stressor

Looking at death as both a biological event as well as an *inevitable source of stress* brings a new perspective to the problems of adaptation. Death is the ultimate stressor for those who survive. We need only examine the descriptions of physical symptoms that often accompany a survivor's grief. They read like a medical dictionary: nausea, insomnia, exhaustion, hallucinations, digestive disturbances, headache, chills, labored breathing, and hot and cold flashes. Chronic stress is the prelude to many disease conditions[14]. For some of us, long term illness, brought on by a complex psychophysical response to death, occurs. Our immune systems are weakened. Alcoholism, emotional disorders, heart and circulatory ailments, and drug overdose or the refusal to take prescribed medicine, have all been linked to stress following the death of a loved one[15]. The pain of loneliness precipitates many self-destructive responses. There are other stress-related behaviors, but this list is representative of the typical problems associated with the grief response.

What we should learn to understand about the stress of death is the prevailing wisdom for managing *any* type of stress: *it is essentially an outgrowth of how each of us perceives and interprets events and priorities.* The way death and loss affect us is primarily a function of how these events are integrated into the developing and changing patterns of life. We can choose to mask the stressors or recognize the limitations *and* advantages that the study of dying holds. For some, the failure to manage this stressor exhausts their energies to adapt. Adaptation energy is finite[16]. But the *will* to adapt must be pre-eminent in any coping style.

Death not only brings to an end the lives of the living but forces survivors in new directions—directions which they often fight against and try to fend off in ways that make living treacherous and continued existence paradoxical. We are never the same once death intrudes into our lives. These endings become sources of relationships between survivors and the unknown[17]. And there are many endings throughout life which necessarily establish new beginnings, new unknowns. Such relationships either bring strength or cause regression as we fail to grasp the complexities of coping with life-death stresses. Deep personal anxiety is a constant companion of the relationship with the unknown, if we choose to limit our awareness of the reality of the death event and its inevitable appearance in every life.

A New Self-Awareness

The important question is: How can we accommodate this inevitable relationship? What can be done to diminish the rigors of the painful trek into the unknown—a trip all must take? Can trauma be better managed? Developing personal awareness of death and the anxiety which follows, understanding the plight of the terminally ill, and their emotions (especially denial, depression and fear), is a start in the right direction. Learning about the common emotions of grieving—anger, guilt and depression—is essential. This beginning will bring us in touch with information that is frequently camouflaged and secreted away.

Furthermore, an examination of the meaning and importance of ritual to survivors, of the various attitudes toward death, and the way children are subjected to the same distortions that have afflicted adults, will generate deep reflection. We can do much to understand the relationship with the unknown—but each of us has to take the initial step. It demands taking risks. However, it is worth the risk if we prevent ignorance from adding to legitimate suffering.

The process of dying, and death itself, is a teacher to be listened to and taken advantage of. Its message is relentless: "I will affect your life in a thousand ways." Perhaps we need to be reminded of Immanuel Kant's centuries-old observation: "It is often necessary to make decisions on the basis of information sufficient for action but insufficient to satisfy the intellect." Developing greater sensory and emotional awareness of options in life is a proven method for enduring radical change and enlarging personal worlds. Overall, it should include the defenses used for coping with life: social support, the unconscious mind, and philosophical and religious beliefs. Too many of us are forced to pursue this inner search at an inopportune time, only when we have come face to face with death, when it has visited us in a most personal way. Then we learn what psychiatrist C. W. Wahl[18] observed: "For it is the consistent experience of psychiatry that any defense which enables us to *persistently* escape the perception of any fundamental internal or external reality is psychologically costly" (p. 19).

Frequently adults, college, and high school students take courses concerning dying and death because of unresolved conflicts based on their past inability to cope with the death of a loved one. A substantial number of my own students fit into this category. They take the course, hoping to find relief. With grief work uncompleted, death anxiety unexplained, with suicidal thoughts, anger and guilt they search for the "why" of the death that has taken a friend or parent. These problems invariably involve limitations of emotional, sensory and spiritual awareness.

Their peers ask: "What study such a topic? What's ailing them?" (Natural questions for those not yet touched by grief and who have neatly suppressed their fears). *Life possesses different meaning for those directly confronting mortality as compared to the typical twentieth-century view of it.* And not everyone needs the same degree of awareness about death. We are at different places in the journey with the unknown.

BREAKING THE CONSPIRACY OF SILENCE

What most of us need is to consider death as a stimulus for learning. At the risk of oversimplification, I must emphasize that the search begins by actively examining death as a legitimate contribution to a liberal arts education, by breaking through the silent curtain that is always drawn as an act of self-defense. This attempt will provide both cultural awareness and mental discipline[19]. It is not easy breaking the conspiracy of silence, but coming together with the common bond of exploring the unknown provides much knowledge, sometimes more than might be expected from the most astute lecturer. A wealth of learning comes from contacts with each other, particularly when the topic is one in which feelings have been repressed for many years. Willingness to share feelings, to flaunt archaic cultural barriers, is essential to the study of thanatology. When emotional factors are excluded the experience is a source of further denying the full meaning of death[20]. Including emotional as well as intellectual content forces an honest confrontation with fear, reassurance that one can cope with the death of a loved one, and that the study of the relationship between life and death is mutually beneficial. Neale[21] suggests that fear of death is linked to life fears:

The conclusion is that our fear of death is basically our fear of life. If our fears were rational they would not prevent us from looking at the inevitability of our own deaths and learning about ourselves and our lives. Since our fears for the most part are irrational, we run away from death, and what we are fleeing as well is our own life. And life is other people. What I am suggesting is that those who are withdrawn from others, who are consumed with guilt, who are too dependent or independent, who are too ambitious or masterful, or too ashamed or proud—these are the ones who fear death the most . . . Our own death is a problem because our own daily living is a problem (pp. 42–43).

Thus, the alliance between life and death is a focal point of immense value. Recognizing and talking about life-death relationships means openly discussing the meaning of life *and* death. How many ways can either be perceived? How is the perception of either related to coping styles? And most important: what gives purpose, meaning and direction to our lives[22]? Answers to these questions will provide fertile ground for developing a new perspective about death.

We must not consider death as a separate entity because life-death experiences are inseparably connected. It is deceptive to discuss death without talking about the life that has been lived, the living which must go on, and the memories which give strength to survivors. Death is surrounded with life; life is surrounded by death. The relationship becomes clear as personal awareness of death increases and avoidance behaviors diminish. (An excellent discussion of the meaning of life and death is found in Kalish,[22] Chapter 3.)

Despite Freud's[23] admonition, "If you would endure life be prepared for death," we play games to veil fears and avoid honest confrontation with a fact of life. As Berne,[24] has frequently suggested, games are a substitute for not facing true feelings.

RECOGNIZING OUR DENIAL

Without authenticity, without being real, it is easy to live the incredible lie, repressing feelings which, if tapped, could initiate an awareness of choices and freedom. And all of this is behavior we have learned previously. What often occurs is that . . . *YOU DENY, I DENY.* Awareness of death always subsists with denial[25]. Death and denial are partners. Daily we read about death or see it portrayed on television. Radio programs are interrupted to bring the news of massive tragedies which happen throughout the world. Death is forever present, but it is not considered real or personal.

After the death of her father, Anna, a student, wrote: "I never saw death as being inevitable—only a distant black cloud that never dared to rain on me or my family's territory. What a rude awakening that was." Death is part fantasy, mystery and intrigue; it is sometimes profoundly unexplainable. But it's out there away from us, happening on another battlefield, not in our lives. And that's a comfortable feeling, since we are able to submerge our natural fears in avoidance created by distance. *We learn to suppress the effect of loss early in life and choose to avoid its implications as we grow older.* Deliberate avoidance is not the same as denial, a defense mechanism of great importance. The former is a choice, the latter operates in the unconscious, while both are parts of our distancing *and* coping techniques.

Distancing Behaviors

It is hard work to preserve this image of indifference. But who are the image makers who ply their trade on the unsuspecting unconscious? The answer is everything in modern society contributes to the deception. Not infrequently, such self-deception offends the dying and "serves to reinforce our own fears"[26]. Consider the following behavior which adds to personal dilemmas.

The extent to which people go to avoid saying the word "death" is almost ludicrous. Do we use the word "death" in our vocabulary? Many of us allude to death with all types of safe phrases such as "passed away," "departed," "went over," or "expired"[18]. (Do people expire or do licenses expire?) We shrink from repeating the obscene words, "She died." Death continues to be pornographic and we dare not mention it as a natural process[27]. These and other euphemisms blur reality, temporarily reduce anxiety and sharply limit self-awareness. They perpetuate denial and avoidance behaviors.

The many professional groups—funeral directors, cemetery salespersons, medical personnel and lawyers, to name but a few—unknowingly contribute to the cover-up. Examine advertisements in your local newspapers. We never purchase a burial plot, we buy a "pre-need memorial estate." A grave is never dug, it's opened and closed. The hearse is a service car. And on and on. Interestingly, it is argued that the play on words may be what people want in order to soften their sorrow at the time of death or during their period of mourning. But the real question is: what does all of this do to individuals when it becomes a way of life as a part of the overall mystique surrounding death? The overindulgence in euphemisms gives death a vague dimension, and as with most euphemisms, it distorts authentic communication—about feelings.

Another distancing technique is utilized when discussions find their way around to the topic of death and many people skillfully change the subject after a very brief exchange. Others refuse to talk about death[1]. They have become experts in handling the uneasy feelings which normally surround such discussions. The easiest way out is to dismiss the topic from conversation, constantly suppress the discomforting tide of thoughts, and intimidate those who refuse to comply. This culminates in an especially devastating consequence when a dying person wants to discuss unfinished business with family members or when the bereaved need to talk about the deceased. The reluctance to communicate provokes additional emotional pain. Surviving siblings may be particularly at risk and forced to suppress feelings[28]. The immediate dismissal of conversation is understandable, given the lack of insight into basic human needs surrounding the dying experience and our ineptness with survivors. However, those who suffer most are those in greatest need of a safe harbor which can be found only in a community of loved ones who see death as a natural event.

Other common distancing (denial?) behaviors find many people putting off making a will, purchasing life insurance, or preplanning funeral arrangements. By and large, survivors are forced to carry the additional burdens and all of the decision-making on ritual when death occurs. Talking about a will or preplanning arrangements is tantamount to admitting that we must reckon with death.

"Protecting" Children

Not infrequently, children are sheltered from death awareness under the guise that they are too young to be confronted with such matters. ("Send the children over to stay with their cousins.") In effect, it is easier to avoid the emotions that would surface in such discussions with them after a loved one has died. It is convenient to tell them that death is like sleeping, the deceased has gone on a trip or that God "needed" the deceased person. These are only a few of the stories that help create confusion and negative stereotypes which eventually must be broken through in a most painful way. Fantasy thinking takes over for children when adults fail to supply honest answers in their attempts to "protect"[29].

Children begin to perpetuate fears just as we perpetutate avoidance and denial.

Denial then is a two-edged defense mechanism: it is an unconscious defense which helps us repress many uncomfortable realities, thereby reducing their initial impact; *denial is necessary for survival.* It has been called "the greatest of all of nature's anesthetics"[30]. Without it, we would have difficulty functioning. At the same time, it is a useful balancing staff, helping in the adaptation to many painful situations.

However, when denial is continuously overused, it becomes an enemy, adding to the difficulties of the trauma connected with death events or other painful loss experiences. Not everyone denies death in all instances. Sometimes we strongly deny and at other times we do not; denial operates at different levels[31]. Although some people are accepting of death, others defy it as exhibited by their daredevil behavior. Still others seem to desire death[32]. Many elderly people, ill for long periods of time, wish that their death would soon occur. At various points in life we may show combinations of the above or switch from one to another, depending on life-change events. A key to personal death awareness is *to analyze our behavior and determine if we are overusing denial* or choosing to avoid what we perceive to be unpleasant. Acquiring this self-knowledge is a crucial step in raising personal death awareness and using the information gained to direct our lives and manage anxiety. Consciously choosing to avoid threatening subjects is one thing, the employment of a very strong denial system is quite another[33].

Accordingly, Freud's view that when we deny we are in fact affirming should be thoroughly studied by all; it provides insight into personal behavior when facing death. A different twist to affirming the reality of death through denying it occurs when we address the topic on a purely intellectual level, strengthening our intellectual armor through study, but still suppressing those tumultuous emotions associated with it. Kastenbaum[34] refers to this practice of self-deception as denial by acceptance.

If we are to overcome being dominated by the social environment that encourages avoidance and denial, it must be confronted and talked about in an open and honest manner. Why is this so important? Because *continuous denial hinders open communication just as suppressing feelings and deliberate avoidance techniques do.* Without quality interchange there is little growth, no awareness of the alliance between life and death.

Since thinking changes emotion, keep in mind that denial or acceptance of death, divorce or any other major loss is not constant, but changes as circumstances and times change. Our experiences, the people we are with at the moment, and the meaning an event holds for us at a specific time, will all impact on the nature and intensity of denying behavior. Extreme denial is the helpmate of fear, and fear can only be conquered by meeting it face-to-face.

In a larger sense then, denial is beneficial at the beginning of a crisis, because it allows time to assimilate the shocking event. But it is not beneficial later, as we finally have to wrestle with the problems and realistic issues that bedevil all of us[35]. Then, persistent denial blocks the process of managing catastrophic change. On rare occasions denial may be the only coping mechanism available if one feels totally inadequate and unable to deal with the event. What fuels denial and avoidance behavior? Can it be changed? Let us examine some possible answers.

INFLUENCES ON BELIEFS ABOUT DEATH

TALK, TALK, AND MORE TALK. Be involved and at least allowed to air ideas and opinions — even if not allowed to participate in the ultimate decision. My parents being more honest with their feelings and fears — and sharing them with me — would have helped me to be more prepared.

> Janine, a senior, on the death of
> her grandmother

Our present beliefs about death are the result of a combination of factors which began early in life. As we examine these factors, the reader may wish to relate them to his/her own life experiences. This exercise will result in an increase in self-knowledge, enhancing the creation of new assumptions about personal death awareness.

Parental Influence

There is evidence to suggest that parents influence the degree of death anxiety in their children[36]. Attitudes and beliefs about death are learned. They eventuate in specific learned responses including depression, fear, anger, guilt, optimism, or hope. Personal experience with death or with others suffering through the grief process makes lasting marks on our memories. If we look back on what our parents have said about death, *or more importantly what they have not said*, we can begin to visualize the origin of our views. Communication occurs whether intended or not: to say nothing is to send a message. Death education occurs one way or another. The entire family plays a significant role in the development of feelings and concepts about death[37]. If parental beliefs about death were filled with confusion, mystery, fear and horror, it is likely they will be passed on to impressive young minds. The power of suggestion on the unconscious mind becomes a terrifying force in this instance.

On the other hand, if death was treated as being a part of life, as an inevitable force in the universe, i.e., an event which gives the lives of survivors meaning, death will form the basis of an important legacy. Were you shielded from death in your family? Was a deceased family member memorialized as though he or she was a saint? Were you whisked off to a neighbor's house when death occurred? Was death a taboo topic? Did non-verbal communication tell you a lot about what your family felt about life-death matters?

Many children are deprived of role models who are open about the reality of loss in its many forms, who believe that loss is a condition of existence. Included in parental influences are the religious and ethnic orientations about death which are part of our overall educational experience. Interestingly, community and ethnic rituals surrounding death become part of the pattern of meaning established about the relationship between life and death. It follows that when we have to participate in ritual which is not clearly understood, or when we are forced to act in a specific way, e.g., touching the deceased, such experiences have a lasting effect on attitudes and anxiety levels.

Myths and Misconceptions

Historically, myths have influenced the beliefs and behavior of people. When bloodletting was considered a sound medical practice, many died (including George Washington). When the world was considered to be flat, only a few persons would venture far into the ocean. Until the advent of the germ theory, curing the sick was attempted by what today would be classified as medical quackery. What is significant to consider for this discussion is that myths and venerable half-truths about death and grief prompt behavior which is fatal to our emotional and physical well-being. *What we believe to be true controls how we behave* [38]. If the basis for action is rooted in falsehoods, responses to death-related experiences will take courses of action of perilous consequences. Fundamental assumptions about death must be based on fact, not fiction. Here are a few common myths and misconceptions which prevail:

1. Crying and "carrying on" over the death of a loved one is a sign of weakness.
2. Men must "be strong" and not show their emotions.
3. Funeral directors always try to take advantage of grieving people. (And they always wear black suits.)
4. Dead people sometimes move or sit-up in the casket because of physiological changes in muscle tissue.
5. When a child dies, parents have each other to grieve with.
6. "Going to pieces" is abnormal grief.
7. To regress, to "act immature" when grieving, is abnormal.
8. Everyone needs to openly express every feeling.
9. Grief can be sidestepped or evaded indefinitely.
10. Children under the age of seven seldom experience "real" grief.

Such mistaken beliefs lead to increased fear and family conflicts when major loss occurs, to excessive drug use, embarrassment, and a host of unexpressed feelings. If you hold one or more of these beliefs, can you determine how they were learned?

Negative Stereotypes

The symbol of death for centuries has been the skull and crossbones or a skeleton carrying a scythe. (We are "cut down" in the prime of life.) Death is the Grim Reaper. For many people, death is always a tyrant— ugly, unnatural, bad, to be fought, and which is never expected. Those images form a pattern of negativism which accompanies many early death conceptions. To illustrate: Toys sold at Halloween for commercial reasons often reinforce a scary, horror-filled message about death at the unconscious level, although they are supposedly designed for laughs and enjoyment. Examples include toys where candy is placed in little plastic coffins stamped "Mr. Bones," or where a skeleton hand comes out of a coffin to snatch a coin placed on its edge. Unfortunately, for some children, economic considerations of the business world negatively influence beliefs about death early in life. Every assumption about death we possess is a product of experiences we have been subjected to in a society which pretends that death is non-existent.

Children also observe some adults cry at a wake and are not sure why. There are no explanations of ritual or the normalcy of emotional expression. Death is envisioned as having nothing to do with life or how life should be lived. It is a visitation of punishment, deemed as something that always steals but never gives in return. It is quite easy to develop great sensitivity to the negative messages which are constantly sent about death and loss. This ready acceptance of death imagery fits into the quest for things—goods, materials, toys—at the expense of the truth that life *does* have its problems.

Opportunities for Open Discussion

One of the most beguiling experiences in youth or adulthood is to have an idea, a story, a joy to share, or a problem to solve and not be able to find someone who will be open and receptive to it. Time and time again the search for meaningful exchange about death is blocked by someone who chooses to avoid the subject, is fearful of discussing it, or has decided that "this is neither the time nor place for such a conversation." Among the most damaging sources of illusions is when the young are unable to receive answers to questions about death. A child's fantasies about death are worse than the most devastating truth[39]. Still, children are left to their fantasies. The reality of death is excluded from the life of the child[40]. There are thousands of stories of children who, having asked a question about a death-related topic (for example, the cemetery they are driving by), have been given a humorous, discussion-ending answer ("That's a granite orchard"). Or, no answer was given; silence was mute testimony. Even dying children view death as an "inappropriate topic of conversation with adults"[41].

Equally perplexing are situations in which meaningful dialogue begins, but as the questions increase and become more difficult to answer, a distraught adult flatly refuses to continue. The conversation usually ends with, "Let's change the subject, I've had enough of this." In the extreme, when one pushes to reopen discussion or brings the topic up on a later occasion, he or she is suspected of being morbid or preoccupied with death. To put it mildly, it is implied that to seek answers about death phenomenon is to be "unusual" or different. The child (or adult) is stigmatized for searching for truth, and the stigma holds for long periods of time. Most professionals associated with the death system (funeral directors, cemetery workers, death educators) have felt a similar stigma.

The inability to find someone to talk with about death at every level of development—from childhood to old age—breeds confusion, suppression of feelings, and fosters the creation of the death-taboo feeling. Conversely, when we find adults who treat the discussion of death as a normal subject of inquiry, who attempt to answer questions about loss to the best of their ability then much of the mystery is stripped away. It helps reduce the number of fears which "unknowns" create. Paradoxically, in talking to children about death, we help ourselves in confronting our own feelings[29]. Open and honest discussion of loss becomes a major influence on early attitude development, and is a powerful force in the formation of coping patterns in later life. Alice described her need to talk and be open in the following way:

> I took a course in mental and emotional health which gave me a chance to learn about death, and to understand my feelings about death as well as the feelings of other people my age. If people could talk about death in a setting such as a classroom (or other) it would bring the whole subject of death into perspective. Everyone will die, so if we realize and accept this, wouldn't life seem more precious and worthwhile, and death seem less frightening and far away?

The words "to understand my feelings about death as well as the feelings of other people my age" is one of the major goals of open discussion. Without it the analysis of death-related phenomena is stifled.

Values

What we perceive to be important and of personal value also gives rise to our conception of death. Religious beliefs, for example, have long been a defense against the fear of death[42-43]. In short, a faith in something outside the self, in a supreme being who gives and takes according to a divine plan, helps place death in perspective. At once, intrinsic faith becomes a transitional experience; the deceased is in a new and higher state of existence; death is seen as a *necessity* to make life meaningful. Those with a clear sense of their own values are much more likely to see death in realistic instead of fearful terms[44].

Social values shape the response of the bereaved, the dying and support networks. Irrespective of religious orientation, whether atheist or agnostic, how one values people, material goods, interpersonal relations, or bank accounts says something about what has or has not been learned from death. Quality interpersonal relationships teach us much about the needs of others as well as ourselves. They provide a refuge in time of crisis, a source of compassion to work through loss experiences, while offering a means of reordering priorities as we experience change. Other people help us learn the lessons needed in order to adjust to life-death experiences, and to be able to see that death perceptions are amenable to change.

The intensity of belief in a particular value system will affect the level of anxiety and fear of death. How we value others reflects the way we use death as teacher. Part of this value comes from the culture we live in. "Cultural attitudes toward war and violence also have considerable impact on young adults. Thoughts about death among young adults have always been influenced by the prevailing cultural climate, including the peace-war status" (34, p. 33). The value one learns to place on the sacredness of life heavily influences behavior, both death related and non-death related.

First Death Experiences

Recall your first experience with death. Was it the death of a pet, a friend, or a relative? Put this book down, close your eyes, and go back in time to recreate that first event; slowly rerun it in your mind's eye. How did the adults around you react to that death, and what did it mean to them and to you. Maybe you have chosen to suppress the event. The death of a close relative, one you loved deeply, inevitably affects your life. A part of your personal world is now gone forever. The support, encouragement and interest that the person previously gave is no longer forthcoming; the continuity is broken. Your self-image temporarily changed. How these experiences unfolded, how you were supported, what was said, and who helped or abandoned you are a part of your present beliefs and assumptions about death. They may have had little impact or they may stand out quite clearly in your mind. But through the years your experiences with death have brought about changed beliefs, mixed emotions, and many questions still to be answered. Of equal consequence is the understanding that childhood fears and dreams may affect us now just as a real death could[40]. The strongest source of beliefs about death is the experience we have had with it (or the lack of such experience). It is also the basis upon which coping skills are developed and tested.

Monumental differences in adult beliefs about death surface when those who have never experienced the death of a close family member are compared with those who have endured the event. Those not yet survivors tend to intellectualize the subject and are often outspoken in their beliefs. Those who are survivors seem to have developed an increased sensitivity concerning their relationships with others and the reality of death; they have acquired a new reverence for life. This is especially true if the individual was with the family member when the death occurred. Jung places this variance in perspective in a statement made decades ago: "The question of the meaning and worth of life never becomes more urgent or more agonizing than when we see the final breath leave a body which a moment before was living." Such an experience brings to consciousness many deep, philosophical considerations.

Age

Increased age is also a common factor involved in the perception of loss experiences and beliefs about death. As we get older, our view of the world takes on many modifications. A considerable amount of research suggests that fear of death diminishes with age[45-46]. The child's attitude toward death, that it is reversible or personified, contrasts sharply with that of a grandparent. The latter's experiences with loss over many years has provided insights which often bring positive changes in beliefs. Not surprisingly, the death attitudes of young people in the prime of life and beginning to think about their life-work are quite unrealistic, as many view their own deaths as a long way off[45].

In the final analysis, the confrontation with death is essentially a *confrontation with our personal beliefs and whether or not we are open to change.* Attitudes and beliefs are the father of the action and are of critical significance in how we *react.* Perhaps our beliefs about death need to be examined and changed, in order to use them as a means to influence life choices. If we continue to believe that dying, grieving, funerals and the like are eerie, bad or unnatural, we will behave accordingly, with avoidance, lies, isolation and blunted feelings. We may even have to continue lying to ourselves as a defense against being hurt and from increasing anxiety which becomes amplified through self-deception.

In his book, *Western Attitudes Toward Death,* French historian Phillipe Aries[47] writes:

> In our day, in approximately a third of a century, we have witnessed a brutal revolution in traditional ideas and feelings, a revolution so brutal that social observers have not failed to be struck by it. It is really an absolutely unheard of phenomenon. Death, so omnipresent in the past that it was familiar, would be effaced, would disappear. It would become shameful and forbidden (p. 85).

The death bed scenes of the past, with the grieving family gathered in the home, have become an exception to the rule. *Currently, over eighty percent of deaths occur in institutions outside of the home* [48]. The most significant result of this evolution from home to caregiving facilities is two-fold: first, there has been a loss of invaluable learning about death as death has been removed to unfamiliar (and often avoidable) surroundings; the death vigil is no longer a part of life experiences. Secondly, many family members are forced to resort to their imaginations about what happens in hospitals and nursing homes and how people die.

When it comes to death, we conjur up devastating horror scenes as death occurs in sterile settings devoid of open exchange. Not knowing the experience by having seen it unfold in secure surroundings leaves us with second-hand accounts from other family members, or (worse yet!) seemingly cold and distant medical personnel. Information passed on by word of mouth has an incredible way of being recast and misinterpreted by both sender and receiver. The result places an added emotional burden on the dying and survivors alike; but more than that, institutionalization keeps death out of the home and neighborhood while closeting it in little enclaves, thus decreasing our individual proximity to it. This displacement of the death scene robs families of opportunities for emotional learning at all ages and keeps a fact of life comfortably hidden. It also feeds into hidden fears.

The Media

At no time in the history of the world have the mass media—which represent essentially the views of others put into print, on television or radio—been able to influence the thoughts and behaviors of others to the extent they do today. Although more often accomplished by design, distortions also occur in subtle, unexpected ways. Fantasized death has achieved great prominence in the mass media[49]. Although, the media can be a meaningful teacher, witness the messages about death which daily come into our homes: "Four Slain in Robbery Attempt," "Mishap Claims Two," "Train Derailment Causes Tragedy" or "Freighter Sinks With No Survivors." These and similar news stories, coupled with television dramas and movies, put across patently untrue messages like the following:

- Death is essentially an accident.
- Grief is a brief one or two hour long ordeal.
- Cancer patients usually die as in "Love Story."
- Death is quickly forgotten by survivors as life goes on.
- Death happens to the "bad guys" most of the time.
- Survivors need little long-term support.

It is unfortunate but true that we are captive of the whims of the media. Furthermore, the secularization of death has led to its deritualization encouraging hidden mourning[1].

There have been many hoaxes perpetuated on people, from the Cardiff giant to the traveling circus side-shows. They pale in significance to the cruel hoax of the present century which makes dying and death a fictitious will-of-the-wisp. In its place comes the media's excessive emphasis on youth, beauty, and instant success. Aging is seen as avoidable and unreal; perpetual youth is king. (Witness the number of face lifts, nose jobs, eyelid tucks, breast implants and similar surgery which cost over $4 billion a year.) So much of advertising takes advantage of the body beautiful, pushing the message that it is easily obtained. Nevertheless, it adds to the presumption of immortality and emphasizes perpetual happiness, free of sadness.

Witness this death message that children are brought up with from television: violence is a major cause of death. By the time a young person has graduated from high school he or she has witnessed thousands of video murders. This is coupled with the message that aggressiveness pays. At the same time, children view numerous advertisements promoting toy guns, tanks, assault craft, and other war paraphernalia. Television has become the plug-in drug[50]. Children usually become immune to violence as they are more and more exposed to it and grow to nurture unrealistic views of life[51]. Such false views affect attitudes about life and death.

Industry and Technology

Industrialization influences people to focus more on products and less on processes. In particular, a technological environment possesses great power to manipulate people. Productivity, the gross national product, new inventions, more efficient assembly line methods, etc., all point to an emphasis on goods, sales and the accumulation of material possessions. Robots have replaced people in the work force, a truly dehumanizing factor in modern life. The greatly increased importance of topping the previous year's quota levels; the incessant competition among members of the business world, and the many stresses which new demands place on people in twentieth century America, dramatically affect patterns of living. We are a truly mobile society. Technology has shortened the travel time between distant points, but at the expense of individual privacy. Technology has made life easier in some ways, but the needs for warmth and sensitivity have given away to further depersonalization[52]. The work ethic has been transformed into the consumer ethic—one can buy whatever is needed, even intimacy. Western affluence and the tradition of rugged individualism tend to eliminate thoughts of death, and minimize the importance of death experiences for improving the quality of life.

While industrialization has benefited millions of Americans, as well as other countries throughout the world, the effects of the affluence it creates tend to divide and create the illusion that interdependence is no longer important for mental health and adapting to change. Rugged individualism has lessened the importance of high quality interpersonal exchange which is essential when we confront problems of living and dying. The danger of this overemphasis on "doing your own thing" is to destroy the interdependence that is so desperately needed in times of massive societal and cultural upheaval.

As we alienate ourselves from each other and become enmeshed in the race for bettering living standards, it becomes evident that we face the danger of forgetting the historical lessons which have evolved from unity in the face of crisis. Technological growth always carries with it the danger of losing our perspective in the face of massive change. Historically, technology has always been a source of anxiety for members of society; it uproots, insulates and isolates[53].

Because we have focused more on getting from others and less on giving to others, we have eliminated avenues of emotional learning which, in the past, came from the intimacy of shared relationships; we have unwittingly allowed technological advances to become the new theology. In a real sense, then, we may rightly ask: "If we can go to the moon, build intercontinental ballistic missiles, and fly faster than the speed of sound, how come we still have to die? Hasn't technology given us 'heroic measures' in the health sciences so that many of the sick and dying are virtually forced to survive (sometimes contrary to their express wishes)?" Given these attitudes, it is easy to suppose that soon death will no longer be necessary, that practical immortality may be "just around the corner." Welcome cryonics.

Because we can project our thoughts, because we can look upon death as we look upon an unfortunate happening (or even as an unfair event and/or a stupid error on the victim's part), we are able to push death into the furthest recesses of our minds. Having even envisioned a life *without* death, and especially since our daily advances in technology cause us to expect another miracle with each new day, we refuse to allow death to interfere with our drinking the heady wine of progress. By intoxicating ourselves with "progress," it is much easier to ignore death and divorce it from its true relationship to life.

A Lack of Intimacy in Communication Limits Awareness

Finally, much of our learning about life, death and how we function and adapt to crises is the product of intimate communication (i.e., gut-level communication with our "significant others"). Through talking to those whom we cherish, we learn important lessons that serve us in time of need. The *quality* of a relationship is directly dependent on the *quality* of communication[54]. Most of us are not skilled in "gut-level" communication. Therefore, our relationships are often shallow. We will observe in Chapter 4 what respondents in the Young Adult Study tell us about the importance of this type of dialogue with family and friends when coping with loss.

Clearly, a major assault on death anxiety is made as we develop skills in communicating feelings. This is a two-way process. It involves learning both how to transmit and receive information as well as being sensitive to symbolic and nonverbal gestures. Once we form meaningful relationships, we are never the same persons again. Honest, open discussion about death-related topics with those who have such relationships break down the myths, stereotypes, and misunderstandings formed in the past. They cause us to reevaluate our positions and develop new assumptions and beliefs about life-death events. Authentic interpersonal interchange heightens sensitivity to the feelings of others, as well as our own, uncovers mutual problems and anxieties, and provides feedback which helps us define where we are and what we need in order to move forward. The price of all of this: we must *risk* sharing feelings.

By not sharing feelings, by repressing the very emotions needing expression, *we become astute performers in stating as true what we are not really feeling.* This is very important to understand because this deception is a protective device learned early in life in order to survive in an impersonal world. By wearing masks which attempt to portray images of strength and control around death, we simply build higher walls and thus become further out of touch with true feelings. As Montaigne once wrote: "We must strip the mask from things as well as from persons; when it is off we shall find beneath only the same death which a valet or a mere chambermaid passed through not long ago without fear." The refusal to unmask burns the very bridges which would span the void between fear and acceptance. This regressive behavior moves in a vicious circle of suppression—stress—renewed distancing—and then more suppression.

Putting masks aside for the moment will allow development of intimate communication and concern—the beginning of reducing death anxiety and fear. A young student put it most eloquently when she said: "When we can honestly share what emotions we feel with another human being, life, and in turn death, has so much more meaning." Fearing death is not abnormal any more than fearing the assortment of unknowns with which we are all confronted. Our negative assumptions and beliefs about death are very much like bad habits, very difficult to get rid of, *but* they can be altered.

We turn next to a "death" most of us have experienced, but for many, one which has long-term consequences—the break-up of a love relationship. And we shall see how the tenacious holding on to faulty assumptions and beliefs about love and relationships leads to a grief response of devastating proportions.

REFERENCES

1. Stephenson, J. *Death, grief, and mourning.* New York: Free Press, 1985.
2. Becker, E. *The denial of death.* New York: Free Press, 1973.
3. Miyuki, M. Dying isagi-yoku. *Journal of Humanistic Psychology,* 1978, 18⁴, 37–44.
4. Bowlby, J. *Attachment and loss* (vol. III). New York: Basic Books, 1980.
5. Lifton, R. *The broken connection.* New York: Simon & Schuster, 1980.
6. Shneidman, E. The college student and death. In H. Feifel (Ed.). *New meanings of death,* New York: McGraw-Hill, 1977.
7. Feifel, H. (Ed.). *The Meaning of death.* New York: McGraw-Hill, 1959.
8. May, R. *Existence.* New York: Basic Books, 1958.
9. Hardt, D. *Death: The final frontier.* Englewood Cliffs, NJ: Prentice-Hall, 1979.
10. Simpson, M. Death education—Where is thy sting. *Death Education,* 1979, 3, 165–173.
11. Leviton, D. Death education. In H. Feifel (Ed.). *New meanings of death.* New York: McGraw-Hill, 1977.
12. Kavanaugh, R. *Facing death.* Baltimore: Penguin, 1974.
13. Peck, M. *The road less traveled.* New York: Simon and Schuster, 1978.
14. Lynch, J. *The broken heart.* New York: Basic Books, 1977.
15. Schultz, R. *The psychology of death, dying and bereavement.* Reading, MA: Addison Wesley, 1978.
16. Selye, H. *Stress without distress.* New York: J.B. Lippincott, 1974.
17. Keleman, S. *Living your dying.* New York: Random House, 1974.
18. Wahl, C. The fear of death. In H. Feifel (Ed.). *The meaning of death.* New York: McGraw-Hill, 1959.
19. Morgan, J. Death education as a liberal art. *Death Education,* 1984, 8, 289–297.
20. Kastenbaum, R. New fantasies in the American death system. *Death Education,* 1982, 6, 155–166.

21. Neale, R. *The art of dying.* New York: Harper and Row, 1973.
22. Kalish, R. *Death grief and caring relationships.* Belmont, CA: Wadsworth, 1985.
23. Freud, S. Thoughts for the time on war and death. *Collected Papers.* London: Hogarth Press, 1948.
24. Berne, E. *Games people play.* New York: Grove Press, 1967.
25. Worden, J. & Proctor, W. *Personal death awareness.* Englewood Cliffs, NJ: Prentice-Hall, 1976.
26. Shepard, M. *Someone you love is dying.* New York: Charter, 1975.
27. Gorer, G. *Death, grief, and mourning in contemporary Britain.* London: Cresset, 1965.
28. Rosen, H. Prohibitions against mourning in childhood sibling loss. *Omega,* 1984–85, 15⁴, 307–316.
29. Jackson, E. *Telling a child about death.* New York: Hawthorne, 1965.
30. Shneidman, E. *Voices of death.* New York: Bantam, 1982.
31. Weisman, A. *On dying and denying.* New York: Behavioral Publications, 1972.
32. Pattison, E. *The experience of dying.* Englewood Cliffs, NJ: Prentice-Hall, 1977.
33. Lazarus, R. The costs and benefits of denial. In J. J. Spinetta and P. Deasy-Spinetta (Eds.). *Living with childhood cancer.* St. Louis: Mosby, 1981.
34. Kastenbaum, R. We covered death today. *Death Education,* 1977, 1, 85–92.
35. Lazarus, R. & Golden, G. The function of denial in stress, coping, and aging. In J. McGaugh & S. Kiesler, *Aging, biology, and behavior.* New York: Academic Press, 1981.
36. Templer, D., Ruff, C. & Franks, C. Death anxiety: Age, sex, and parental resemblance in diverse populations. *Developmental Psychology,* 1971, 4, 108.
37. Wass, H & Scott, M. Middle school students' death concepts and concerns. *Middle School Journal,* 1978, 9,¹, 10–12.
38. Maltz, M. *Psychocybernetics.* New York: Pocket Books, 1969.
39. Kliman, A. In the movie *What man shall live and not see death.* Films Incorporated, 1144 Wilmette Ave., Wilmette, IL. 60091.
40. Gordon, A. and Klass, D. *They need to know.* Englewood Cliffs, NJ: Prentice-Hall, 1979.
41. Bluebond-Langer, M. *The private worlds of dying children.* Princeton, NJ: Princeton University Press, 1978.
42. Templer, D. Death anxiety in religiously very involved persons. *Psychological Reports,* 1972, 31, 361–62.
43. Martin, D. & Wrightsman, L. The relationship between religious behavior and concern about death. *Journal of Social Psychology,* 1965, 65, 317–323.
44. Dacy, J. *Adolescents today.* Santa Monica, CA: Goodyear, 1979.
45. Kalish, R. & Reynolds, D. *Death and ethnicity: A psychocultural study.* Farmingdale, NY: Baywood, 1981.
46. Fiefel, H. & Branscomb, A. Who's afraid of death? *Journal of Abnormal Psychology,* 1973, 81, 282–288.
47. Aries, P. *Western attitudes toward death from the middle ages to the present.* Baltimore: Johns Hopkins University Press, 1974.
48. Bok, S. *Lying: Moral choice in public and private life.* New York: Pantheon, 1978.

49. Corr, C. Reconstructing the changing face of death. In H. Wass (Ed.). *Dying: Facing the facts.* New York: McGraw-Hill, 1979.
50. Winn, M. *The plug-in drug.* New York: Viking, 1977.
51. Sharapin, H. *It's happening right there in your living room.* Speech delivered at the third annual conference of the Forum for Death Education and Counseling, Kansas City, MO, 1980.
52. Preston, J. Toward an anthropology of death. *Intellect,* 1977, April, 343–344.
53. Boorstin, D. Tomorrow: The republic of technology. *Time,* January 17, 1977, 36–38.
54. Powell, J. *Why am I afraid to tell you who I am?* Niles, IL: Argus, 1969.

Chapter Three

THE BREAKUP OF A LOVE RELATIONSHIP AS A "DEATH REACTION"

The essence of everything is letting go of the past.
        Gerald Jampolsky,
        "Love Is the Only Answer"
        in *Creativity In Death Education and Counseling*

All living relationships are in the process of change, of expansion, and must be perpetually building themselves new forms.
        Ann Morrow Lindbergh in *A Gift From The Sea*

Our lives and our behaviors are much more profoundly affected by the beliefs we hold unconsciously than by the beliefs we hold consciously.
        Willis Harman and Howard Rheingold in
        Higher Creativity

I spoke with an Episcopal priest who does counseling. I also had a very intimate discussion with my mother and a close friend. All told me to deal with each day individually and to vent all my energy into projects which could be easily finished that day. This was in order to develop a feeling of worth—and that the world was not at an end.

Perhaps being more realistic about life in general would have prepared me. I was in a fantasy and was not facing reality. Life is tough and one does not escape it. One must deal with it. It may feel overwhelming but you can survive.

        Don, a college senior, on the breakup of a
        love relationship

Love is a force which affects everyone's life in some way. As many people have experienced, the severing of a relationship which had been a source of happiness and security for months or years is often catastrophic. And as Don and most others realize, albeit too late, most people do not look at their relationships realistically. They are based all too often on questionable assumptions and beliefs. At the same time, however, there are many breakups due to the dramatic shifts in attitudes, values, and interests which occur during these ever-changing years[1].

In this chapter I suggest that some breakups result in a grief response as intense as those associated with the death of a loved one due to the illusions of romantic love and the childhood beliefs they are based upon. Having compared data from survivors who have experienced losses through death or a breakup, similar physical and emotional reactions become apparent. The implications for relating to those grieving a breakup as well as our own personal response to this type of loss is explored.

EMOTIONAL AND PHYSICAL RESPONSES

If loss is a central theme of life, as I suggest, then its impact will vary depending upon the individual's unique traits and learned coping skills. Of particular significance are the effects different types of losses have on the same individual. Our fantasy that only death is a major loss and all other losses are of secondary importance leaves much to be desired. There is compelling evidence to suggest quite the opposite. A major reason for this are the illusions and faulty assumptions about love relationships which an individual holds. They are similar to those surrounding death.

It can be argued that *any* separation from a loved one, through divorce, the breakup of a love relationship, a temporary geographical separation, or separation from divorced parents produces a grief reaction for *some* individuals that is as intense as a death reaction is for others. Indeed, marriage counselors and therapists argue that divorce is as devastating as death for those involved[2-3]. A young woman writing to me about her divorce shared the following.

> A friend who had taken a death and dying course said, 'It might be like dying' and explained Kubler-Ross' stages to me. I said, 'It's worse than if he died because he *consciously chose* to leave,' and at that point I knew that K–R's stages apply to grief over any loss, not just loss of life. Knowing about these stages and being able to apply them to myself helped more than I can say to convince me I wasn't going crazy; that I was reacting and behaving normally.

(Kubler-Ross's "stages" provide a model depicting how some individuals die, and is also considered the dying person's grief.) What is important to draw from this anecdote is the devastating effect rejection had on this woman, in view of her perception that her husband had consciously chosen to abandon her. She experienced many physical reactions: chest pains, hyperventilation, lower backache, and pain from the back of her head into her neck and shoulder blades. The harrowing fear that she could not help her children cope and would not be able to obtain money for basic necessities was overwhelming.

Other people see a breakup of a love relationship as equally overpowering as 21-year-old Sonja suggests.

> Preparing for the end of a love relationship is different because often the end is unforseeable. It's hard to imagine not being together. Death is easier to prepare for and I think that courses offered at school are a great help to people who have either encountered the death of someone close or will eventually do so in the future. Understanding basic loss patterns, and seeing yourself pass through each phase, helps you know you will get over it.

Sonja's remarks are obviously debatable, but they *represent beliefs which strongly affect the nature of the grief response.* We scoff at the idea that anything except death can be devastating, but that is only because of our inordinant view that death is unnatural, a force which destroys but never redeems.

The large number of breakups which occur among the young are perceived by them as major loss events[4]. During the critical adolescent-young adult years, when an individual is establishing an identity, a breakup takes on special meaning. It is a "death" in the true sense of the word. However, the tendency of parents and older adults is to dismiss the serious disorganization and chaos accompanying it. From the griever's perspective there is a fundamental difference when a breakup is compared with the death of a loved one: the support system is considered inadequate because many support persons minimize the intensity and depth of the loss. It is commonly perceived by parents and other adults as simply a part of a person's growth and development, an event that everyone experiences. Therefore, the end of "puppy love" is to be expected and should be easily assimilated. (Why isn't this rationale used with divorce among older adults or the death of a loved one?) However, this does not ease the searing pain that accompanies many of these breakups. Nor is it an event that can be quickly forgotten, as the individuals return to the mainstream of living again. Like grieving a death, much time is needed to adjust without the presence of the ex.

If we ask an older person with whom we have a particularly close relationship to tell us about the first love in his or her life, we are amazed at how similar the story is to the one which we or one of our younger friends, might tell. Examine the following reactions to a breakup to underscore the devastating toll that it takes.

(1) It just took lots of time to forget and not until almost 1½ years after am I comfortable to date again and I still think of him. I was the one who broke it off and felt *so* guilty and took it hard.

(2) When I broke up with my boyfriend, I stayed in bed for *two weeks* without eating or moving—I just cried. My two best friends stayed with me the whole time talking to me . . . I really was in terrible shape, and I don't think I would have made it without them.

(3) I was determined to cope by largely forcing myself to become more independent and self-reliant. Friends at first were helpful, although the novelty of helping a friend cope (big ego-builder for many) soon wore off. So, I compensated by turning to alcohol and drugs. I write, take walks, read, drink, and smoke pot when depression hits. I have become much more wary and cynical concerning future love relationships.

(4) I always felt nauseous and lost my appetite completely. One month had gone by after we broke up and I had not eaten a thing. I lost twenty pounds and went to the family doctor. I was really weak and could not do much of anything. I slept a real lot and never went out of the house.

These examples illustrate not only the death-like response to severed relationships, but several other notable factors as well. There is often deep shock and loss of self-control. Physical reactions are extremely intense; one seeks security, supportive friends, ways to cope with strong feelings. The crushing loss of self-esteem maximizes the struggle to adapt.

Common problems of guilt are experienced much more by women than men. Whether the woman initiates the breakup or not, she often feels guilty. In the latter instance, she feels that the breakup is her fault even though the male may have initiated it, and if she had acted differently, it could have been prevented. There is some evidence to suggest this may be due to woman's greater interpersonal sensitivity. Given this sensitivity, these feelings are seen as being normal, when in truth the guilt is not cause and effect guilt but rather neurotic in origin and expression. Neurotic guilt parallels many grief responses associated with death as well as a breakup.

On balance, perhaps the most damaging of all emotions to deal with are the insecurity and fear which are experienced. Many believe that they are unable to face life without a companion and immediately feel the pain of loneliness. The intensity of these feelings is difficult to understand if we have not recently experienced them or been around someone who is trying to deal with them. These individuals may not want to be left alone for long periods of time and believe they will not be able to cope with their pain. They need the comfort of trusted friends; the experience is catastrophic.

A COMPARISON OF REACTIONS

The important but controversial question remains: "Can the breakup of a love relationship have an impact on an individual similar to the death of a loved one?" For some people, it obviously does. In interviews with young adults who have experienced both types of losses, and in the comparison of their physical and emotional responses to both kinds of losses, the evidence strongly suggests that a "death reaction" to a breakup occurs[5]. First, a wider variety of feelings is often expressed. For example, our research indicates that more young adults reported anger, guilt, loneliness, hatred, rejection and depression. We additionally observed evidence that frustration, self-pity, emptiness, reduction in self-confidence, and a feeling of being lost were more associated with the breakup of a love relationship than with the death experience. Two of these feelings are of special significance: rejection and a reduction in self-confidence.

Although mutually agreed-upon breakups occur, they are the exception, not the rule. Most breakups are initiated by one of the two people involved: it is not mutually agreed upon. Sometimes a breakup comes without warning. At other times it is expected, but that does not especially lessen the pain. (The same is true when death is expected.) The outcome is that one of the two is filled with feelings of rejection. Rejection is a most powerful psychological force in shaping loss responses. This was emphasized by a freshman who wrote: "Nothing has really helped me. I thought I had started to get over him, but I haven't. He left me for someone else, and I can't deal with the rejection. When I got back up to school I was looking for love in everyone." To be rejected is to lose all self-esteem. This is especially destructive if the individual had low self-esteem to begin with. Joyce put it in the following perspective: "Rejection seemed to be twice as bad because I didn't like myself enough to bounce back." Betty described it this way:

Another person I am associated with experienced a similar loss. Her philosophy was that she was never secure in herself, never liked herself; would she ever be happy with a man? She began to see good things in herself and this rubbed off on me. We realized, together, that *we* are the only persons that we *have* to live with, so we should care about ourselves.

It is helpful to recognize that rejection spawns anger and hostility in the person rejected. Venting these feelings and recognizing them as an expected outcome of rejection proves healthy in the grief process. When anger is not directed outward it may be experienced as guilt, lowered self-esteem or depression[6]. Regretably, anger is sometimes vented on innocent friends who misinterpret the action and assume it is directed at them in a very personal way. In fact, this is not the case; it is simply a response to feeling stripped of dignity and importance. Anger expressed by people in crises should always be considered as a coping anger, never as personal. Rejection, coupled with low self-esteem, usually indicates a longer, more intense grief response. Jo Anne explains:

> Time away from the guy helped to dull the pain of not being with him all the time, but still, every time I see him now all the hurt and rejection comes back and mostly a sense of wanting him back desperately.

Notice the inherent assumption that Jo Anne holds: "I cannot live without him." This default assumption and a lack of self-confidence goes hand in hand with low self-esteem. It becomes apparent that when crises occur, those lacking confidence in their abilities to overcome and confront the reality of their breakups have increasingly difficult times in adjusting to them. In looking back on their experiences, many young adults felt that they would have coped more successfully if they had been more self-confident. Meg, a freshman, explains: "I would have been able to cope with the loss much better if I had had more self-confidence or someone to help encourage my self-confidence. As it was, only one person was really concerned and she had no *real* comfort to offer."

The reaction to being devalued as a person is withdrawal from the world. This withdrawal heightens anxiety and prolongs pain, but is a natural response, found in numerous interpersonal conflicts. "If I had been conditioned to believe," said Sara, "that I too am important and worthwhile, I don't think I would have to work so hard at believing it each time I suffer a loss. I would be able to put my energies toward coping instead of withdrawing." Talking with others is a lifeline to rebuilding self-confidence: their continued support maintains it.

In terms of physical reactions, twice as many young adults reported that vomiting accompanied their breakup as compared with those who had experienced the death of a loved one. Obviously, this is reflective of great emotional trauma. Respondents undergoing a breakup also reported they suffered from insomnia to a greater extent, and experienced more digestive upsets besides vomiting. These two symptoms are common in grief responses associated with the death of a loved one, but appear to be *more intense* for many young adults when a breakup has occurred. Are all of these physical and emotional reactions the result of a kind of tunnel vision in which individual perspective regarding what is really important has been diminished? Hardly. They are the result of beliefs and assumptions held about relationships, the prospect of recovering from loss, and the fear of not finding enduring love.

CAUSES OF INTENSE RESPONSES

Here are some examples of the assumptions and beliefs in the words of respondents in the Young Adult Study which are part of the excessive reactions to the severing of relationships.

1. There's not really any way to rationally cope with love.
2. Most people don't look at reality within the relationship.
3. For everything I did I needed to have his approval.
4. I think we both grew up and were afraid to let go.
5. Sometimes I think I will never get over it.
6. I thought of it (the breakup) as a failure.
7. I was willing to take any chances to win back his acceptance of me.
8. I had the feeling that most of the blame for the breakup was on me.
9. I always had thought our relationship would never, ever end.

There are many unquestioned assumptions about love relationships that lead to excessive suffering and pain. The most common faulty assumptions associated with extremely intense reactions are: (1) I am not a worthwhile person, I am not loveable; (2) He or she was the perfect person, the *only* person for me; (3) I will never find someone like him/her again; (4) I could depend on him/her for everything; (5) Our relationship will never change, it is perfect; and (6) Life will never be happy for me again.

Where do these assumptions originate? Probably from a combination of sources: unfulfilled childhood needs, (love, understanding, security, etc.) romantic notions from movies (Top Gun), the media, (Soap Box Operas) fairy tales, (Cinderella), novels (Danielle Steele's), comparisons to ideal others, (Romeo & Juliet, Princess Grace & Prince Ranier, etc.) and strong feelings of insecurity. Some unquestioned assumptions lodge in the unconscious and persist for a lifetime. This is especially true of romantic love. It is not unusual for married couples to assume that they will not change nor will the nature of their relationship through the years. They refuse to accept the fact that new interests and experiences bring challenges and potential enrichment to a relationship.

In particular, unconditional love allows the other to grow *and* change in some marriages, and it is considered desirable in this regard. The notion of romantic love however, keeps the couple trapped in time. These and other convictions about love relationships are the basis for negative expectations when a breakup or a divorce occurs and for the feelings of helplessness and hopelessness that follow. Accordingly, the individual must abandon the belief system: "I can't live without her." This type of thinking becomes the basis for sickness and long emotional upheaval unless it is given up. The unrealistic beliefs which pervade a severed relationship contribute to loss of interest in school or job and subsequent inability to concentrate and earn good grades or maintain productive job performance. It also results in absenteeism and feelings of alienation from others, not to mention prolonged depression. The internal message to the unconscious mind, "I can't live without her" must be replaced with "I AM coping with this change in my life as millions of others have. I AM worthwhile and capable. I AM living without her."

A number of breakups are preceded by a great deal of rationalization. This defense mechanism, often referred to by professionals as "unconscious self-deception," is used to keep from facing the inevitable pain that permanent separation brings. On many occasions, one or both partners finally realize that they have very little in common, or one partner may feel that the other has become too dependent, and that it would be better for both if they went their separate ways. However, the fear that one will hurt or anger the other, that one will not be able to find another relationship, or that family and friends would not approve of the breakup, causes many young adults to deceive themselves. They rationalize that "things will get better," or "she doesn't mean to act the way she does," or "he is just under a great deal of pressure." The few strengths of the relationship are emphasized, the many weaknesses are overlooked or minimized. Elaine explains.

> My suitemates and friends helped me to realize certain things about myself and our relationship that I knew deep in my heart, but didn't want to believe. I tried to make myself look good even if I felt bad. I

knew what was happening to our relationship but I refused to accept it because I needed someone there. This only made things worse because I didn't get the satisfaction that I needed anyway.

In other instances, self-deception gives way to exploitation of the other. This is illustrated in the angry response of Jill who said:

Last week, over break, I broke up with my boyfriend of three years. I am not finding it very difficult to live with (it was coming for a long time) in that I don't miss him in particular. But I do desperately miss a companion. The weekends are especially difficult because all my friends pair off, and I feel like a fifth wheel. Also, my ex-boyfriend, this first weekend apart, jumped into bed with another girl. I just feel so degraded, repulsed, and used. It makes me extremely angry for allowing myself to be used and that for three years I was only something for him to get his rocks off with.

So far I haven't let on that I know anything about it, and I have acted as if nothing was really wrong, but sometimes I just can't help feeling that it is not fair that he shouldn't be feeling any repercussions. I realize that no one ever said life was fair, but sometimes it would be really nice. I find myself regretting the last year of the relationship because I had numerous chances to go out with guys who would provide me with what I was looking for in a relationship, and I didn't take them because I was too scared and too comfortable with what I had. Right now I just take it a day at a time and try to stay very busy. But its funny, I can't motivate myself to be busy doing something constructive (school work, etc.). I just needed to tell someone who had no connections to either me or my ex-boyfriend.

Feelings of exploitation bring deep regret and bitterness for some. A numbness and listlessness prevails quite similar to reactions when a loved one dies. Finally, once the relationship does come apart, added pain is experienced. Shelly advises:

My own thoughts greatly helped me cope, although the relationship was on the way out for a while, and for two years I was apathetic. I found it difficult to cut it off. For a couple of years I hung on to it while the other party was much more involved—it was more habit, dependency and family that kept me from ending it sooner. The actual hurt came months later, during the first month of school, when I found that my ex-boyfriend couldn't continue to be friends, where I had hoped we would stay in contact. I felt a part of me, a good friend, had died.

The refusal to heed warning signs, coupled with the insecurity of one or both partners, appears to result in strong feelings of rejection. Most traumatic, however, are the sudden, unexplained breakups. It is extremely difficult for most individuals to let go of the relationship early, probably because, for at least one of the partners, the relationship symbolizes security and wholeness without which one believes she/he cannot function. Ironically, parents and friends often see the breakup coming, but their warnings fall on deaf ears. "Listen to the advice of others," said Paula. "They can see things that you often can't. My family and friends could see the inevitable breakup with my six-year boyfriend. I refused to believe/listen to them and was in for the shock of my life."

We turn now to the aftermath of a breakup, coping strategies employed, and the beliefs associated with normal recovery.

BELIEFS ASSOCIATED WITH UNCOMPLICATED RECOVERY

In ridding the self of thinking which perpetuates additional emotional and physical pain it is useful to understand at the outset that overdependence is a major factor that must be dealt with. Overdependence on another is a form of addiction. All addictions make a person a slave to something outside the self. On the other hand, mutual dependency is a common need in the development of relationships[7]. A balance of dependence and independence is at the core of healthy relationships and mental health. Unfortunately, many developing relationships result in one partner giving up freedom of choice and decision making and allowing the other to assume all responsibility. Much overdependence can be traced to unmet childhood needs. The eventual severing of such a relationship is a tragic reawakening as the dependent person not only loses a loved one but must establish a new identity at the same time. (Widowhood often carries the same burden.) Regaining a sense of independence with the help of friends and family gradually rebuilds personal identity and permits an individual to obtain a sense of control over life.

Overdependence on another person not only minimizes the development of personal skills to deal with the many stresses of life but it also reduces the number of supportive relationships which normally would develop. Asserting oneself to gain a degree of independance is not an easy task when we have been overdependent, but it is essential in rebuilding our personal world. It means learning to take risks in what we do for ourselves. However, if we believe that not risking or avoiding rejection are non-negotiable conditions of life, then we have closed the door to existence by isolating ourselves from important social interaction.

There are a number of convictions about the self and the breakup which are associated with normal grief work in recovery. First, and by far the most critical, is the belief that: "I shall overcome this massive change in my life." The certainty that we can prevail regardless of the nature of our loss is essentially a product of successful experience with change early in life coupled with determination and positive self-esteem. Self-esteem (the subject of Chapter 6) can be enhanced by the nature of our support network, the development of new coping skills (see Chapter 7), a reinvestment in life interests, and through the love of family and friends. Significant others are the catalysts for the griever to believe "I AM making it through this difficult period in life." The continuous replaying of that thought heavily influences coping behavior through the power of the unconscious mind.

The second major conviction associated with recovery is: "I AM worthwhile despite what has happened." It is significant to understand that we have been rejected in a relationship not because we are not loveable and worthwhile but because our *behavior* and beliefs are not agreeable with the perceptions of the other. Coming to and dwelling on the conclusion that the rejection by one person is not an indicator of being devalued by all places the breakup in perspective. Little thought is initially given to the fact that relationships change continually and for many reasons. That one person chooses not to continue the relationship does not mean the other person is not worthwhile. It may well be that there were no common interests and goals as originally thought. Not infrequently, the concept of love varies immensely between couples and this divergence accentuates itself over time since it is never a subject of discussion.

Thirdly, the belief that: "I have not been singled out for this tragedy, it happens to many people" sets the stage for a reduction in self-pity. Self-pity immobilizes the individual and at the same time eliminates action to counteract the isolation and feelings of loneliness which commonly accompany a breakup. The realization that relationships end for a variety of reasons, and that it is not a punishment for previous transgressions by a vengeful God, assists in the process of acceptance. Reconstruction of an environment without the former friend cannot begin until acceptance occurs both emotionally as well as intellectually.

A fourth conviction associated with successful coping is a positive belief about the future. Many individuals ultimately conclude, to use their expression, that "there are other fish in the sea." Not surprisingly, this belief frequently comes to pass sooner or later when a new relationship is established. Among the most fundamental convictions for dealing with separation is faith in the future. Those who can look ahead and visualize good things happening, who have learned from the past, and create new interests and goals, commonly resolve their grief with few impediments. On the other hand, it is those who believe all is lost that suffer the longest. This view can be changed when we force ourselves to reengage life, *believe that the past is history and can no longer influence our feelings,* and act out these beliefs.

Now let us examine specific ways people in the Young Adult Study coped with their breakups. These techniques reflect their assumptions and beliefs about their dilemmas and of equal significance their faith in the future.

COMMON COPING STRATEGIES

Friends are the answer to losses. More friends means "less loss." Talking about the loss and having friends close by (comfort) is the cure to any loss.

Ed, 21 years old, on the breakup
of his love relationship

Just as negative beliefs about our ability to deal with a breakup prolongs grief work, so can positive beliefs that managing separation is possible shorten the period required to resolve and adjust to it. When we firmly believe we are still loveable, that we will find another special person, that the event was a learning experience, and everything has a reason for happening, or that it was "better for both of us," we begin our adjustment on solid footing. "My belief," Fran mused, "is that the ending of the relationship was meant to be and was probably for the better." Jody adds, "Most people told me it was better this way and I have come to believe that." It is just such beliefs that are the basis for letting go of the past and not being trapped within it.

Given the severity of a broken relationship, approaches to coping with it and managing grief work are many. We begin with the observation that *there is no single best way to deal with separation.* Rather, there are usually several means of coping which form a pattern, an individualized coping pattern. Some of the most common forms of adjusting, as suggested by our research follow, not necessarily in the order of importance.

1. Just as in coping with the death of a loved one, friends who provide a willingness to listen and *show empathy* (not just sympathy)

help us to examine reactions and feelings. "I live with my sister," said Danielle, "and she would always listen to me no matter how much I repeated myself." Phil adds, "The thing that helped me the most was being with people to try to get my mind off it. When you are alone, you can't help but think about your grief." Non-judgmental listeners not only facilitate the release of emotions, but help normalize responses which seem abnormal to the griever. Tracey explains the importance of a new male friend who listened:

> No matter what I said or how many times I repeated myself, he was always there to listen. He and I became very close (partly due to this) and have been the best of friends ever since. Another female friend was always there to be sympathetic and tell me I was right, which helped my self-confidence and self-esteem a lot. It's good to know there are others that have gone through the same experience and survived just fine.

In other words, friends are reality checks. In this instance they reinforced decisions which were made and helped Tracey understand that she could survive. Doreen put it this way: "Getting out with friends distracts you as a replacement activity and it starts building self-confidence about your ability to interact socially on your own." Friends heavily influence our thoughts about our ability to survive.

2. Time is a key factor in recovery. Diane observes:

> When it first occurred, it seemed that there was no hope in the future. After a period of time I realized how erroneous that assumption was. Time was the definite factor of coping with the loss. *One tends to think irrationally at such times and not until rational thinking reappears can any loss be dealt with.* (Ital. added)

The phrase, "It seemed that there was no hope in the future" is identical to the descriptions of despair evidenced in the deaths of loved ones. Consequently, the time span between the change from irrational to rational thinking is a painful one wherein much social support is needed. In addition, time can be an enemy if one is unable to break the thought-addictions to the former friend. Here is where using self-talk and keeping busy are essential in focusing thoughts away from the ex-boyfriend/girlfriend.

3. Keeping busy by joining organizations or participating more in those in which one is already a member was helpful ("I was doing a lot of acting and singing at the time—keeping busy"). Others became more involved in student government on campus. "I joined a sorority," Edie wrote, "which helped me meet new people. I

budgeted my time to keep up with my studies and to do things I never did, like playing tennis and reading a lot of good stories." Beth said, "Composing my music was the biggest release of tension." Notably, friends also keep the griever busy by taking the rejected lover to concerts, plays, on short trips, or to parties. These activities are significant because they are a part of the critical process of adapting—changing old routines, with new more productive ones which do not include the former partner. This social contact is the basis for affirming life and the importance of the self.

4. Some individuals take a part-time job. This helps to take up much of their free time and provides opportunities to develop new relationships. Work also forces an individual to assume responsibilities, relate to others on the job, focus on work objectives, and restore a sense of worth. It combats social withdrawal. Part-time work is a significant way to reengage life by reducing reminders of the breakup and introducing new thoughts and assumptions about one's capabilities.

5. Many people spend more time on school work or going to the library. "I found myself in the library every day for 5–6 hours," said Sue. "Doing this, I was able to totally involve myself in my school work and, for me, this gave me a rest from the horrible thoughts I was feeling." Not thinking about the other person is an ages-old method that works. As a thought about the other comes to mind, it is replaced with something more positive ("I have many trusting friends") or negative ("He was a bad influence on me").

   Even talking too much about the ex helps feed the hope of return for some individuals. Therefore, using the technique of thought replacement is a method of relearning how to live without the other. This is work and demands patience but yields a significant dividend over time. Perhaps most telling is the reduction in depression and sadness that thought replacement brings.

6. Paradoxically, the need for support is tempered by the need to be alone to think about options and choices. "I like to be alone," said Jackie, "at this beautiful lookout point that overlooked the Hudson River. For some reason it makes me feel better." It is during these times of silent contemplation that decisions are made and new beliefs are born. Ted explains:

   I more or less went deep into myself and reflected on all of the past memories, then looking onward with hope to learn from my mistakes. . . . It's O.K. to feel sorry about the past, but to belabor the issue is counter-productive. I focused on the future instead of the past. It also helped to reflect on the past and look at all the good things you've had instead of dwelling on the bad.

Ted's belief system, coupled with support from his family and friends, was instrumental in his acceptance and resolution of his breakup. It is noteworthy that many breakups are sources of education about people and relationships. Ted recognized this.

Consider Ned's beliefs. "I thought that I was still young and had my whole life to live and that I could find another girl who had some of the same qualities — love, affection and appreciation — and most of all, a personality." So much of adjustment to a breakup depends on beliefs and expectations about the self and the future. Looking ahead to all of the good things to come, of the opportunities to grow, is a part of recovery ("I coped by visualizing my post-graduation plans, taking me away from loss to new people and interests, hopefully").

7. Ideally, finding others who have had breakups and realizing that they have survived and carried on has special meaning, as Mitch suggests. "Hearing about people who had been in similar situations and had gotten over it was a big help." It was especially helpful to *talk* to others who have been through the same type of breakup ("Each friend I have talked to revealed their own heartbreak relationships and their problems in their relationships which helped me not to feel alone or abandoned"). The technique of finding others who have experienced the same type of loss is important in normalizing behavior. Realizing that emotions which seem out of control are not necessarily abnormal is stress reducing. Another significant result of finding others with experience in the same loss is that it aids in the search for meaning. Major losses are always accompanied by the question "Why?" The answer to why a breakup occurs is frequently found in conversations with others who have had similar experiences or with older adults. Coming to a conclusion with regard to the why of the breakup is important in completing grief work.

8. The need to find new relationships and the meaning which evolves from them assists in overcoming rejection. "I developed *women* friends who were a great help since the relationship had been with a man," Laura wrote. "It helped me to see that I could have a

world which would not fall apart when an intimate relationship was no longer there. It is very important to be involved in things and with people—to keep a feeling of an O.K. person on your own." Our self-worth does not have to depend on one person: This is among the most fundamental beliefs for coping well with any breakup. Mary Jo adds: "I kept myself as busy as possible. I forced myself to go out and socialize and the new attention I received helped strengthen me."

9. Turning to religious beliefs and accepting the loss as a part of life is a very common and effective coping technique. Nancy put it this way. "My religious beliefs and attending church really helped. I was looking for guidance and support, and I received it." Twenty year-old Erin said: "Part of what helped me cope was telling myself that God's ways are mysterious, yet must be accepted. Also, the saying: 'With faith, there is no fear and with fear there is no faith' helped." Possessing timeless alliances with spiritual or religious wisdom transcends most relationship losses.

How Counseling Helps

In situations where a griever was unable to find support persons who understood what was being experienced, it was important to seek professional help in dealing with readjustment. This strategy is not a sign of weakness. On the contrary, it is a wise choice, inasmuch as professionals, whether in the community or on the college campus, have consistently shown high success rates in helping grievers overcome this type of loss. They are strong sources for altering false assumptions and creating new beliefs about change and the self. What do young adults say they receive from their counselors?

First, counselors give grievers a sense of direction in attacking their problems. This is because they help *set up specific goals to work toward in the immediate future.* By defining where we are going, and how to get there, we sense regained control over life. Problems can be solved if we obtain assistance in planning strategy. "After realizing that I was not doing a good job coping with my breakup," said Betty Lou, "I sought professional help. I feel this was most beneficial to me because my counselor helped me look at the situation more objectively, and helped me realize that I was worthwhile." Emotions do hinder wise choices, although professionals help grievers realize that they can make it alone, without having to be attached to a particular person.

Second, counselors help grievers identify emotions which often seem to be in complete disarray. Some counselors will provide the griever with lists of affective words which aid in pinpointing feelings so that a closer examination of their meaning and intensity occurs. Understanding what is being experienced while recognizing the normalcy and acceptability of emotions (given the circumstances) eliminates the stigma of "being different because I feel this way." One often has a special need "to develop an autonomy and functional outlook toward not blaming myself (no guilt)." Betty Ann said: "My counselor finally told me that I would have to accept the fact that I had lost a friend, and that not everyone would like me for what I am."

Third, counselors provide dependable lifelines. June put it this way: "My counselor gave me her phone number and let me know I could call her at any hour. This was so supporting. She also let my sessions run longer if I needed them. Her schedule was second, I was first. She also gave me material on how to be assertive." We all need lifelines at various times. We can find one in a friend or through professional persons, although the latter usually do not take calls at all hours. Regardless of choice, this action is an important step in regaining control of life. No problem is insurmountable. There are always ways to deal with loss, and frequently the biggest challenge is finding out where that wisdom, that assistance can be found. Most of the time, that wisdom lies within us, and what is needed is someone who will help bring it out. In the final analysis, changing our internal environment is the solution to any external problem.

10. It has long been acknowledged that turning to skills and interests helps restore feelings of being worthy and capable. This is an extremely important coping technique. Ted said: "I was able to cope by turning to my hobby of woodworking to tell myself I am still a good person and have good things in me." Others utilize athletic or recreational skills or turn to drawing or painting. What seems to stand out in many of the coping patterns for dealing with a breakup is the need to reestablish a sense of stability and direction. This occurs in part through accentuating skills and interests with the resulting restoration of confidence.

More than ever the grieving person needs to know that, "I am okay, I am a good person." Jill adds: "It also helps to have things to do to show that your life goes on. . . . " Showing that "life goes on" means giving up the past, refusing to allow it to be a constant source of emotional pain and anxiety. The solution to most problems of breakups lies in the willingness to give up the past.

11. The return to interest in a member of the opposite sex is another turning point in recovery. The budding of a new relationship is very helpful in regaining a sense of importance. ("I found a new girlfriend who helped me to forget.") Finding a new relationship is a frequent way of coping. Sometimes it happens that one finds another person who is also on the rebound. ("I was lucky enough to find a young girl in the same situation as I, just the reverse. We helped each other.") It should be noted that quick replacements also result in additional problems when another separation occurs.

    There are clearly a number of young adults who report that a member of the opposite sex was very helpful as a listener. These individuals were *not* replacements for the partner they broke up with, just good friends.

12. Expressing feelings of anger and sadness is a basic coping technique. Crying becomes an important outlet whether it occurs when one is alone or with others. June said, "Music helped me cry (i.e., certain albums did so). It helped me get a lot out of my system." Finding emotional outlets aids recovery by reducing physical tension ("If you feel like screaming or yelling, then do it"). Don adds: "My art and my music became a great release for my internal emotions. My guitar will always listen and take me away. The same with my drawings. They let me escape." It is important to remember that crying or playing music are not male or female responses; they are human responses, coping tools of immense value, suitable for either sex. Another way that anger was diffused occurred through the use of humor and minimizing the qualities of the other partner as Clark explains.

Through a joint effort of my friends putting down my ex-girlfriend I was really able to accept the breakup. By a lot of sarcasm, jokes and put-downs, I got to laugh, and realized the old adage about plenty of fish in the sea. I think my personality accepted the badgering as a kidding session and I didn't need the passive, consoling care. I think it helped me. I don't think I'd like to have it occur all the time with other losses, but in some circumstances, it is very helpful.

This is an example of becoming disillusioned with a former friend by thinking about his/her shortcomings. It is also accomplished when the person is alone and thinks about how badly he/she was treated by the other. In fact, by thinking of the person in a humorous or absurd way the previous bonds of attachment are slowly cut.

13. A final coping technique used involves convincing oneself that the negative aspects of the relationship were good reasons for the breakup. This is coupled with not allowing oneself to dwell on the good times. Claire expresses it:

> I honestly feel that dwelling on the *bad* things, making yourself think about these things, is the best thing to do. After a while you convince yourself that thinking about the good things is *not* helpful. It hurts too much and it is wise to wait until later to do this. Also, don't listen to the radio too much. It sounds absurd, but I'm serious. There are too many songs about breaking up, being in love, etc. It's depressing.

This technique is also a good example of how this 21 year-old changed her belief from "I can't live without him" to "I'm better off without him."

Notice the positive assumptions/beliefs that these coping techniques are based on:

1. Finding trusted listeners helps reduce anxiety.
2. Going out with friends is important to keep from dwelling on past thoughts.
3. Keeping busy and organizing time helps develop new routines.
4. Replacing thoughts of the past with thoughts of the future is essential.
5. There is so much more to come in life. Life can go on.
6. Finding new relationships and attention from others restores confidence.
7. I can make it through anything with God at my side.
8. Professional help is not a sign of weakness.
9. Reengage life by using skills and becoming involved in new pursuits.
10. I can express feelings through music as well as friends.
11. Dwelling on the bad parts of the relationship convince me that the breakup is acceptable.
12. All love involves risk and growth.
13. Accept that which cannot be changed.
14. Reach out for help, do not go it alone.

In summary, in order to cope with a breakup it is vital that we maintain contact with others, stay visible, develop new friendships, seek healthy emotional outlets, and establish and use helpful coping techniques. We would also strongly suggest ridding oneself of all the reminders of the lost relationship: letters, photos, gifts, ticket stubs, and favorite records. Gather up all the momentos, put them in a box, and store them out of sight. These only serve as reminders of rejection or sources of guilt. Changing whatever is a reminder must become part of a new routine to follow. This means initially avoiding places which are reminders of the other and scheduling time on weekends and holidays so as not to be alone dwelling on the loss of the relationship.

This does not mean that one no longer speaks to the ex-boyfriend. While many relationships are severed without the wish to remain on speaking terms, there are some breakups where the former partners remain friends ("My ex-boyfriend helped too, because we are still on friendly terms, at least for now, and we can still talk about how we feel"). The past must be looked upon as a growth experience. Individuals must reach out to the future and the possibility of new relationships. Be good to yourself. *You are important.* ("The relationship had been one of giving and taking—I gave and he took—I had to think about me for a while.") Above all else, allow yourself the freedom to grieve, we are told by Christina:

> You must learn that most losses are not your fault . . . Life is very unfair and it has nothing personal to do with you. You must learn to take things in stride. Vent the anger and frustration. There is nothing wrong with being emotional and venting feelings. I think that this is the most important factor in coping with any loss.

There are many philosophical positions taken when we look back on a breakup and attempts to cope with it. There is always a risk taken in loving another: the risk is the possibility of the relationship not working out. But as Al said, "When you love someone you have to take the chance of getting hurt. Accept it, if you can't change it, and keep living." This is, of course, easier said than done. But *accepting that which cannot be changed* and going on living is the most positive and productive option possible, as hundreds of young people agree. They have called on their strengths, with the help of others, to adapt to new circumstances. Most of them realize they can overcome their setback. This was exceptionally well stated by Sheila, a senior:

> Everyone must try to keep in mind that what they have makes them what they are. Their strengths, beliefs, and talents have not been taken away. They may lose a lover or a family member—but by realizing

one's own strengths we become less dependent on these things that are so subject to change.

Maureen tells us to focus on what you learned, on what you have gained. "My loss trouble didn't last long because I don't really think in terms of loss. I have been raised to be optimistic and constructive with my problems and feel that I have concentrated more on my gain and have grown and found greater peace because of this."

For those who have suffered through the recent death of a parent or some other loved one, it is probably most difficult to imagine that the breakup of a love relationship could come anywhere near paralleling the pain of that death. Moreover, the suggestion that anyone could consider them to be equal may have even stirred anger. However, it is equally difficult to understand the deep emotional ties that people have with animals, and their ensuing grief responses when a pet dies. Still, pets provide much needed companionship and are positive influences on the health of owners[8]. All responses to severed relationships depend in large measure on the nature of emotional investment in the object of loss.

Certainly not all breakups include an intense grief experience any more than all deaths do. (There are high grief and low grief deaths)[9]. Clearly, many breakups seem to alter one's sense of identity and demand the reestablishment of oneself as a "single" person. Those who enter a romantic relationship often do not feel whole, adequate, or important unless they continuously have that relationship. They feel worthy and alive at the time, but when it ends, they revert to past feelings of inadequacy, as being unworthy and incomplete. To venture forth once again alone, feeling helpless and unable to function, is indeed a major life challenge. This condition, coupled with the great sense of loneliness and distrust which pervade breakups, causes a very serious crisis. Nobody except the rejected partner knows what the relationship has meant and how much energy had been invested.

All of this points to what has been previously stated: the perception of loss and grief are in the "heart" of the beholder. Yes, *some* individuals deeply grieve over non-fatal losses, as though a death had occurred. *Powerful childhood beliefs about romantic love are devastating in adulthood.* What should be learned from this fact is that these grievers need as much love and concern as do grievers suffering from a death of a loved one. Peers who give care need to maximize their caring just as they would for those who are grieving a loss through death. These grievers have not "gone off the deep end" in their behavior. They are attempting to build a new identity with the feeling that they possess very little to start with.

Can any of this trauma associated with the death of a person or a relationship be minimized or eliminated? Can we learn to cope in healthier ways? This is our next consideration.

REFERENCES

1. Freedman, J., Carlsmith, J. & Sears, D. *Social psychology.* Englewood Cliffs, NJ: Prentice-Hall, 1970.
2. Hafer, W. *Coping with bereavement from death or divorce.* Englewood Cliffs, NJ: Prentice-Hall, 1981.
3. Tanner, I. *The gift of grief.* New York: Hawthorne, 1976.
4. LaGrand, L. *Coping with separation and loss as a young adult* Springfield, IL: Charles C Thomas, 1986.
5. LaGrand, L. The breakup of a love relationship as a "death reaction." In C. Carr, J. Stellion & M. Rebar (Eds.) *Creativity in death education and counseling,* Lakewood, Ohio: Forum for Death Education & Counseling, 1983.
6. Worden, J. *Grief counseling and grief therapy.* New York: Springer, 1982.
7. Reiss, I. Toward a sociology of the heterosexual love relationship. *Marriage and Family Living,* 1960, 22, 139–45.
8. Freedman, E. & Thomas, S. Influence of animal companions on human health. *Death and Life,* Newsletter of the Thanatology Program, Brooklyn College, 1985, 3, 4–6.
9. Fulton, R. Death, grief, and social recuperation, *Omega,* 1970, 1^1, p. 27.

Chapter Four

CAN ANYONE BE BETTER PREPARED?

What people really need is belief in themselves, confidence in their own ability to take on the problems and opportunities of life.
John Powell in *Unconditional Love*

The greater your loss or frustration is in life, the more philosophic you must force yourself to become in regard to it.
Albert Ellis & Robert Harper in
A Guide to Rational Living

I learned that when we acknowledge our feelings, we are able to make a choice to act or not to act. When we deny our feelings, they take control.
Pat O. in *Afraid To Live, Afraid To Die*

No, not when it is someone as close as my father. I don't care what any "high roller" tells me. My father was sick for ten years and I still wasn't prepared even though I knew he could have died at any time.
Grace, a senior

Yes. Be thankful when you can — be aware of everything around you. Spend time and appreciate your parents, friends and others. Make good times and friendships and memories to remember when your time of loss does come. Actually, I smile when I remember my Dad. Think of the good times.
Jeanne, a sophomore

Preparation for loss, particularly a death or a breakup, appears at first to be a purely metaphysical question. Many young adults think quite differently; they are keenly aware that some people are better "equipped" to cope with loss than others. In this chapter, I emphasize the importance of social interaction and honesty as critical components in dealing with crises. Among the most telling observations supporting this posture are those graphically illustrated by suggestions of young adults who conclude that preparation depends much on the degree of self-awareness, beliefs (as reflected above by Grace and Jeanne), and quality relationships with others *before* loss occurs.

CHANGING OUR PERCEPTION OF DEATH

An important and controversial issue presents itself: how to best help ourselves deal with the deaths of loved ones and the many losses that are part of life. Several questions need to be addressed: Why do some individuals cope better than others? Is preparation possible? Is it worth the effort to change our behavior before death occurs? How can we accomplish the task?

Generally, to increase knowledge of any aspect of living expands conscious awareness of it, and gives some foreknowledge of factors involved in transition. Accordingly, it is argued that knowledge prepares us for adversity and excludes the shock of complete surprise which, in loss experiences, maximizes pain and suffering. Nevertheless, disbelief when loss occurs will still be dominant to a great extent, regardless of how "knowledgeable" or "prepared" we might be.

But first let us consider the opposite question: what happens when a myopic view is nurtured, when we choose to define our personal realities only in terms of the joys and good tidings of life? We are left ill-prepared for becoming fully human, prevented from becoming all we are capable of being when time takes its inexorable toll. And unfortunately, a significant portion of human experience is totally ignored. Indeed, we live in an unrealistic world unable to view death as an integral motivator in living.

Dr. Donald Irish[1], speaking at the Hamline University Symposium on Death Education, provided rare insight into the contribution that foresight provides when he said: "The purpose is to release creativity by *engendering a larger love of life* rather than a deeper dread of death. When fully developed, this position would neither begin nor end with a hedonistic 'eat, drink, and be merry, for tomorrow we die' view of life; instead, life could be more sensitively savored throughout, more like a continual smorgasbord than a Bacchanalian binge," (p. 47, ital. added).* In short, death and loss experiences make more important the tasks accomplished each day; they further intensify the meaning of all the virtues—like love, honesty, hope, trust, and the gift of self. Most important: they challenge and release creativity.

As important as knowledge is about death and what to expect when it

---

*Nowhere, to my knowledge, is the issue of preparation for loss more eloquently and profoundly stated than by Donald Irish in this presentation. Although his focus is on death education as preparation for living, I believe it applies to the entire spectrum of loss experiences. I recommend it highly if you wish to explore the importance of preparation for loss and affirmation of life.

happens, it does little to guarantee that the most desirable behavior will actually occur any more than knowing the mechanics of the tennis stroke will make better tennis players. As usual we must experience what has been read and talked about, to "try on," as it were, the tactics of confrontation. Unless we've been through loss or death experiences, we often do not believe they are real. Now we all have experienced separation, what theologian Paul Tillich calls "small deaths." But have we truly learned from those separations, or have we simply dismissed them as unfortunate occurrences to forget as soon as possible? Dealing with separations, death included, takes time, patience, energy and persistence — and the return is emotional learning.

We cannot "get over" the death of a loved one on command any more than we can speed up the period of pregnancy before a child is born. We can lessen feelings of insecurity, loneliness and self-consciousness by learning that much of what society declares to be "individual weakness" or "lack of self-control" is, in fact, the total *human* response to parting with someone or some object which we have held dearly. In short, death education minimizes "secondary sources of anxiety which stem from cultural norms." Some of this anxiety is generated from a lack of understanding of the grief process[2]. This is a critical truth to understand, because we are bombarded by pressures from a production-oriented society which demands impeccable control of behavior under the most difficult conditions. This is illustrated by the increased stress placed on grieving people who cry, and are told they are being selfish for crying because the deceased was very old.

Learning about death and the ensuing grief which accompanies it should be looked at in the same way that we view education about any other subject: as a means of enhancing the quality of life. A point of focus is to visualize death and grieving as events which provide both practical and theoretical learning. Overcoming the objection that death never has positive outcomes, that it is not an integral part of the life cycle, is the very first step taken. Once we accept the opposite premise, a host of ideas open up for dealing with death anxiety.

I have spent much time thinking about the question of whether anyone can become better prepared to cope with death and other separations, whether sudden or anticipated. This is not an easy question to answer. As the father of an infant who died from SIDS (Sudden Infant Death Syndrome), as one who conducts support groups for those with life-threatening illness and has been with many dying people, and as one who was with his own father as he took his last breath of life, I am convinced that we can prepare for death experiences just as we can prepare for any type of experience that is an integral part of life; we inherently possess that capacity. Parkes[3] has suggested that it is useful to have gained as much acceptance of death as possible when we finally encounter the death of someone we love. I would add that the acceptance of losses other than death is equally critical when those losses occur. This implies that we must be more aware of the universality of loss and death. Interestingly, such awareness is as contrary to contemporary lifestyles as is the use of nuclear weapons to any peace-loving human being.

A FORGOTTEN TRUTH—A BEGINNING

Everyone needs to deal with the simple truth that all relationships end in separation. This reality holds great potential wisdom for all and its implications should be the subject of deep thought and discussion. However, it is almost never at issue. What emerges clearly here is that separation *is* a fact of life, and a pervasive influence. When a person dies, when a divorce is final, when a breakup occurs, when friendships end, a part of us dies. We grieve that dying. In building close friendships, in loving others, we invest a part of our life in those persons. We will mourn for those investments as we mourn for the significant person who is no longer there.

Indeed, separations and their impact should be discussed in an atmosphere free from labels of "this is morbid." At an appropriate time and place *before* separation occurs we should be allowed to consider the implications. To begin this task let us recognize an attitudinal frame of reference which predominates in a positive approach to the problems of living and dying. We will examine this attitude through an analysis of success in dealing with several life crises.

There is a considerable amount of data in the literature on adjustment to life crises to suggest a very strong relationship exists between certain life events and psychological and physical symptomatology. That is, some people react to a crisis in ways which cause them to become incapacitated and unable to function for long periods of time. In some cases, their maladaptive behavior has lead to self-destruction. Why is it that some individuals are driven to extreme forms of behavior and others are not? More specifically, why is it that individuals experiencing any traumatic life change, or series of changes, do not develop the same degree of impairment? Why are some individuals better able to cope than others? A brief review of some of the literature on longevity and life changes will be of help in answering these questions because *hope* is not merely the crucial factor in extending life, it is also part of the specific mental attitude that is behind efforts to overcome other tragedies.

HOPE, A POSITIVE BELIEF SYSTEM, AND COMPANIONSHIP

Hope is strongly associated with faith in something outside the self. We need only turn to the many accounts involving being a prisoner of war to discover that those who gave up hope, who never tried to escape or tried to resist the brainwashing, who believed all was lost, succumbed very quickly to confinement. Those who survive keep their imaginations busy particularly with affirmative thoughts of the future and their loved ones. They cling to beliefs tenaciously, whatever their content. They do not dwell on the past and what happened but what must be done with the present to make their futures. Hope is like a wonder drug to them. It is noteworthy that faith in something always precedes hope, the faith may be in the self, others, God, the goodness of things, or that everything works out for the best. Faith is a catalyst to hope. All of this suggests a commitment to prevail.

Phillips and Feldman[4], in their examination of death and birth dates of 1,333 famous Americans, found that their deaths occurred most often in the months after their birthday and least often in the months preceding a birthday. The desire to reach a particular milestone in life, to live to that next birthday, is suggestive of the power of hope in the face of personal crises. It strongly implies that some individuals postpone the day of their deaths. They decide when they will die. Furthermore, the researchers presented evidence of a dip in the death rate before presidential elections and Yom Kippur, both of which support the notion that the power of expectation and hope in postponing death is prevalent.

This same phenomenon is reported by many hospice personnel working with dying patients who are told they have six months or less to live — and these patients frustrate the predictions of the experts and live for months longer. I remember visiting a middle aged man with lung cancer who was told by his physician that he had a month and a half of life remaining. Eight months later he was still going strong, no longer bed-ridden and even driving his truck. He had made up his mind he was not just going to lie there and die because the physician said he would.

He had coped with the most stressful event of his life—the assumption that death was imminent—by his *desire* to live on. And he did—for a year and a half. When I asked him why he got out of bed, he thought for a moment and replied, "I was sick of people waiting on me. I never had people waiting on me in my life." These are *not* isolated incidents; they are reported time and time again in the literature on loss. Thoughts either lengthen or shorten lives.

HOPELESSNESS

On the other hand, hopelessness has been shown to increase symptomatology and to hasten death. Many studies suggest that hopelessness, depression, and loneliness are precursors of serious illness. Weisman and Hackett[5], Kubler-Ross[6], and Kastenbaum[7] have all reported that patients who expect to die, or have a "will to die," *do die sooner than expected.* And, from a medical point of view several who died had no indications of their imminent death owing to present conditions. The attitude formed toward circumstances to be confronted is the pivotal factor in how we cope with crisis. Furthermore, hopelessness, a negative evaluation of the future, has been linked to suicidal intent[8].

Lynch[9] assembled a variety of studies and anecdotal data to show that social isolation, a lack of human companionship, the death or absence of parents in early childhood, a sudden loss of love, and chronic human loneliness are significant contributors to premature death. His work points out that widowed, divorced and single individuals have higher mortality rates for all causes of death, have more chronic and/or debilitating diseases, require more physician's visits and spend more days in hospitals than married individuals or those living with others where human companionship and love is normally found.

Companionship and/or strong interpersonal relationships significantly influence the general lifestyles of individuals to the extent that they are better able to cope with crises. Lynch[9] maintains that it is social isolation in both childhood and adulthood which contributes to increased interpersonal difficulties and a pervasive loneliness which impinges upon the ability to deal with life stresses. "Human companionship, in turn, can significantly change physical and psychological reactions to emotional stress," (p. 100). He concludes that the aversive conditions which each individual must confront throughout a lifetime are far more perplexing and upsetting to those who lack someone with whom to share them. Of particular importance for our consideration (i.e., being better prepared to cope with a major loss, especially death) is the importance of shedding the image of total self-sufficiency in order to develop the type of human companionship best suited in the management of life-change events. Strikingly, a fundamental source of hope comes from those around us and their caring attitude.

Myers et al.[10] found that the degree of social integration—being married, being satisfied with a career or occupation, having high social status—influenced how individuals dealt with certain life events and whether or not they developed psychiatric symptoms. Those most affected by the crises in their lives were the widowed, separated, divorced, and single people never married as well as those not satisfied with their roles as homemakers or with their work roles. Once again, the importance of human contact as a wellspring of hope, particularly during times of duress, appeared to be a dominating factor in coping with various life-change events.

As a brief aside, it should be noted that not only social class but income can affect how some people cope[11]. Whatever the stress, economic independence tends to help one through the difficult adjustment periods, as suggested by widows who are left with substantial assets as opposed to those who must go on welfare, seek work, or limit their attendance at social gatherings because of a lack of income.

Returning to the question of whether we can be better prepared to cope with the death of a loved one, or other major losses, seems ludicrous to some people. To begin with, it is argued, who would want to think of sad happenings, when joy and happiness are so much more to be sought after? Why bother? Simply reading such a statement brings a reaction of, "How crazy!" or "Who would want to prepare for tragedy?" As we note the opposing viewpoints of Jeanne and Grace which opened this discussion, where both suffered through the death of a parent, there is much for us to think about and consider. Their responses indicate how belief systems, formed before death occurs, create either additional chaos or lead to eventual resolution. And these are beliefs which can be altered as we go on living and will naturally affect coping styles throughout life. Before we analyze the possibilities for preparing to cope with the deaths of loved ones, let us first examine what we are told from the Young Adult study about being better prepared to deal with a breakup.

PREPARATION BEFORE A BREAKUP

The implication clearly emerges that there are similarities in bereavement whether it stems from death, divorce, or the breakup of love relationships. Because of these similarities, I have listed a number of statements, indicating how an individual could have been better prepared to deal with the breakup of a love relationship. Each of these statements would be worthy of discussion by those entering or presently committed to a relationship. They appear with but slight editing, just as they were written by some of the nearly 1,000 individuals who were asked how they could have been better prepared to cope. Many of their suggestions are also quite applicable to the argument that it is indeed possible for us to be better prepared to cope with the death of a loved one.

1. Have a more open relationship with people who have some sort of control over your life. Also, don't take someone for granted.
2. You must be aware of the signs that occur before the breakup happens. Do not ignore them. If I had looked more objectively at the situation in the beginning, rather than let my feelings rule, I would have been able to end the relationship *before* it got so involved, thereby preventing a great deal of pain. You have to look at things as they really are and not as you want to see them.
3. You can be better prepared to cope with a breakup by being on good terms with your family, your friends, and also yourself; this is of major importance.
4. Don't look so far into the future. I was crushed when it didn't work out. Now I take each day one at a time and try not to look so far ahead.
5. Consider the unexpected and how you would deal with it (i.e., mentally prepare yourself). A person should be aware that a relationship can end at anytime.
6. If in some way our society could convey the idea that loss is a part of life—it would then be easier to accept.
7. Appreciate each moment with the rationale that the person may not always be there.
8. Throughout the relationship, it is always better to talk everything out and then there will always be a better understanding.
9. Be honest about your feelings. You have to be secure in yourself.
10. Accept the facts. Don't try to change situations which cannot be changed. Always think of the good times and the better alternatives.
11. Realize that some of your reactions to loss (such as overeating) are as destructive and may be even more destructive than the loss itself.

12. Don't let yourself get involved with anyone who treats you poorly one day and great the next.
13. In the loss of a love relationship, one could be better prepared to cope if one is more aware of the things to be expected from the relationship and if one is also aware of his or her own needs.
14. In this kind of loss, I would suggest to always leave yourself in a fairly good, independent position. Never lose your sense of personality, individuality, and self-reliance.
15. It is best to believe that a problem or loss is only what you make of it. And if your mind is together you can handle it. Let's face it—some degree of loss is an everyday ordeal for most people. You have to learn to accept the change, because if there can only be one winner, there have to be an awful lot of others who didn't win, at least that day.
16. You could be better prepared by developing enough of yourself so that when you are left alone, you have the strength to go on.

These statements were written with one basic assumption: we can learn to better cope with a breakup. On the other hand, they also provide guidelines for the strengthening of existing relationships which, paradoxically, are at the core of dealing with all major life changes, including death itself.

Perhaps the most significant admonition is the call for self-development. What we can learn from this data is that there is obviously a great deal of self-deception preceding many reported breakups. Frequently, one or both partners refuse to recognize they are incompatible, that their interests are completely different, and that one does not meet the other's expectations. Nevertheless, they continue to see each other and attempt to perpetuate a relationship which will never work. A very similar self-deception occurs with our confrontations with death: we choose not to recognize its impact on our life and how best to cope with it. Most of us do not look at death or other separations in light of the suggestions just offered.

PREPARATION BEFORE A DEATH

When the question of preparation for coping with the death of a loved one was addressed in our study, there were a variety of responses ranging from "I don't know" to "Impossible." Generally, most answers to this question fell into three broad categories.

The first reaction to the question of preparation stated unequivocally that, "I was prepared." In this instance the death was expected, the person who died was older, and the expectation of death seemed to be accepted because of age and the fact that the deceased had lived a good and full life. Notice that the naturalness of dying when one is old and life is complete seems to be a pivotal element in acceptance and the belief of preparation. Interestingly, in this view of preparation, the individual *knows* the nature and seriousness of the illness which precedes the fatal event. This is a critical piece of information, as we shall see later. This view also includes the importance of having had a good relationship with the deceased and the feeling that nothing was left unsaid. A striking example of this concept was expressed by Janette: "The only way that one can cope with the loss of a loved one is knowing that the time spent with this person was well-spent. One needs to feel that the relationship was positive. There can be no regrets about what should have been said or done." The quality of interpersonal transactions are fundamental to how death is accepted by survivors. When the deceased was younger (i.e., considered not to have lived a full life) then the person doing the reporting experienced an even greater sense of loss, even though the death was expected.

The same idea of preparedness was expressed by some persons involved in breakups, separations, and divorces. The individuals realized that romantic loss was impending, and when the final moment arrived, it was often difficult to accept; it was still seen as being unreal. But there was general agreement that forewarning is useful. ("If the loss is obviously coming, then some grief beforehand helps.")

In the second answer to the question of preparation, a number of people said it was impossible to be better prepared for the death of a loved one. Briefly stated, their responses were as follows: "No, death is tragic; there is no way to prepare for it" or "There is no way to be better prepared for a loss. The only way that I can see that it would be easier is if the person stayed sort of detached from all of the things that can cause pain from a loss of some sort." To follow this advice would simply place one in a world void of love and caring by withdrawing from life itself. Most young people who were associated with a sudden death were especially insistent in their stand that no one can deal with death in that type of situation ("Be serious. How can one be better prepared for the sudden death of a family member?") Moreover, their rationale hinged on the beliefs that "no one ever expects a loss to happen to her," and that which cannot be controlled cannot be prepared for. A final reason given for the impossibility of being better prepared was that each loss was in some way different, and so coping with losses necessarily differed also.

The third group looked at the experience of a loved one dying and said "I wasn't prepared—but I could have been better prepared if only I had known this or that beforehand." The door was left open for greater acceptance and understanding. What were the factors that would have led to better preparation, to greater acceptance, and a better way of coping? There are many such factors. I will list a number of these, again, as written by respondents. And in the pages to follow, we will analyze them in greater depth:

1. Be aware of yourself.
2. Talk about death as if it were like any other topic.
3. The only way to be prepared for loss is to deal with reality and know that it can happen at any time. Realize that young people are capable of dying.
4. Courses on death and dying in high school and college—of which I had taken none.
5. I think a major factor in coping with a loss is the ability and availability of people to talk with and who will communicate their feelings concerning the loss.
6. Yes, by having a close family and having some kind of a belief in God.
7. Our society tends to deny death and thereby fosters our individual denial of it. I believe society could help us by preparing us better to face our grief.
8. Accept things as they are with no regret, and continue on after the loss.
9. Yes, by accepting and identifying the signs which were apparent but overlooked.
10. Knowing how to relax more easily and not push myself to exhaustion.
11. Yes, don't hold in any feelings. Let friends and other people help you with your situation.
12. Increase your knowledge of how to help others deal with it.
13. Have discussions about the death of various people close to you. Talk about what you would do if they died and have the person tell you the way he or she would want you to feel and what they want you to do.
14. Be more realistic when dealing with children and their upbringing. Education!
15. Do what your heart tells you; when your heart says go to see someone or say something nice, do it. Don't put it off because you're afraid or tired.
16. Realize that time heals all wounds.
17. Be glad for what you had, don't regret what you didn't receive.

The first 13 statements came from those who had experienced the sudden death of a loved one, including deaths of parents. Combined, all 17 statements are representative of the rationale given by young adults to support the position that one can be better prepared to cope with the deaths of loved ones. It would be appropriate at this time to go back and compare these statements with those given for dealing with a breakup. What similarities and differences exist? And what types of beliefs do these representative statements reflect? How does one increase awareness of the self?

From the anecdotal data supplied by respondents, a majority believed that we can be better prepared to cope with death—and it need not involve a morbid preoccupation with the subject. Rather, it entails a willingness to allow death to become a genuine topic for discussion, a force which reshapes the quality of life. It also involves a willingness to challenge the present social mythology which blocks necessary dialogue.

Obviously, some people cope better with the deaths of loved ones than others. How they do so, we believe, is in part a product of their nurturing and the choices made in being an open person. There are as many ways to cope as there are differences in approaches to living. Since we are all at different places in the search for how death fits into the scheme of life, personal death awareness varies immensely. However, two of the criteria for becoming "prepared" to enjoy life as well as cope with major loss are essential: awareness of self (which includes *inner* resources), and the development of coping styles to endure as a survivor. How can these criteria be met?

Evidently, the argument that one can become better prepared to cope with the death of loved ones focuses on four basic approaches: (1) increasing knowledge about death-related phenomena, (2) increasing communication skills, (3) developing strong interpersonal relationships which enhance the self-concept, and (4) developing a belief system which integrates death into life. How relationships evolve to facilitate these approaches, and the development of the self-concept, are complex questions. We will try to shed some light on them as we turn to more specific information that respondents say is needed in order to better cope. In exploring this line of thought, we will examine characteristics of interpersonal relationships which are critical factors in preparation for loss: (1) establishing and maintaining trust, (2) being honest, especially with ourselves, (3) being willing to risk in a new personal relationship, (4) establishing and maintaining *open* communication, and (5) receiving support and, in turn, giving it to others.

Before turning to these issues, it is appropriate that we conclude the first part of our discussion of the question of preparation by returning to the points raised in the beginning of this section and the positive remarks of Jeanne (p. 75). Consider her beliefs about preparation in terms of the importance of concentrating on quality memories which in turn, imply loving relationships. Happy memories are positive grieving tools. And recall her emphasis on *appreciating* loved ones—but most important— her directive, "be aware of everything around you." That is, increase our awareness of all that we possess, for it is that greater awareness that sets the stage for acceptance of that which is taken away. There is great wisdom in her suggestions. There is also much wisdom in the remarks of Mitch, a senior, who, in his positive view that we can be better prepared to cope with the death of a loved one, sets the stage for our examination of the specific factors involved:

> Yes, keep friendships and relationships free from discord. Make amends. Communicate feelings daily. Forgive. Forgive. Affirm those you love. Accept your faults and the faults of others. Live each day as though it were the last day on earth.

Does Mitch sound too idealistic? Can we *communicate feelings daily?* His suggestions are presently being followed by many who have experienced the pain of loss as well as those who are sensitive to what builds or destroys self-esteem. The willingness to resort to the cliché "that's too idealistic," is another way of saying "I refuse to live that way. I refuse to accept help; I refuse to change."

WHAT YOUNG ADULTS SAY IS NEEDED

> *Students our age tend to fail to perceive the future in concrete terms. We don't understand the mortality and reality that life thrusts upon us. Basically, if we were more aware of death and the loss that accompanies such a tragedy, then we would be able to better cope with it when it actually occurs.*
>
> Gino, a senior

Being aware of all that life entails, including the living that goes on before and continues after the loss caused by death, is largely a matter of experience and education. It takes time and patience to learn from loss, particularly losses of those who love us. But there is one factor which stands out in the confrontation with death which influences reactions to it regardless of past experience: By and large, the nature of our patterns of communication with the significant people in our lives is the pivotal element in determining which direction efforts to survive will take. This is best expressed in the following statement by 21 year-old Murray: "I've found that living *each* day one at a time and trying to do all I can to insure that others understand *me* and I understand them has helped me prepare myself for future loss. *Communication* is extremely important as well as an openness to share and experience each other."

There is one profound implication for dealing with all of life's trials that should be noted from this observation: loss can be confronted, defused, and used—if we are able to share our *innermost fears*, hopes and joys. To live in an environment in which feelings are allowed to be shared non-judgementally, an environment which is free from strong recriminations, is the foundation for developing understanding of ourselves and deep respect for others. Respect is a neglected factor in reactions to loss, yet it is the basis for being able to engage in non-judgmental dialogue when helping someone who is grieving. Obviously, it is not easy to accept the feelings and beliefs of others with whom we disagree. But we do not have to accept their beliefs, simply acknowledge their right (and need) to express them, and recognize that they believe in them as strongly as we believe in ours.

Why is all of this so important? Because it is open exchange of feelings early in life, this habit of self-expression, that nurtures the critical ability to relate to someone else on a very intimate emotional level when crisis occurs. Although death is inevitable, "meaningful communication is within the power of each of us"[13]. This type of communication is risky simply because it leaves us vulnerable to rejection. We either maximize our lives through a willingness to be vulnerable, by chancing rejection again and again, or we crawl into a little shell eliminating chances for growth, both intellectual and spiritual.

Communication is learned behavior. If our communicating skills are weak they can be relearned; we can build new skills and learn to listen to feelings, not just words. For the grieved, this bond is a link with life itself[14].

In any case, this has special significance for all of the goodbyes that have to be said in a lifetime of separations. I contend that the ability to communicate on an intimate level creates a mind-set that significantly reduces death anxiety and the fears that lie behind it. Those who live without regrets, who are fully alive, see death as another life event. Orville Kelly, founder of *Make Today Count* and fighting lymphocytic lymphoma, spoke about how his disease had made him appreciate life so much more that he would not want to return to his previous lifestyle. Helping others with cancer had transformed his life. "Because of my way of living during the past three years," he said, "it will be easier to say goodbye." The same may be true in coping with all major losses, including death. The issue is one of valuing the *processes* of living more than the products; it is living at the center of our relationships and not on their periphery.

Interestingly, this risk is well worth taking when we look at what happens when intimate dialogue is absent:

> For approximately one year I was counseled by a social worker. As I look back I wish that I had started counseling before my father's death—he was dying for nine months. I am the only one in my family that did go for counseling and I am the only one who can now talk openly about his death. I believe I'm the only one who has come to terms with it.

> Joyce, 21 years old

Learning to communicate at a level of deep feelings facilitates the emotional exchange so critical in dealing with life crises. When this is encouraged and practiced as part of our overall communication style the ensuing climate of candor and openness reduces conflict and anxiety. The alternative, when intimate communication is not practiced, is the suppression of feelings or the need to turn to professional help or to strangers, as Dawn explains:

> I sought professional help because I couldn't talk to my family about it. This was a person I didn't know and I felt I could express my feelings more openly and easily with this person. Later on I thought about the situation more on my own because I was blaming myself sometimes. I had to find out "why?"

It is a rather common reaction to feel guilt as well as deep anger when a loved one dies; these emotions need to be acknowledged and ventilated in order to allow us to deal with indecision, lack of initiative, and all of the tensions that result in trying to maintain composure. The close knit family is a powerful source for coping with traumatic change because members possess the ability to communicate at a very intimate level and permit therapeutic release.

Just how important is the family and what does dialogue among family members mean for survivors and the dying? Again and again subjects in the study point out that family members are the wellspring from which flow examples of love and motivation as well as healing and support that is so important if growth is to evolve from tragedy. Doreen, a senior music major, gives us the following example:

> We had enabled my grandmother to die at home. This brought all family members home which reunited us—bringing us together (fighting together for a similar cause)—making her happy. We were able to discuss dying openly with each other—and her. She accepted death, which in turn made us accept death. We are a very close family and being with her when she died tied the knots even tighter.

These types of relationships become the sources of continuity which, in turn, generate strength in the face of adversity. As young adults tell us, people who need each other and believe in this mutual giving bring openness and acceptance to the death event. Doreen's statement not only presupposes an awareness of death as one of life's turning points, it further highlights the results of employing openness and mutual support as critical factors in coping.

Equally significant in the support network are friends. In fact, it is not uncommon for the griever to turn to friends as though they were surrogate parents, as though they were fully prepared to provide nurturance and love so desperately needed. Consequently, roommates, boyfriends, and girlfriends give initial assistance because of their proximity to the griever who is away from home. Strikingly, this assistance is in no way a superficial, stop-gap type of support, as friends usually have more contact with the griever for longer periods of time than does the family. ("I think friendships are, at this stage in life, one of the most important things in coping and I do rely on them heavily.") This is especially true in coping with the breakup of love relationships and friendships, as many grievers believe that peers are more aware of the dynamics involved than their families. When they do turn to family members, the mother is most frequently the major support person mentioned.

Friends contribute heavily to the restoration of self-confidence during the grief process through supportive behaviors ("They showed me they really cared"). Friends are also the source of insights about loss, changing the way it is viewed ("They gave me other sides of the situation which I could not/did not want to see"). The following characterize specific behaviors that had a positive effect on the course of mourning.

1. A friend of mine held me while I cried.
2. The unconditional acceptance from others helped me.

3. Friends were willing to keep me busy. They took me out to keep my mind off of it.
4. They gave me a sense of security.
5. They encouraged me.
6. They listened when I wanted to talk.
7. They helped me feel that things always get better.
8. She alleviated some of my self-pity, *loneliness,* depression, and fear.

These expressions of verbal and non-verbal support are integral parts of the support systems of many reflecting signals of importance and dispelling fear that they are alone in their sorrow.

WITHOLDING THE TRUTH

If one is willing to consider that death is a natural part of life, that it is all right to grieve and be sad, that emotions surrounding death are not out of place or abnormal, that is the beginning of development of a belief system which sees death as a teacher—a source of deep emotional learning. This understanding is an important part of minimizing the fantasies and fears which intensify and complicate coping responses. The lack of this type of death education is reflected in behavior in which reality is distorted.

Not infrequently, information about death is routinely withheld or incompletely provided in order to supposedly prevent emotional upset and preoccupation with thoughts of what might happen if a loved one were to die. What is forgotten is that eventually, when the truth does emerge, those who have not been completely informed feel betrayed. Young people argue that reversing the tradition of never discussing grief and/or bereavement, would have helped them better cope with the final outcome.

To illustrate, let's examine four responses in which important information was withheld.

1. In my case I was led to believe the dying man would recover. I was completely shocked when I got a phone call saying he had died. I would have been much better prepared if I had realized the severity of the situation.
2. I was told that this person was going to recover from her sickness. When she died the next day, I felt that the doctors were covering up something. It would have been better if I was told that I may lose her than to have them saying otherwise and subsequently losing her.

3. Yes, we knew my grandfather had cancer, but only right before he died, and nobody told us how serious it was. I couldn't believe it had really happened. Also, I didn't know what to do about it, either. Maybe if our parents hadn't been afraid to tell us the truth from the beginning it would have been a little easier for me.
4. I never found out she was sick until two weeks ago. She died the day before Thanksgiving and no one ever let me know she was that bad off. I don't believe in withholding important truths in order to protect.

Keep in mind that these responses were given freely. They were on the minds of individuals involved in the deception and stood out as being important enough to write about. What is apparent is that in each situation it was believed that *the truth would have made the experience less difficult to cope with.* As usual, when the facts are later revealed, we feel shock and anger for having been deceived; sometimes the anger and distrust lasts for years. This happens in far too many loss experiences, and in each situation the pain is *not* lessened but is increased. The importance of honesty and reverence for truth must never be underestimated.

HONESTY

Let us pause for a moment and consider Beverly's reaction to the romantic breakup with her boyfriend, resulting in a very intense grief experience especially because of the dishonesty that prevailed. "Honesty in everything is *so* important. I know that if this person I lost had been honest with me throughout our relationship, all of the time, I would have been so much more prepared. I wish I could have cried right away too. I couldn't cry about it for three of four months." Obviously, when deception occurs it hinders normal grieving, and the additional affront (along with the original loss) causes the individual to harbor emotions which, under other circumstances, would not dominate recovery. Furthermore, the withholding of information from members of the family tends to create a sense of isolation eroding personal security so essential in working through grief.

Occasionally, this same situation occurs between those who are dying and survivors, resulting in even more serious ramifications for the bereaved as we shall see later. The major contribution of quality communication to loss resolution is not simply truth-telling in the face of crisis: Rather, it is the fact that openness and willingness to share allows for better management of emotional trauma in the face of life's major transitions. Effective communication occurs when the listener is able to convey to the griever, mostly in non-verbal ways, that her feelings are legitimate, that she need not be embarrassed by them, and that trust and confidentiality will permeate the exchange.

Honesty prepares us just as it limits shock, anger, and guilt by allowing us to relate to the dying and to other family members in ways which are personally meaningful. As Fran said, "I was quite well prepared as I was told all along that her health (i.e., the grandmother's) was rapidly failing. Honesty was helpful!" When we are completely informed about a crisis, it makes us feel a part of it rather than excluded from it, that we are with the family and not divorced from it, and that we are considered capable instead of incapable. Openness and honesty helps eliminate needless suffering[16].

An additional problem occurs in families that have experienced the death of a loved one but who refuse to talk about the deceased once the funeral has taken place. Young family members suffer considerably when they are unable to ask questions and get answers about the death itself. Most damaging for survivors is when the dominant figure in the family refuses to discuss the death, even refusing to allow other members of the family to mention the deceased. ("To this day my father cannot be spoken to about the death of his oldest daughter—it's an unspoken rule.") When one is unable to bridge the gap of silence, not only is the normal process of sharing hurt stymied, but for some family members it adds new sadness and even more depression because a lack of discussion is typically interpreted as "she will now be quickly forgotten."

This misinterpretation often spawns resentment towards those who refuse to discuss the deceased person in normal conversation, thus narrowing a support base. Debbie, a 20 year-old junior, tells us why she thinks continued support is so critical: "We can all be prepared to cope better with any loss—big or small—if we are able to vent our feelings without much hesitation. If we can talk to those close to us, without embarrassment, etc., it helps relieve the pain." Of course, *this type of exchange presupposes openness within the family long before a death has occurred*, and it is a significant source of preparation for dealing with any loss.

FAMILY RELATIONSHIPS

It follows that the quality of interpersonal relationships within the family is a key resource in preparation for loss experiences. An awareness of mutual love and concern and *freedom to seek support* are predictors of positive resolution of major losses. The freedom to seek assistance must not be minimized, for all too many family members, plagued with ambivalent feelings, are unsure of how they should react. ("My mother told me it was all right to cry.") The quality of the bereaved's relationships with the deceased person is equally instrumental in the course of grieving and acceptance of death.

Over and over again we were informed of situations in which there was some type of unfinished business with the deceased, which, if it had only been cleared up, would have helped the griever in the coping process. Or there were problems brought on by the death of the deceased which culminated in strained relationships among the surviving family members. Here are some examples:

1. In my case, I knew the death of my grandmother was imminent. If I had another chance again, I would be much more open with her. I would talk to her about it. I think this would have helped me to be able to better understand how she had accepted her death and in turn helped me to understand it too.
2. I was totally unprepared for a loss. It was my freshman year in college and I really had no idea how to respond except by crying and saying, "why grandma, why now?" I think I felt an emptiness mostly because we were closer than my brothers and sisters, and I wanted her to see me graduate from college.
3. My boyfriend was my main support. Without him I don't believe that I would have adjusted so quickly, even though it took a year or so. My hatred and anger that I felt kept me from my family because it was directed toward them.

Relationships among family members are sometimes strained when there is a long sickness preceding the death and respite care is not available. One family member may feel that another has not done her share of helping during this difficult period.

Differences among grievers in showing their emotions is another potential source of conflict. A young woman who came to see me after the death of her father was especially distraught. One reason for this was that the rest of the family felt she had displayed too much emotion and had overdone her caring gestures. What they did not know was the strong feeling that she had had for her father. "He was the only person that understood me," she recalled. "He let me be a child again when I was around him. I loved him so much." The lack of open and intimate communication within this family, which had prevailed for years, was a contributing factor to family conflict when death occurred. Conversely, when strong caring relationships exist among members of a family and friends, when we are encouraged to express emotions, then even the most difficult situations can be overcome, as suggested by Rena:

> Last year, four people died in four weeks. I think the things which helped me the most were my friends and my mother. For over a month I was in a state of shock. My friends spent a lot of time with me and pulled me out of the shell I had crawled into. Finally, I started going out again, and with time and all the support I got from others, it doesn't hurt as much.

The impact of these four sudden deaths, and Rena's subsequent readjustment, point to the need we all have for high quality interpersonal transactions with significant support persons. There is little doubt that although relating well does not guarantee we will be able to cope well with a particular death, relating well is the framework within which strength and self-understanding generally lead to recovery and the integration of loss into life[17].

What if our family is not open with its feelings, and we have been taught to "go it alone?" Recognizing how important interpersonal transactions are to mental health, it is essential to seek someone to share feelings with for peace of mind. It may mean turning to an understanding relative or a close friend. This is a time when it is perfectly legitimate to be *interdependent.* If we fail to find someone to listen, it becomes difficult to put thoughts into perspective, to realign priorities. In some instances, this energy-consuming conflict with our feelings escalates into long-term problems, as Mary reminds us after the death of her sister. "Five years after the incident I still had problems and felt I wasn't coping—I had a great many guilt feelings. I had a very close friend who allowed me to speak out freely—she made no judgments, no answers, just honest listening." Note that the ultimate listener was a friend and not a family member, as death in her family was not to be discussed, and Mary had chosen to carry her guilt for five years until it became too much for her to live with.

NEEDED INFORMATION

Next to having open relationships and the dialogue which accompanies them, a lack of death awareness was a consistent theme expressed by many respondents as a reason for being totally unprepared to deal with the event of death. As a result, their reactions were total disbelief, sometimes fierce, and always energy-draining. What specific content about death was lacking in frustrating the adjustment process?

First, they needed to know that grief was *natural* and that it was all right to let emotions flow. This was contrary to the common belief that becoming "emotional" was a sign of weakness. It also implied that they understood what emotions are, how they should be interpreted, and what their protective function is. Knowledge about the grief process was totally absent in the initial confrontations with death and led young people to question not only their own feelings but also the propriety of sharing them with others.

Second, it was necessary to understand how the person who was dying felt. If they were able to understand the needs of dying people, their fears, and the emotional changes they experience, such understanding would have removed some anxiety in terms of what to say or do when visiting. Knowing what to say to one who is dying was especially perplexing.

Third, they needed to be familiar with death rituals. Because many young adults had not been permitted as children to participate in death rituals of family members, and be involved as part of the family, they had been deprived of the opportunity for experiential learning. Clearly, ritual helps establish the reality of death[18]. In not knowing what to expect during the crisis, their anxieties had increased at the time of their first wakes or funerals.

Fourth, they desired to know what loved ones had wanted in terms of funeral arrangements *before* they became ill or died. Because so much had to be done in a short time after the death of a loved one, it was increasingly stressful to have to make decisions regarding services and burial with the surviving parent or relative. If there had been a willingness to discuss preferences beforehand, the pressure of decision-making would have been lessened and conflict between some family members reduced.

Fifth, it was essential to learn how to cope with the stresses surrounding death events. Because they had felt so overwhelmed by the sudden realization that someone who has been alive was now dead, they experienced extreme difficulty in dealing with anxiety and tension.

Sixth, they needed to talk about death *before* it happened within the family and to understand that when death occurs, each person's feelings are valid, regardless of *the manner in which they are expressed.* It would have been important to know that they did not have to follow the grieving behaviors exhibited by other family members. There must be respect for different modes of expression. The most frequent suggestion made was that death and other relationship losses be talked about *before* they take place.

What is basically inherent in many of these statements is an obvious need to experience deep emotional feelings early in life in order to develop tools for self-understanding, and experience the dimensions of emotionality in others. Direct, early experience with stress-laden events is the primary learning force in the development of coping patterns and the acceptance of emotions accompanying loss. Sadness, for example, must be characterized as a *normal* part of separation; we need to reintroduce the true affective dimension of loss, commonly removed from death events by media coverage and the reduction of ritual.

It is all right for adults to cry in the presence of their children or even cry with them. Simply: *Total* humanness must be expressed. When we have experienced the death of a loved one as a primary mourner, and given equal consideration with other family members, the death becomes an event promoting community, a feeling of belonging and solidarity, while at the same time preparing us for the tribulations connected with future losses. What we so frequently learn for the first time on such occasions is that there are many people who feel the way we do, that there is nothing wrong with us or the emotions being experienced. Gerri placed the importance of experience in the following perspective: "I do, however, think that death is easier to cope with the second time. When you realize everybody dies, after a while your depression becomes your own selfishness." Her statement is arguable, although there is a new found self-awareness when we are tested in that manner. We also learn the importance of reinforcement from others who are loved and respected. Nevertheless, there are many people who would not agree with Gerri's observations. They would be right to suggest instead that it may not be easier in terms of the pain, and that one does not become depressed out of self-interest.

To pursue this issue further, we might ask ourselves why we have grieved the death of a loved one, and perhaps reach the conclusion that selfishness is involved to some extent, as we tend to overemphasize what *we* no longer have (i.e., are you feeling sorry for the deceased or more for yourself?). We refuse to give up that which we have cherished, and self-pity is expected. After all, grieving the death of a loved one includes the death of part of the self as well.

Jackson[19] has suggested that there are three major reasons why we grieve: there is fear of what lies ahead, there is a sense of insecurity in the face of our loss, and we are sorry for ourselves because we have been deprived of our loved one. I believe there is a fourth reason. We often feel the deceased has been cheated out of life, the retirement deserved or the experiences that would have been so joyful and hoped for. Nevertheless, the experience of successfully grieving the death of a loved one helps us recognize one basic fact: having used coping mechanisms that work, we are now better able to reduce our fears of the unknown and fantasies surrounding death.

Let us conclude our discussion of preparation with the following illustration of what the young or old can attain when we believe we can prevail and death is no longer a taboo. Dawn advises:

> The thing that helped most in coping with the loss of my mom was that I was prepared for it because I knew in advance she was going to die. So my grief work was basically finished before the actual event. Also, I had always told my mother how much I cared for her and loved her—so nothing was unfinished when she died. I had no regrets about not saying things to her I should have when she was alive. . . . I coped fairly well, I think. Although my mom died at a fairly young age (56 years old), she was always such an active, vibrant person and I felt she utilized all her time to the fullest while she was alive. That's why I was able to cope with her death.

What Dawn and many other young people tell us is what Leo Buscaglia has often stated and what many of us tend to forget: If you live, love and trust, it is easier to let go.

You might ask yourself at this point, when was the last time you told someone very close to you that you loved him or her. Why are you putting it off? This is a difficult question to answer, but it is critical to confront. If we can slowly begin the process of expressing feelings, if we can reconcile ourselves to the fact of mortality, if we can admit that death gives meaning to life, our agenda for preparing to cope with the death of a loved one becomes our agenda to find new meaning in life.

That new meaning in life implies that each of us make a ruthless self-assessment with regard to what we value. Just how important are people in our lives? What connections do we have to things that do not change, that are eternal? How strongly are we committed to our goals and interests? Essentially, what we are being told by young adults is: *We need roots, timeless connections, endless bonds in order to survive when our world collapses around us.* They are saying that the risk of post-bereavement illness and trauma is clearly lessened if we possess a wide variety of connections to people — values, and interests which are not transient and fleeting. Study these responses.

Annie: "I feel the significant base of values, influenced by my parents, is an important source of strength, especially when dealing with tragedy in my life."

Alice: "We are not here forever and we should always keep this concept in the back of our minds."

Andrea: "The most effective method I've used to prepare myself for losses is developing my interests and potential goals (career and other)."

Dan: "Accepting yourself for who and what you really are before a loss occurs, can always ease the shock of any loss. Most people, I find, have forgotten or maybe never learned who they are."

Maureen: "One should not have just one or two things that they feel they could not live without. Rather, having many loved ones, interests, and activities will help when you lose someone or something."

Michelle: "Just know that God was and is always there. He will never let us get into a situation, which through Him, we cannot cope with."

Arthur: "To be mentally prepared, I believe, is the key factor in dealing with loss."

Julie: "I think now that it is important to have your own life and have a good sense of your own self and worth before you can really have a good relationship."

In the final analysis, it is the spirit and resources within each of us that is the core of survival, and the more we develop what is within, the more we use our unconscious minds, the better prepared we will be to deal with death and other loss events. This all presupposes a willingness to *accept* the discovery that our focus on life is too narrow in scope and that much more can be accomplished with the talents and abilities which lie dormant.

REFERENCES

1. Green, B. & Irish, D. *Death education: Preparation for living.* Cambridge: Schenkman, 1971.
2. Preston, J. Toward an anthropology of death. *Intellect,* 1977, April, 343–44.
3. Parkes, C. Bereavement: *Studies of grief in adult life.* New York: International Universities Press, 1972.
4. Phillips, D. & Feldman, K. A dip in deaths before ceremonial occasions: Some new relationships between social integration and mortality. *American Sociological Review,* 1973, 38, 678–696.
5. Weisman, A. & Hackett, T. Predilection to death. *Psychosomatic Medicine,* 1961, 23, 232–256.
6. Kubler-Ross, E. *On death and dying.* New York: Macmillan, 1969.
7. Kastenbaum, R. & Kastenbaum, B. Hope, survival and the caring environment. In E. Palmore & F. Jeffers (Eds.). *Prediction of Life Span.* Lexington, MA: D.C. Heath, 1971.
8. Minkoff, K., Bergman, E., Beck, A. & Beck, R. Hopelessness, depression and attempted suicide. *American Journal of Psychiatry,* 1973, 130[4], 455–459.
9. Lynch, J. *The broken heart.* New York: Basic Books, 1977.
10. Myers, J., Lindenthal, J. & Pepper, M. Life events, social integration, and psychiatric symptomatology. *Journal of Health and Social Behavior,* 1961, 23, 232–256.
11. Parkes, C. Determinants of outcome following bereavement. *Omega,* 1975, 6, 303–323.
12. Sullivan, H. *The interpersonal theory of psychiatry.* New York: Norton, 1953.
13. Shephard, M. *Someone you love is dying.* New York: Charter, 1975.
14. Moro, R. *Death, grief, and widowhood.* Berkeley, CA: Parallax, 1979.
15. Kopp, E. *An end to innocence.* New York: Macmillan, 1979.
16. Brantner, J. *Positive approaches to dying. Death Education,* 1977, 1, 293–304.
17. Parkes, C. & Weiss, R. *Recovery from breavement.* New York: Basic Books, 1983.
18. Stephenson, J. *Death, grief, and mourning.* New York: Macmillan, 1985.
19. Jackson, E. You and your grief. In D. Berg & G. Daugherty (Eds.), *The individual, society and death.* Baltimore, MD: Waverly, 1972.

Chapter Five

BELIEFS ABOUT THE DYING: ESTABLISHING RELATIONSHIPS

What is essential is invisible to the eye.
                        Antoine de Saint Exurpery
                        in *The Little Prince*

Miracles are not contrary to nature. They are only contrary to what we know [believe] about nature.
                        St. Augustine

There were times when I wanted to get sick (from the radiation and chemotherapy) but I would not permit it.
                        Jeff Blatnick, 1984 Olympics Gold
                        Medal winner

If you are dealing with the terminally ill, spend as much time as possible with them. Be there to hold their hand and hug them when they need it. Most important — be there when they die to say goodbye to them — something I missed, and I still resent it.
                        Jane, 20 years old

Everyone is terminal. Those who have been declared so by a physician simply have a more compact time span to consider than others. Therefore, thoughts about personal death are farthest from our minds. And rightly so. Although death seems remote, eventually we will be called upon to be with a dying friend or loved one. At that time, our fear of death will exert a powerful influence on how we relate to the dying person. We will either use our energy to be fully present or use it to fend off fear.

To the perceptive observer, the literature on death in western society is replete with descriptions of dwindling relationships between medical personnel, family members and the dying person as death draws near. In this chapter we examine the needs of the dying and how we as potential survivors can best meet these needs. Discussion of the Hospice movement, with the emphasis on affirming life until death, is followed by an analysis of the stages model of dying and how we should respond to various emotions in the dying process.

This material is especially important to survivors and the dying as assumptions and beliefs about death and prolonging life are dramatically illustrated in the behavior which occurs. These assumptions and beliefs affect the quality of life of the dying person and the subsequent grieving of survivers. It is well known that the beliefs of the dying affect the results of treatment used in fighting their diseases. That is a primary reason why some cancer patients have severe side effects from chemotherapy and others do not.

FEELINGS OF INADEQUACY

The anecdotal data in the Young Adult Study suggested great feelings of inadequacy and frustration when one was confronted with the expected death of a loved one. This is a near universal experience. Questions such as, What can I say? What should I do? or Should I go and visit at this time? were most puzzling. These queries are to be expected, given the cultural distancing of personal death. However, keep in mind that these questions and the fears they are based upon are a direct result of the beliefs about death we formed as children. Our death fears (beliefs) deeply affect our behavior around the dying.

Recall our earlier discussion of a profound and simple truth that most people refuse to believe: *all human relationships end in separation.* Indeed, all relationships of every type end in separation. This is profound because if we study and contemplate its meaning, it possesses far-reaching implications for living and developing attitudes and beliefs which govern behavior toward those who are dying. The simplicity of this truth lies in the realization that since the beginning of recorded history, separation has been the most predictable factor in human behavior. Little is said about the experience that relationships inevitably end. Throughout life, there is a refusal to allow the truism to develop to its logical implications.

When the thought of death comes to conscious awareness, it is rationalized as an event many years in the future and nothing to be concerned about in the present. Yet it is the present—day by day, month by month, year by year—which prepares us for the future when separation inevitably comes. Sometimes, this truth strikes home through a confrontation with the death of a loved one, as it did with Annette after the death of her father. "I do believe that healthy grief yields an end-product: you become more of an individual in realizing that nothing lasts forever; the people around you won't and neither will you." At the very least, the frank and open discussion of separation, which naturally comes up but is curtly dismissed, could save unnecessary suffering. How we separate from life is as important as how life has been lived. Talking about this prospect will enrich our final days. Silence will strip us of personhood. Moreover, the beliefs of family, friends, and caregivers at this time will play crucial roles in our final separation.

ASSUMPTIONS/BELIEFS HELD BY EXCEPTIONAL CAREGIVERS

How do caregivers help the dying? How can we facilitate the creation of a caring, open relationship with the dying? What skills do exceptional caregivers possess? Why are some caregivers more at ease with the dying than others? Can anyone develop the ability to deal with the conflict of expectations which often occur between the dying person and the family? The answers to these important questions are found in the attitudes and beliefs caregivers possess about death, the dying person, and themselves. The following, though by no means exhaustive list, represents the range of assumptions and beliefs associated with effective caregiving by family members or professionals. They provide insight into the attitudinal frame of reference demanded in establishing caring relationships when death is considered probable.

1. Each person's dying is individual and reflects his/her lifestyle.
2. The dying are *living* the remaining days, months, or years of their lives.
3. The dying must be allowed to be in control of their lives in so far as they choose.
4. Death is a universal, natural event which gives meaning to existence.
5. Family members have needs to be met as well as the dying person.
6. The dying should be treated with the same respect given to dear friends.
7. Encourage the expression of feelings of the dying person and the family.
8. Never underestimate the coping ability of the dying person or family members.
9. Emotions such as anger and rage expressed by the dying toward individuals are *never* considered personal attacks.

10. Never reinforce helplessness by doing for the dying what they can do for themselves.
11. The use of physical touch (handshake, hugs, etc.) is more significant than what is spoken.
12. Hope must be maintained.
13. The *consistent presence* of those who care is the key to comfort and dignity for the dying.
14. Unconditional love is a powerful coping force for the dying and their families.
15. Openness and honesty are basic essentials in living and dying.
16. It is important to involve the family as a cohesive unit in caring for the dying family member as circumstances permit.
17. Listening is a part of the art of loving.
18. Change is a condition of existence.

This list would make a significant source of discussion questions for family and caregivers. These positive assumptions and beliefs are the basis for building relationships during crises because the dying person is *always* considered the most important person in the drama of death.

How can anyone begin to develop new viewpoints about caring for the dying? Can we change our beliefs and overcome the fear and apprehension surrounding the dying event? The answer is "yes" to both questions. Specifically, these changes occur by being open to and modeling the behavior of exceptional caregivers. It means asking questions of these professionals and choosing to participate in the care of others. It means realizing that the greatest gift we give to the living and the dying is ourselves and our presence.

Furthermore, we must recognize that misinformation and non-information are potent sources of behavior, perhaps as effective as any of our family or social traditions[1]. Therefore, we must eliminate the half-truths, fables, and falsehoods about the dying which affect our behavior around them. In this way, we develop relationships which facilitate the massive transitions dying demands.

In the pages to follow we will examine how these relationships develop through greater awareness of the needs of those coping with life-threatening illness.

DYING STYLES

There are many variables involved in the process of dying so that even though dying is much the same for all of us, it is also unique to each person, for it reflects the way each has lived [2-4]. Thus, some people choose to die in silence. Even between husband and wife, sometimes nothing is said about dying. Others will be fighters, as Dylan Thomas suggested ("Do not go gentle into that good night,/Rage, rage against the dying of the light"). Their fighting includes changing their lifestyles radically, resolving life-long conflicts, taking responsibility for their disease, changing attitudes, and obtaining peace of mind for the first time in their lives. This group often obtain long-term remissions or cure themselves of their illness.

Still others believe that on hearing the news of their life-threatening illness nothing can be done, and they go home to wait for death. Some choose to keep up a good front and go on as if nothing has happened; others deny to the end.

Of course, there are a number of individuals who participate very little in their dying. They make minor changes, but essentially leave *their* dying in the hands of the physician.

Many others will choose to have one special loved one or their family with them most of the time. *Some will have no choice at all;* they will be subtly manipulated in their dying by family and physician. Dying styles are diverse and individual and therefore as different as lifestyles.

THE DYING ARE LIVING

The belief that the dying are living is simple yet profound. Everyone agrees this is basically true but they do not *believe* it. For example, the dying search for honesty from friends, family or physicians but are often thwarted because of the fear that pervades the relationship. If we are honest with the dying, they can cope with anything—honesty is therapy. Often, those around the terminally ill are afraid of the symbolic meaning of the disease, not the person, afraid of the possible outcome and the reactions of the dying person. Fear always affects the quality of care given by family and friends. They love the person very much, but they cannot be truly honest about what is happening. In his book, *Someone You Love Is Dying,* psychiatrist Martin Shephard[5] writes:

> Again and again, I return to the theme of open and honest communication as the most useful element in helping someone to die in comfort and dignity. Failure to communicate honestly not only prevents full sharing of thoughts and feelings but deprives everyone of an opportunity to plan for the future.

Yes, the dying especially should be allowed to plan for their immediate future needs and seek an advocate in medical matters. The fear they sense in those around them is sometimes interpreted as "a fear of me—that I am unloveable." It follows that when we feel different from those we love—we feel estrangement as well. However, most people crave structure in the face of crisis, that is, a sense of direction. Family and friends give the dying structure, that power to cope by their willingness to treat them with respect and dignity. We underestimate their inherent ability to cope with their dying, an ability everyone possesses. There is always coping ability—if it is fed truth.

LEARNING FROM THE DYING

The deathbed scenes of old, which Philippe Aries[6] so aptly describes, were not merely open and accepting family rituals but also potent sources of beliefs about death. Much learning was passed from the dying to survivors. Death was visible. The family, the source of mutual support, was acutely sensitive to the wishes of the dying, helping them live their lives to the end.

The scene has changed considerably since then. The dying are not as often in charge of their remaining hours. Unless they are especially vigilant and lucid, or have families who place a high priority on allowing them to maintain dignity, they may not be consulted or allowed to die in a way which is in agreement with their wishes. However, each of us has but one death and one dying style and it seems most fitting that we should, in so far as possible, be the main figure, the center of concern, the one who is to speak and to be listened to. Should people die according to the expectations of others, or will their need to maintain self-worth be honored? Surgeon Victor Richards[7] answers: "The first thing to remember about dying patients is that it is *their* death" (p. 326).

The observation that there is no need for unnecessary suffering should be a central theme for those attending the dying. Significantly, they do not suffer just physically; they suffer emotionally because they are not related to as living. Ironically, emotional pain affects the intensity of physical pain. This is critical to understand if we are going to help and give comfort. The nature and impact of relationships enjoyed in living and dying bear heavily on a happy death as they do on a happy life.

Why is it then, when it is obvious that people are dying, they are subtly declared "different" and are related to as non-persons? Could fear, negative stereotypes or the reminder that we, too, are mortal drive us to separate ourselves from the dying and in doing so, isolate them from connections to life? Because a person is labeled as "dying" it does not mean that his individuality ceases to exist. The dying are still whole persons. They teach us—"that we have only NOW"—if we are willing to listen and not allow fear to dominate[8]. They teach us monumental lessons: we possess more than we appreciate; trust is a critical lifeline; we can cope with any loss; it is all right to behave as a child again; and there is strength in love which is eternal. This learning cannot take place unless the living-dying relationship is an open one. Therefore, we must take special care, whether family member or medical personnel, not to submit to the temptation to use deception as therapy[9].

This brings us to the question: What is there to talk about with the dying person? Here is a list of subjects which many dying people wish to discuss during the course of their illness. To be sure, these topics place a premium on communication and a persistent, caring relationship. They are:

1. Discussion of what occurred today, the type and amount of pain experienced, the exchanges with friends and caregivers, the results of tests administered and treatment received. Noteably, caregivers should be aware of the danger of reinforcing negative beliefs about treatment. The importance of participating in treatment, believing in its efficacy as well as the power of a positive attitude, should be stressed.

2. A review of past life events, a survey of projects finished, of friendships enjoyed, of business left unfinished. We can provide the time for this personal reflection on the meaning of life.

3. A frank and open discussion of the disposition of personal effects, money, special bequests, the payment of bills, or the upkeep of a home or equipment.

4. A discussion of unknowns, of what to expect in treatments/ medications to come, of fear of death. Sometimes there is great fear associated with how one will die. Will it be by suffocation or choking? Will it be painful? Most of us fear the process of dying and not death itself.

5. A discussion of immediate desires or needs, such as something from home that is familiar and useful. It could be reading materials, an electric shaver, or a special piece of clothing.

6. A discussion of funeral arrangements, pall bearers, clothing, of people coming back to the house. (Not all may wish to discuss arrangements, but many dying people do).

7. Whether the visitor should stay longer or leave, talk or just sit

quietly. Many sick people need to rest or be alone at times that conflict with visits by friends and family. This has to be discussed openly. (My father, dying of emphysema, would often tell my brother and me that he wanted us to go—he was tired—even when we had only been with him a few minutes. This type of situation could be misinterpreted if family are not aware of and open to this need).

8. A discussion of philosophical issues which have become real. The meaning of pain and suffering is frequently an issue for discussion. The question "why?" is a difficult one to answer. (A dying person once said to me, "I never thought He [God] would give me such a cross to bear.") We do not have to have "answers" as much as we need to help the person verbalize what pain and suffering may mean to him/her. We may share our beliefs if appropriate, but never present them as the final answer for the person, simply our philosophy of suffering.

9. Hope. A dialogue about hope in the days ahead, or hopes of an afterlife are often subjects of concern. The hope that they will "live on" through what they contributed during their lifetimes, or through their children or grandchildren, are a part of life review. This may be coupled with fears for the hardships survivors might face[10].

10. How one's children will fare is frequently a subject of concern. How they will be cared for and by whom and how they may react to the death are significant issues.

11. And last but not least, the dying often want to talk about everyday events and issues. A favorite superstar or professional team, a new building being erected, the weather, or a friend who has made news are examples of topics of conversation.

In answer to the question "What is there to talk about?" we answer "The same that we talk about with the living." Physician Cicely Saunders[11] said: "Humiliation and exposure are the lot of many of the very ill. We can help them to feel valued in the way we give the things of everyday life" (p. 165).

The problems of dying in America, therefore, are essentially problems of interpersonal transactions. In a word, alienation. These problems involve questionable forms of interpersonal exchange between the dying person, the family, and medical personnel. Despite this unfortunate condition there is evidence to suggest that meaningful relationships are significant factors in how long dying patients live[12]. In some respects, relating to dying people is different, but, in some ways, it is also common sense: We never degrade a person by telling him/her that the illness is not serious, by saying we will visit again in two days and then not return, by talking down to him/her, by lying or by keeping a person waiting for long periods of time. The issues which evolve are essentially issues of truth, power, trust, fear and self-worth.

To put it another way, there are conspiracies of silence, battles of denial (by the family and some medical personnel as well as the dying person) and the complete refusal on the part of survivors to recognize that the dying *possess the same basic human needs as "the living."* That fact is critical to understand. The needs of people in life-threatening crises are simply manifested in different ways. Their basic needs, now more than ever, must be honored. The dying possess the same rights as the living.

Consequently, *the great challenge for family and other caregivers is to find out how the dying person wants to cope* with the present circumstances. The dying possess the ability to cope, if we treat them fairly and promote self-determination. Psychologist Therese Rando[13] puts it this way: "We have the power to structure schedules and surroundings so patients have a sense of security and control over life and their environment. If we have a non-judgmental, warm attitude, we can elicit the feelings and thoughts they need to communicate" (p. 267).

NEEDS OF THE LIVING AND DYING

There are two dynamics which operate in all interpersonal relationships: the needs of the people involved and the reason or goal for coming together[14]. Unless we give detailed attention to the former, the latter will never be properly addressed. That is to say, in the desire to do all that can be done for a dying loved one (bringing comfort, love, and a reduction of physical or emotional pain), guidelines for action must focus on *their* priorities. We begin by recognizing that when death threatens, a person experiences heightened sensitivity to his or her world and those who are in it. Basic needs and the taken-for-granted treasures of life are magnified through the lens of illness.

Much has been written about what people need to feel good about themselves and make a contribution to the community in which they live[15-17]. Most taxonomies of needs begin with the biological necessities, for without food, sleep, and shelter, other concerns are of little importance. Nevertheless, it is not unusual that due to the nature of an illness biological needs are not met. Some individuals are unable to keep food down, while others feel nauseated at the smell of food. Nor do many dying people sleep on a regular basis. Both of these factors contribute to physical unrest and especially to emotional disposition.

Next come feelings of security. We all seek protection from possible danger. Control over the environment gives a sense of security which minimizes anxiety and fear. Security is sought after in many forms: economic security, safety from violence, or the security among friends. Over time, the sense of what is important to feel secure about changes drastically. However, everyone needs the stability which secure surroundings provide. For the dying, this means people and places—people who can be trusted and places of familiarity. When feelings of powerlessness prevail, everyone else becomes a power figure in life. And when the dying finds themselves in a hospital or nursing home (occasionally in their own home) where they sense they are "just another patient" and not "special" to at least one caregiver, the core of security is uprooted. There are additional fears to manage.

According to Maslow[17], when biological and security needs have been met love from others and affirmation of self-worth is essential for each person. These are *supreme needs*. To realize that at least one other person loves you, not because of what you do but just because you are you, is an all-consuming need. As suggested earlier, unconditional love is central to feelings of self-worth; everyone needs to feel important. This sense of worth is strongly influenced by the way others treat us. How are the needs of affection and worth manifested in daily life? Recall the "little things" that are freely given by a loved one, and how good that makes us feel. The living *and* the dying sense the same unconditional giving or lack of it in relationships that build or destroy feelings of self-worth.

The need for recognition is often met by a mere phone call, the greeting of a friend, the mention of our name, a handshake, a "Hi, Mom" or a pat on the back by the boss for a job well done. The living *and* the dying need this attention expressed in a variety of forms and gestures. All these signs are affirmations of positive regard. For the dying, recognition needs must continuously be met by sincere attention from friends and family and by short but *consistent* visits especially as the disease takes its inexorable toll on physical features.

Recognition needs of the dying are further met through review of life experiences and the willingness of family and friends to seek their opinions and wisdom on appropriate topics. Attention is shown in many ways: a single flower, a piece of mail, the offering of a sip of water, a favorite possession brought to the hospital room, even the soft whisper of one's name. Recall how you have felt when attention was lacking in your life. Can you remember a time when you were ill and didn't feel that friends and family were spending enough time with you, or that they had so many other odd jobs to do that they were unable to show the concern you expected? Multiply those feelings by the circumstances of a final illness and you will begin to appreciate the importance of sincere attention.

UNCONDITIONAL LOVE AND THE DYING PROCESS

Physician Bernie Siegel[18] has suggested that love is the most powerful immune stimulant known to medicine. Interestingly, it is much more than a biological force for it possesses the power to change the emotional disposition of patient and family members alike. The importance of unconditional love in healing and prolonging life must never be underestimated. Nurses and hospice workers often report how the course of life-threatening illness changes when a dying person receives unconditional love through the sacrifices, commitment and care unselfishly given by others. The fundamental message is: loving attention *prolongs* life.

I remember visiting with a young AIDS victim who told me about his recent trip to a medical center for tests. One evening, a 61 year-old nurse who was taking care of him said: "I work with a lot of elderly people who are dying and I can understand that their time has come. But I can't understand someone dying who is so young." He looked at me and said: "I knew she *really cared.*" The care of that nurse, her manner, her touch, and her expression of love was a deeply refreshing experience for this young man who had endured excessive discrimination because of his illness. It was deeply touching to have someone care and he needed to share that highlight of his journey to the medical center. "I knew she really cared" is an intriguing message for all caregivers to give emotional needs the highest priority in their relationships.

Alice provides the following anecdote of the power of caring and unconditional love in prolonging life.

My uncle, age 82 was declared terminally ill by many doctors and told he would die within the next six months. My aunt did not give up hope and took my uncle out of the hospital and took it upon herself to help him. At that time he could not walk or go to the bathroom alone. My aunt rolled his back with a *rolling pin* harshly, gave him bodily massages, and made him try to walk daily. My aunt was 80 years old at that time and had more life than anyone I knew. Needless to say, within a year, my uncle could walk up to a mile before having to rest. He ended up dying at age 88 but he had six extra precious years to watch his neices and nephews growing up. The hospital even sent my aunt a letter of recognition, declaring it was a miracle.

This was a miracle of unconditional love by Alice's aunt. Needs concerning love and worth are met by the *way* we share it with others. This often means the gift of time to the dying, which involves the commitment of presence when *they* choose to talk. If you wish to establish strong relationships with anyone — *give them more than they expect.* What is more precious to give than time?

Meeting needs further implies that caregivers remain sensitive to ways that help the dying stay in control of living. Too often they are thoughtlessly stripped of their dignity by the refusal to allow them to use skills they still possess. Family members may assist them in eating or reading, but need not take over and do everything thereby reinforcing further inaction. Caregivers should take time to assist the person to the bathroom instead of insisting on the use of a bedpan. To be able to get up, to move, means one is still in control. This is life affirming. Most important, it is an accomplishment that enhances self-esteem[19].

A related matter is the fact that some dying people often undergo role changes. They no longer see themselves as father, mother, breadwinner, professor or student; and their change of status drops as the routine of hospital procedure is enforced. There is a tendency to forget, amidst all of the overwhelming changes brought on by disease, that the dying person's self-worth walks a tenuous line of ups and downs. To understand this fact is to understand behavior labeled as "not being like her." There are many reasons for a dying person to be angry, not the least of which is to feel, "I'm no longer the person I used to be."

NON-VERBAL COMMUNICATION

Touch becomes a major vehicle for destroying the "I am a non-person" assumption and conveying affection and admiration. When we allow the loved one to place his hand in ours, or when we reach out as we greet the person during conversation, touching becomes a symbolic bond giving assurance and feelings of sincere concern. The place of tactile communication in physical and emotional health has been well established, as it conveys feelings and attitudes in ways which have a stronger impact than the spoken word. It also enhances communication when used in conjunction with verbal exchanges. This is especially significant in relating to people who are seriously ill, as it has been suggested that anyone in an unfamiliar setting, such as a hospital, reverts to more primitive forms of interaction such as touch[20].

From my own work with the dying, I am convinced that human touch is clearly the most significant though underused way of conveying sincerity and caring. I always make an effort to shake hands, touch the hand, or if appropriate kiss the person, depending on the individual circumstances of each visit. While not everyone wants to be touched, the vast majority of seriously ill people are most accepting to this form of communication. The act of touching helps remove the stigma that they are "different."

Two other components for conveying love and warmth are eye contact and body position. The eyes reflect strong emotion to both the living *and* the dying. Eye contact says, "My interest and concern is with you and your plight." The dying person's value is reflected in our eyes. It is not easy to maintain eye contact with the dying (and it can be overdone) when we are confronting strong emotions. The fear is that we may "break down"; although there is nothing wrong or unbecoming with sharing emotion. It may well be the most appropriate expression to cry together. On the other hand, to help maintain composure, keeping attention on the purpose of the visit is useful.

Most importantly, we need to be aware that our own physical positioning says much to the dying person. Do we stay near or do we draw away? Do we stand looking down on the person or do we search for ways to convey equality and empathy. The message of conveying equality can be accomplished in part by sitting in a chair or on the edge of the bed so that *our eyes meet on the same level.* To have to look up to a visitor or to have someone hovering over you does nothing but oppress and in some instances infuriate. We inadvertently play power games by this behavior. Standing over someone merely emphasizes inequality and decline. Caregivers need to be both spontaneous and vulnerable to the dying person. This is especially true of men who tend not to allow emotions to show.

Does everyone die in isolation created by the inability to relate? No. It is evident that some people wish to die alone, do not want to talk about the prospect, or choose to relinquish control to others. But most people die when they decide to die[21]. There are numerous examples of this choice. Michelle's father is illustrative of this phenomenon:

The doctor told us (two months ago) that my father would pass away the next day. He lived for three weeks after that because he wanted to help my mother prepare herself.

There are numerous individual reactions by caregivers to the reality of death. Thus, we cannot relate to every dying person in the same way. It is critical to recall that there are as many styles of dying as there are styles of living. Our challenge in helping the dying live until they die is to understand the indicators to be found in their lifetime habits. How do they choose to live their dying? Above all, we must never take away their hope in the quest to facilitate their choices.

Finally, it is tempting to overgeneralize what is known about *some* dying people to *all* dying people. This is an avoidable trap. If one has lived as a fighter, it is quite likely he/she will die fighting that which is perceived as the adversary. Others choose to slip away in peace and with acceptance. The lesson is clear: despite our knowledge, emotional learning occurs again and again and we must always be open to it—if we truly *believe* that every dying person is unique.

WHOSE DEATH IS IT?

All death-bed scenes are not poignant, serene, and acceptable. The healthy-dying fantasy (that everyone dies accepting death) turns into a devastating dilemma, increasing anxiety for survivors and caregivers alike[22]. It is not easy for survivors to stand by and observe circumstances unfold with which they do not agree. However, who is the major focus in the drama of death? Is it not they who are dying? We must not force others to die our kind of death, although we may help them alter the way they look at dying. Should we not allow the dying to pick and choose who they want to be with at such critical times? Instead of forcing our expectations, we need to be attentive to their cues.

It follows that we should not be offended if the dying loved one refuses to share certain information with us that he willingly shares with another. A dying person chooses to share with others for several reasons: to "protect" us, out of love, out of fear we will not understand, or perhaps because of embarrassment. Sometimes the nature of the disease clouds memory or precludes any conversation which would have been the normal opportunity to disclose information. There are many answers to this dilemma: nevertheless, we should allow loved ones that freedom of choice unencumbered by our personal preferences.

Special Needs of the Dying

In times of crises, special needs arise which on examination are an intensification of the *security* and *ego* needs that are constantly at the root of human behavior. Security and ego needs become very special when existence is threatened. The search for safety becomes one of the first concerns of societies as well as individuals. Sterile hospital settings coupled with poor quality relationships between medical personnel and patients, or patients and families, often spawn feelings of powerlessness in the dying person. Powerlessness often adds to depression.

Dying is frequently organized and controlled by institutional goals and bureaucratic rules[23]. Therefore the dying search increasingly for characteristics in nurses, doctors, and family members which give them a sense of hope and trust. To some, the humanness exhibited by hospital personnel is lacking because it is clothed in the garb of "clinical efficiency." To others, helping professionals become strong power figures that are either to be challenged, or treated gently out of fear of alienating a source of help.

TELLING THE TRUTH

Like most patients in the hospital setting, the dying forget that they employ the physician to work for them. They demand little in the way of medical personnel accounting for their actions, and along with their families the ill become victims of intimidation through medical jargon and time barriers. However, most patients seek nothing more than the truth, as do their families. They want to be able to assess and direct their remaining days. Dignity is at the center of security. The fear of increasing dependence and loss of control over the direction that life is taking, especially with the normally self-reliant person, becomes a major source of anxiety[10].

When extreme patterns of conduct or evident indifference are introduced into their lives by others, including members of their family, additional stress is introduced. We subtly invite social calamities in the hospital room by frustrating the human desire to be treated as an equal. There is no "patient power," but there is a tendency in society to strip the dying (as well as the elderly) of their rights to make their own decisions. We are *not* referring to decisions regarding self-destruction, but decisions about care based on truth regarding their condition and prognosis.

Without truth, all is lost[24]. The reason we lie is to avoid the pain of confronting change and heightened emotional responses.

The ill express much anger at being sick. As Leslie put it: "I'm sick of being sick." Anger sometimes becomes the substitute for crying for both sexes, as few dare cry or be honest with feelings in an atmosphere that is so perilous. What patients are saying is: they sense the nature of our presence, whether we are "warm and sincere" or "detached and professional." The ill are saying that we, the so-called living, are half the relationship and therefore are half of the problem.

I asked Kathy (at twenty-three, dying of leukemia) what was the most important thing the living must learn in order to relate better to the dying. She replied: "Be *honest;* be honest about what you're feeling. The main thing is to realize when you walk into a sick room how you are feeling and why." This is a near-impossible task for medical personnel and families alike because it presupposes that they have consistently evaluated their actions in terms of beliefs about death and attending the dying. This is a major undertaking in which most of us sadly lack experience. What Kathy was implying is: if the caregiver's energy and attention is focused on his or her fears, or saying the wrong thing, he or she will find it impossible to be fully present to the dying person. This brings us to the issue of truth-telling.

Many physicians argue that to tell a person he is dying will only hasten his demise because the ill lose their will to fight. However, psychologist Charles Garfield[25] asserts: "Ambiguous or dishonest communication imposes needless emotional pain on patients and families facing life-threatening illness" (p. 110). Being honest with the dying has strong meaning for their unfinished business: "How can we say good-bye, if we are not told early in the course of the disease?" or "How can a dying person say good-bye, if those who provide care will not show recognition that separation is at hand?" How can a person adjust, get his affairs together, make amends if need be, or live as he would choose for the remainder of his life if there is a conspiracy of silence? Nora, a senior, witnessed this very situation: "I felt bad because no one told my step-father that he was going to die. He was not prepared and neither was I. I felt it was very unfair to him."

Is the lack of telling the dying the whole truth designed to protect the patient, the family *or the doctor?* Most terminally ill people eventually realize at the end that they are not going to recover[26-27]. We can only imagine the feeling of distrust that many must harbor when they come to realize by themselves that they are not going to get better, or when they are finally told the end is near. Lee, a first-year student, makes a strong plea for honesty when she says:

> I am continuously amazed at how often "truth" is the best solution to a problem. Honesty seems so simple. Yet, when one is put in a given situation, it can be difficult to be honest. It seems like I've become used to protecting others, saying what I think they want to hear, and thinking what I "should" think rather than being honest with myself and with others about my feelings. By trying to "protect," I do myself as well as the other individual a great injustice. I get much more satisfaction now because I'm making a conscious effort to be completely honest with myself.

There is much to ponder in her remarks.

Some professionals argue that telling the truth about the diagnosis of a terminal illness removes hope and promotes attempts at self-destruction. There is no scientific evidence to support such a contention. How people learn of the nature of their illnesses (with gentle concern, not brutal frankness) is a crucial factor in their response. As Charles Corr[28] reminds us: "The key, as so many have pointed out, is not the content but the manner of communication" (p. 17). People who are terminally ill possess the courage and strength to confront their condition and deal with it, especially when honesty, with compassion, prevails.

Whenever we are ill (being in a dying condition aside), there is often a change in self-image. We feel no longer loveable. As important relationships diminish, as familiar surroundings are replaced by the hospital or nursing home setting, and as immobility inhibits contact with loved ones, the amount of positive feeling toward the self is lessened. This is accompanied by the normal fears concerning treatment and the probability of recovery. Like many losses that occur in life, the ego is assaulted by changes the person is forced to undergo. For those who provide care, attention must be paid to how we can *minimize the great differences*, real or imagined, *that exist between the living and the dying.*

Much thought should be given to how social contact is maintained, especially involving significant others. These concerns should include children as well for they frequently are able to add a quality of authenticity, spontaneity, and care which does much to lift the spirits of the ill. In the words of philosopher and poet Kahlil Gibran,[29] "You give but little when you give of your possessions. It is when you give of yourself that you truly give", (p. 20). Frequently, the mere presence of someone at the bedside will have a strong positive influence. It diminishes the overpowering fear of abandonment.

Participation or Observation?

Ultimately, the dying need *attention* and *acceptance* as persons in a world that is now filled with the clinical efficiency of the helping professions, and the technological machinery involved in so-called "heroic efforts." As noted earlier, the constant availability of important people in the life of the dying person is the cement that holds together the emotional transitions encountered. The key question is: *Do we wish to participate in our loved one's dying or simply be observers?* This is not an easy question to answer for survivors who are having trouble dealing with their fears. Still, various forms of assistance and involvement can be helpful to our grief work[30]. At the same time, active participation and "acceptance of the dying" means that we are willing to endure changes in behavior of the dying person that may be upsetting.

To better understand this behavior consider your mood swings which accompanied a recent illness. Perhaps you were in a lot of pain and discomfort and neither wanted nor recognized much of what was around you. However, the next day when feeling better your mood improved accordingly. Similar changes and others of an emotional nature must be understood within the context in which they occur. Dying people are grieving their approaching death[31-32]. Negative remarks or silence are not directed personally toward any survivor. These unfortunate responses must be viewed as simply ways of coping with an event which has never before been confronted. Survivors have to accept behaviors which are normally among the most difficult to accept; they must tolerate the intolerable. There is a need to be prepared for continuously fluctuating behavior and the confusion which it generates. At times, this creates a tense situation, one that demands great patience.

Sometimes the dying feel they are burdens to loved ones, adding unwanted stress in their lives[33]. The elderly often perceive this experience as a loss of control[34]. Moreover, the silence of the dying person is often misinterpreted as depression, suppressed anger or fear of death, when in fact just the opposite is being expressed—he is trying to spare survivors additional pain. All of these interpersonal transactions point up the need for great sensitivity on the part of family and the refusal to act on outward appearances alone.

Unfinished Business

Perhaps the greatest sensitivity is needed in determining if and when the dying wish to speak about those subjects for which they need to find resolution or about which they express concern. There are some individuals who choose not to talk about their dying or other self-involving matters. This is a reflection of their wishes, habits, and learned coping mechanisms, and is most difficult for caregivers to accept, because it fails to meet their expectations. However, forcing the dying person to respond to questions is both degrading and stressful.

Conversely, there will be times when the person may hint at wanting to discuss unfinished business: Changing a will, care of a child, the gift of a painting, funeral arrangements. Someone must be at the bedside, willing to listen, not judge, to encourage the expression of hopes or disappointments, not minimize them. The dying are going through the major grief experience of their lives, and like all grievers, they are searching for someone to understand their pain and concerns.

Sometimes the dying and survivors have to give each other permission to do many things: cry, rage, remain silent or tell of their deepest fears[35]. Then they begin to know each other on a level never before realized. This development must never be thwarted because it results in a beautiful intimacy, a mutual bond, a bond that death itself cannot sever. Clearly, intimacy and good relationships are associated with longer survivals[36].

Non-verbal Communication

The dying are also astute readers of non-verbal communication. Experts in the field of alcoholism say that an alcoholic brought into an emergency room for treatment can "smell" hospital personnel's disdain and revulsion of them, without their having to speak a word. I would argue that the dying and most hospitalized patients possess the same ability. They are acutely sensitive to how they are treated, if they are liked by their nurses, and if there is *sincere* interest in them. A man I visited in the hospital and loved very much said, "I can't control my bowels and I've just had a bowel movement. Would you find a nurse to clean me up? And don't go. Some of them can be pretty rough. They won't be, if you are here." He had sensed many days before that there were few people interested in a dying old man wrestling with his emotions in a crowded general hospital.

FEARS WHEN DYING

There is a tendency to forget that often there are many fears to be confronted in the dying process. E. Mansell Pattison[37] describes fears associated with the loss of identity, loneliness, sorrow, the unknown, loss of body, and a host of others. Avery Weisman[27] states that: "Fear of dying consists of different types of vulnerability—*helplessness,* to be without options; *hopelessness,* to be alienated from our distinctive reality; *guilt,* to have fallen from the expectations of our ego ideal; *truculence,* to be in danger and to be angry about our plight; and so forth" (p. 114).

Cancer patients in remission live with the fear of recurrence of their illness. I recall a young woman with cancer of the lymph glands, whom I had come to know quite well from one of my support groups. I had occasion to call her about a speaking engagement she had wanted me to make. When she answered the phone and realized it was me, I sensed her immediate disappointment. She went on to say she was hoping it was her physician to give her the results of tests completed the day before. It was not until several days later that she indicated the great fear confronting her—maybe her remission had ended.

A more tragic and difficult time comes when one's worst fears come true—a remission ends and the disease reappears. Once again the emotions associated with the original diagnosis have to be dealt with. Family members and other support persons must be made aware of the many fears the dying person encounters, including the fear of what will become of the family. Will they be taken care of? Will the death cause great hardship? We can help allay these fears[37].

Initially, the fear of death is overpowering, some would argue universal, because it poses questions involving fear of the unknown. Throughout life, there are many unknowns which we all must confront, causing apprehension and anxiety until reasonable ways of dealing with them are found. There are other fears which family members can help the dying overcome: the fear of abandonment and the fear of losing personal identity. These twin fears are quickly born and develop rapidly, depending on interaction with friends, loved ones, *and* medical personnel. The person's social value is often at issue; socially valued people are treated differently than the less socially desirable[38].

The classical situation occurs when prolonged illness takes its toll on the number of people who normally came to visit. As he or she begins to fail and appearances change, the person becomes aware that there are now fewer contacts with friends and family members. This awareness of isolation is augmented by the lack of time which medical personnel spend with the person. Often, the individual needs to talk to these power figures. This shattering awareness is also felt when the patient pushes the call button for the nurse and she does not respond for a long period of time. I once was called to visit a hospitalized cancer patient, and during our conversation I asked, "What bothers you most about your being here?" She replied, "When I call for the nurse it takes a half hour before someone responds." Nurses are very often overworked because they have to care for too many patients. They are burdened with paperwork and other duties as well, but the fact remains that the seriously ill person interprets the lack of response as indifference. We can safely conclude that indifference is equated with rejection.

Although social isolation stems in part from the nature of the illness and withdrawal by the dying person, avoidance by those in close proximity is the most significant cause[39]. If visitors are lacking, and attention from those who come in contact with the dying person limited, one feels deserted and unimportant. The loss of self-esteem and identity is a crushing blow. To experience this near the end of life can only be more painful. In giving care we must be aware of the symbolic meaning of human contact. *Presence means we care, especially when we persevere, and are regular in visiting.* Of course, this can be a major sacrifice, but for the dying person it is crucial in the maintenance of self-esteem and the feeling of being loved. There are few experiences more devastating to the dying than feelings of abandonment and rejection[40].

Visualization

Because of the great anxiety often generated by fear, shame, or relationship problems, as well as problems accompanying the management of pain, both patients and families often need opportunities for diversion, to rest and relax. One approach, helping to provide rest and relaxation and at the same time aid in treatment, is the use of visual imagery audio tapes. There are many to choose from. Some have been made to allow the ill person to visualize scenes that are created to fight the disease (cancer)[41-42]. Visualization in conjunction with conventional treatment therapies has proven highly successful with many people, leading to long-term remissions *and* cures.

I have had positive results in using these in our Hospice program. They promote relaxation as a prerequisite to visualizing shrinkage or removal of the cancer by white blood cells or other agents. Some of these tapes result in changing the patient's belief system from that of being powerless to having control over the disease. Family members may listen together with the patient or use other tapes for themselves. Most report strong relaxation responses and a more positive attitude towards their struggles. Further discussion on this topic is found in Chapter 7.

Our Own fears

To fear a dying person is not unusual. We all seek connectedness: to people, to places, and to things. Therefore, when this continuity is threatened or ends, fear invades. Some family members and friends are so fearful that they cannot visit the dying person regularly, especially when the end draws near[43]. I remember a father who could not talk to his dying daughter, a son who could not totally engage in conversation with his father. My brother, who visited our father more than any of the other children during his four months of hospital confinement, was absent on the evening of his death because he was unable to confront the emotional turmoil of the death vigil.

There is nothing weak or abnormal about having fears which keep us from the dying when the end is near. Many of these fears result from the lifelong societal camouflage of the natural inevitability of death. To watch a loved one die recalls a complex assemblage of experiences, perhaps even a reminder of our own mortality which forces withdrawal. We should be reminded here of Kavanaugh's[44] remark: "The basic mask all humans put on is to call ourselves 'the living' when we are equally 'the dying' " (p. 24).

In coping with the tendency to draw away from the dying, to shorten a visit, to cancel the next trip to the hospital, to avoid emotion-laden conversation, it may be helpful to consider the following points when facing an agonal situation. First, it has long been acknowledged that survivors who have not been able to relate well to their dying loved ones experience increased difficulties in adapting once death occurs. Second, in deciding on the course of action to take in relation to visiting throughout the final period of declining health, it would be wise to ask ourselves this question: "Can I live with what I do now—after my loved one has died?" Much guilt evolves from what should have been done.

One young woman confided that before her father died she had accomplished all that she thought she could in relation to being present and showing her love for him, so that now: "I feel good when I think of my father. I did all that I could. I thought of that key question when I was tempted to run away and it helped me to stay. I'm better for it now." We cannot miraculously overcome our fears, but we can slowly confront them openly and share them with those we trust.

Respite

One final suggestion. In caring for a dying loved one family members must acknowledge that they are not superhuman; it is impossible to do everything, be everything and provide everything. Mistakes are made, exhaustion sets in, and sometimes the hope that the vigil will end flashes in one's thoughts. It is important to accept those traits for what they are: integral parts of our finite reactions under stress. This admonition of human limitation easily goes unheeded when we become immersed in the commitment to the dying person. But to come face to face with our breaking point, to recognize our limits, will save untold frustration and guilt at a time when every bit of energy is needed. Therefore, we have an obligation to meet our needs too: seek the help of others, make a work schedule, share the work load, take turns visiting, and make time to be alone. It is the only way to continue caring without becoming ill.

HELPING—THE HOSPICE WAY

The word *hospice* comes from Latin *hospes,* meaning "host." During the Middle Ages monks operated havens for destitute people, including travelers, the homeless, and others who were in need. This ancient practice of giving assistance evolved into the present-day focus of assisting dying people. In 1879, Mother Mary Ackenhead, who founded the order of the Irish Sisters of Charity, began an intensive program of care for the dying. More recently, Dr. Cecily Saunders founded St. Christopher's Hospice in London in 1967. She is responsible for the current interest and development of the Hospice movement as we know it today. These and other unsung heroes possessed the vision to realize that the psychosocial needs of the dying and the management of their pain are best met in an environment where the time of medical personnel and volunteer workers is devoted to one purpose—to help the dying *live* until they die. As Herman Feifel[45] in *New Meanings of Death* wrote: "It is the *living* rather than the *dying* of the person sick-until-death which requires prolongation. The quality of life, not mere insentient survival, stands in need of our worship" (p. 352). Hospice therefore, is a journey of intensive caring.

The Hospice program includes the coordinated efforts of medical personnel, clergy, social service workers, and volunteer caregivers who help alleviate emotional and physical pain and provide support services to terminally ill patients and their families. It is a team journey of caring. There are over 1,400 hospices in the United States which have as their primary goal the care of the dying in surroundings which promote quality living until death. This means conscientious pain management (*before* pain becomes intense) and emotional support that maintains patient dignity and provides for individual needs. The Hospice program allows the dying person *to be in control of his or her life* as much as possible. Providing *what the patient wants* is an essential element in giving control[46]. The family is also given support before and after the death of the family member.

The great need and importance of this work is reflected in a pioneering approach called the "Host-Hospice program." This involves people who are willing to take into their homes a dying person, provide meals, a bedroom, and needed companionship for as long as needed. While one of the goals of the Hospice program is to allow people to die at home, if they choose, some dying people do not have a family or close relatives to provide these services. The Host-Hospice program is the answer: love and care are given freely by others not related to the dying person at a time when it is desperately needed. An option to dying in a hospital setting is now available even when one has no immediate family.

There are several other types of hospice settings: (1) home care only, (2) home and hospital care, (3) free standing hospice where all services are provided in one building, (4) a self-contained hospice wing in a hospital, and (5) a hospice team in a hospital setting.

The goals of the Hospice program comprises a total caring—physical, psychological, social, spiritual—for the dying person and family.

1. Death in secure surroundings, especially at home, if appropriate.
2. Pain and symptom control as needed and/or requested as part of an individualized treatment plan.
3. The training of family members to provide physical and psychological care.
4. Social support and bereavement counseling as appropriate.
5. Respite time for family members.

6. Giving assistance to the dying in completing any unfinished business they may have.
7. Facilitating positive relationships between the dying person and all caregivers.
8. Listening.
9. Coordinating efforts to insure "death with dignity" and quality living until death occurs.
10. Community education.

THE STAGES MODEL OF DYING

In talking about the process of dying, no one person has been written about or received the attention of the public more than the Swiss-born psychiatrist Elisabeth Kubler-Ross, who has worked with hundreds of dying people. She has suggested that there are five stages—denial, rage, bargaining, depression, acceptance—through which dying people progress[47]. Although misinterpreted by many people, her theoretical contribution provides many insights into the emotional dramas played out in the lives of the dying and their survivors. The five stages create an initial framework for understanding the dying process, even though they are void of descriptions of other emotions which have to be dealt with.

Before examining how to facilitate the emotional reactions involved in the stages model it is important to realize that they are *not a prescription for death*. Not everyone dies according to Kubler-Ross, nor did she imply they did. It should be noted that other authorities disagree quite strongly with her and take issue with the sequential stage theory[25]. Criticism focuses on the highly subjective nature of data collection and interpretation, the lack of replication of her findings by other researchers, and the fact that each stage can be interpreted from a different perspective. Many other styles of dying have been suggested[37, 48–49].

Nevertheless, the stages model has remarkable application to many of life's crises other than death and allows for a broad understanding of part of the emotional patterns associated with loss. Furthermore, it is an excellent starting point for listening to patients and understanding their behavior[23]. This five-stage model may be applied to loss experiences other than dying. The reader may wish to apply the model to a recent major loss to better understand its versatility. Our emphasis will be on what we can do to help those who are experiencing the emotions suggested in the model. We can be significant influences for increasing the ability of both the dying and survivors to cope. Our contribution depends essentially on *how* we relate to them and whether fear gets in the way of compassion.

Denial

Sudden or anticipated loss often places us in the position of denying the reality of massive change. When learning that death is near, it is quite normal for a person to say: "Not me. It can't be true." A fundamental law of survival has always been to deny information that is unacceptable. This applies to many of life's crises and is quite normal. Denial surfaces in many ways and with different intensities of emotion. One may scream, "no!" or the denial may be kept inside to be discharged later.

What can we do in the presence of outward denial? Agree with the denier by remaining silent, or with a nod of the head. Our most important contribution is to be there. Allow denial; that is coping. Disassociating oneself from the reality of loss is a coping mechanism used by young and old alike. It is needed so that we may slowly assimilate the catastrophic news. And until the person allows himself to become consciously aware of the seriousness of his illness denial must be honored[25].

Rage

According to Kubler-Ross, what follows or accompanies denial is anger and rage. It is often directed at God ("He can take it," she says), or nearby medical personnel: "These doctors don't know what the hell they're talking about. They're no good. Why are they doing this to me? Why is God letting this happen after all I have done to be good?" Anger may be directed at a loved one ("See what all of my hard work for you has gotten me!").

Later, anger emerges from the frustration of physical weakness, receiving "get-well" cards, or from the observation that the senders represent life, health, and happiness. As with denial, anger should be allowed to run its course.

We must be prepared to hear swearing or cursing in rare instances. This behavior should not be interpreted as a personal attack or a lack of respect for God. It is an expected outcome for someone who has a hurt which has never before been experienced ("I'm going to die!") and is emotionally distraught. As Monsignor Kellogg[50], a priest who has worked extensively with the dying, says: "People have to breathe in the face of tragedy; let Dad get mad at you." In this instance "breathing" comes in the form of anger and rage, and we must bear with it. It is not a personal anger, *it is a coping anger.* When one is facing such persistent frustration, coupled with fear, anger is a natural response. Do not respond to anger with anger. Let it run its course. Survivors resort to this same coping anger on many occasions.

Bargaining

For many people there is a need to bargain, to ask for something by being willing to give something in return. "If I can only go home or visit my sister, I promise to take all of the treatments," is a way of bargaining. One may also bargain with God—for more time, just a little more time in order to finish a project, or to see a newborn grandchild, or to go to a favorite vacation site. Bargaining is extremely important for the dying because it means that they are maintaining their dignity; they are holding on to life.

Accordingly, we must be careful about taking away their hope, for without it they are defenseless. Faith and bargaining maintain hope. For survivors, the suggestion of a particular bargain must *always* be grounded in reason and honesty. We never promise anything unless we can deliver. Imagine the following when a loved one is promised that she can come home from the hospital for the holiday. Everything has been planned, and the dying person is looking forward to it, confident he will make the trip. However the doctor has never been consulted, or the person has never been warned that any such trip depends on his response to treatments, his present condition, or whether the course of treatment can be continued at home. The day arrives and the patient's hopes are shattered. He is not allowed to leave the hospital. The result is a major emotional setback, one which survivors have contributed to by not making wise preparations.

Depression

In depression, thought and body processes seem to shut down; fatigue is pervasive. There is a temporary closing off of the self from others. Hopelessness temporarily invades. The dying become depressed for many reasons, not the least of which is the realization that they are losing all of their relationships, anger has turned inward, or they recognize they are growing weaker. Depression waxes and wanes. In fact, depression can be assumed to be a time in which we recharge our psychic batteries, to prepare for the next difficult adjustment.

What can the caring person do? Again, simply be there, for the person's spirits are affected by our presence and patience. This is a major test of our endurance. At the proper time, we initiate conversation and get the person to think anew, when *he* is ready. But our healing presence must prevail—it is our nearness, patience, and consistency which are vital to the dying person in this circumstance. Should our loved one turn his back on us when we enter the room or refuses to speak, remember, he is not trying to hurt us. *Sit down and wait.* Just listen. Say, nothing. Those in crises often mask negative feelings with behavior towards others that is less than kind and appropriate (it's called "displacement"). The person is reacting to, coping with, dealing with the major confrontation of life. The dying need maximal compassion and reverence in this confrontation. The depression will lift, though it may later return. Through it all, sensitivity to what the dying person wants is essential.

Acceptance

For many dying people, acceptance comes with an optimistic "I'm ready," or they may choose to talk only in the past tense. Still others indicate their acceptance of the situation non-verbally, through a smile or holding hands. Some will choose to talk about their funeral, the arrangements for it, and what they would like done. Conflict occurs when the family is not ready to accept death but the dying person is. The family may refuse to acknowledge the situation or to discuss what the dying person would like to talk about. Here is where priorities must be rearranged and caregivers must accept what has already been accepted by the dying person.

Other Emotions

The emotions and thoughts involved in the dying process certainly are not limited to those just discussed. Depending on individual circumstances, there may be feelings of shame as the dying person loses basic skills, grows weak, or is unable to control bowel function. Withdrawal, regression, or childishly demanding behavior may emerge. Feelings of injustice, guilt, or of being punished may be expressed. So much of a dying person's behavior is a product of past experiences with crises, beliefs about life and death, and his value system. Unfortunately, there may be gross misinterpretation of behavior by caregivers. For example, with denial, a dying person may *seem* to be denying the fact that he is dying, when in reality he chooses to protect his family, or maintain relationships with others on his own terms[51].

The five stages are sometimes experienced by members of the family as well as the dying person before and after the death event. There is often conflict between the family and the dying person because they are at different emotional places (stages) in the dying process. What must be reemphasized is that the emotions expressed are normal; they are a means of coping. These stages do not necessarily occur in a fixed order. Some may be skipped or repeated and not everyone reaches the stage of acceptance. Above all, we must never underestimate the coping ability of a dying person. Each person possess inner resources that lie dormant until called forth by impending circumstances.

Priorities

Ultimately, the priorities of the dying are focused in the here and now, because they have fewer friends and a finite future. We can assist by refusing to take away their need for power and control (in so far as they are able), by allowing them to be "productive" and by never failing to listen. For when they find there is no one to listen they feel there is no one who cares. Which is the greater hurt—to die alone, or to die with loved ones nearby who choose not to speak about the realities of life, the future, and separation. The terminally ill are often victims of devaluing behavior by the living who themselves are unaware of their seeming callousness.

I recall a woman with brain cancer who told our support group of an experience that meant a great deal to her. When she would visit the hospital for treatments, the non-verbal behavior of the doctors spoke volumes to her. She told us: "One was tall and towered over me. The other two, women doctors, sat down on the edge of the bed or in a chair to talk to me." The very act of taking the time to sit down had impressed her; it was perceived as "I want to take the time to explain. You are important." Their actions made her feel that she was not just another patient.

In crises there is always need for a sense of security, love, worth and recognition from those who are in positions of power. Devalued self-worth is a product of depersonalized care. Caregivers should lower defenses which normally keep them at a safe distance. They must learn as much as possible about how their healing presence becomes part of the coping ability of the dying.

That same healing presence is needed when the dying choose to cope by denial. This may be a person's strongest ally right to the end. We will help immeasureably by not forcing our way through that denial. It is also essential to consider that some individuals may not wish to speak about their dying. It may be so distressing that they choose not to discuss it[52]. Though such persons are in the minority it is indeed crucial that we honor their wishes which can be assessed in early conversations. Later, they may give us new cues that indicate a willingness to talk about their impending death. It is not easy to do all of this. Frustration is not uncommon. Despite these difficulties, in the final analysis we will have made love transcend fear and sorrow. There may even be times when we will be surprised at how a loved one beats the odds. This is occurring more and more: the person is supposed to die within a month but lives for over a year. Or, amazingly, the cancer shrinks and disappears. This happens for many reasons. It has long been known that illness means we have to take a new road in life[53]. This means change our entire lifestyle— nutritionally, spiritually, emotionally and in terms of physical activity. When these miracles occur they not only give rebirth to our loved ones but to caregivers as well. Truly, the power of belief brings new enthusiasm for life and meaning to existence.

CAN THERE BE A GOOD DEATH?

In summary, what we have been discussing is essentially how to help someone die a good death. The words "good death" may seem mind-boggling because they appear strongly contradictory. The contradiction develops when death is considered an evil and not a natural reality. Because of this stigma, it is assumed that there is no such thing as a good death; every death is bad. Unfortunately this belief influences the way the dying are related to. Perhaps the "good death" terminology needs to be changed since many people feel that the only possible way that their death (or any death), would be acceptable, is if it occurred gently and suddenly—like the turning off of a light. The vast majority of deaths, nevertheless, tend to be just the opposite; they are of a chronic, long-term nature, where there is time to prepare[39].

Weisman[49] has suggested that we might die an appropriate death, though few people are fortunate enough to do so. The conditions for an appropriate death are first, we are relatively pain-free, with suffering managed and controllable. Secondly, emotional and social conflicts are kept to a minimum: no unfinished business, emotional deprivation, lack of attention due to social class, or communication problems within the support network. Next, we are given the freedom to engage tasks which, under the circumstances, we are still capable of performing; interpersonal conflicts are to be minimal with both family and medical personnel; and ours wishes are honored in relation to and consistent with our self-esteem.

Finally, we are allowed to choose the significant person or persons in life whom we can yield control to as the end draws near. At the same time, we have the freedom not to be with those we do not feel comfortable with, whether they are medical staff or family members.

Can individuals die an appropriate death? Only if those around them will permit it. That is, each of us must put the dying person first and personal desires second; we must not lay out our agenda for their dying. In retrospect, it implies three basic assumptions: (1) one of our main objectives is to learn how to help the dying maintain their dignity; (2) we must recognize that people are individuals when dying, just as they were individuals when healthy and free from disease; and (3) discussion of whether certain treatments and life-prolonging technologies should or should not be employed must precede the dying process.

The big question remains: Will we be able to translate theory into practice? It is relatively easy to discuss what should or should not be done in our attempts to help one separate from life. But when the time comes, when we must face the death of a loved one, theory seems to become irrelevant and we are left to our own inclinations. By way of review, here are some reliable guides to assist in this task.

1. *Be there.* Your healing presence is a resource with incalcuable impact. Life emanates from your presence.
2. *Be reverent.* Let the dying person be in charge, free to tell you when to come and go, what she needs, and what will be the topics of discussion.
3. *Expect regressive behavior.* There may be times when the person is demanding on the one hand and overly dependent on the other. Do not become alarmed at such mood swings.
4. *Maintain dignity and hope.* Do not take away the power and control that one still possesses. Without hope no one can cope. Maintain hope to help the person reach little goals.
5. *Let honesty prevail.* There is a difference between being honest and blatantly truthful. Each of us can deal with our trials and assimilate the truth when it unfolds a little at a time.
6. *Practice empathy.* Place yourself in the position of the dying person when you are not sure of what to do. What must it be like to be losing all of your associations with the world? What does it feel like to be treated as though you are useless?

7. *Accept anger as coping.* Persevere in the face of anger. What your loved one is saying is, "If you love me enough, you will let me be angry at you.

8. *Silences are as important as words.* When your question goes unanswered — let it be. It is good to be there without saying anything as well.

9. *Listen.* Our greatest contribution may simply be to listen when the dying person wishes to talk, particularly at night. Night time seems to accentuate loneliness when coping with life-threatening illness.

REFERENCES

1. Brown, B. *New mind, new body.* New York: Harper & Row, 1974.
2. Ufema, J. *Brief companions.* Fawn Grove, PA: Mullisan, 1984.
3. Cappon, D. The dying. *Psychiatric Quarterly,* 1959, 133, 466–489.
4. Powell, J. *Unconditional love.* Allen, Texas: Argus, 1978.
5. Shephard, M. *Someone you love is dying* New York: Charter, 1975.
6. Aries, P. *Western attitudes toward death from the middle ages to the present.* Baltimore: Johns Hopkins University Press, 1974.
7. Richards, V. Death and cancer. In E. Shneidman (Ed.) *Death: Current perspectives.* Palo Alto, CA: Mayfield, 1980, 322–330.
8. Kubler-Ross, E. (Ed.). *Death: The final stage of growth* Englewood Cliffs, NJ: Prentice-Hall, 1975.
9. Bok, S. *Lying: Moral choice in public and private life.* New York Pantheon, 1978.
10. Mount, B. *Palliative care of the terminally ill.* Speech presented at the annual meeting of the Royal College of Physicians and Surgeons of Canada, Vancouver, British Columbia, January, 27, 1978.
11. Saunders, C. Dying they live: St. Christopher's Hospice. In H. Feifel (Ed.). *New meanings of death.* New York: McGraw-Hill, 1977.
12. Worden, J. & Proctor, W. *Personal death awareness.* Englewood Cliffs, NJ: Prentice-Hall, 1976.
13. Rando, T. *Grief, dying and death.* Champaign, Il: Research Press, 1984.
14. LaGrand, L. Communicating about death: A model for reducing anxiety. *Selected proceedings from the First National Conference of the Forum for Death Education & Counseling.* Lexington, MA: Ginn, 1979.
15. Erikson, E. *Identity: Youth and crisis.* New York: Norton, 1968.
16. Sullivan, H. *The interpersonal theory of psychiatry.* New York: Norton, 1953.
17. Maslow, A. *Motivation and personality.* (2nd ed.). New York: Harper & Row, 1970.
18. Siegel, B. *Love, medicine, and miracles.* New York: Harper & Row, 1986.
19. Kalish, R. *Death, grief and caring relationships.* Belmont, CA: Wadsworth, 1985.
20. Hardison, *Let's touch: How and why to do it.* Englewood Cliffs, NJ: Prentice-Hall, 1980.
21. Hutschnecker, A. *The will to live.* New York: Simon & Schuster, 1983.

22. Kastenbaum, R. New fantasies in the American death system. *Death Education,* 1982, 6, 155–166.
23. Benoliel, J. Talking to patients about death. *Nursing Forum,* 1970, 9³, 254–268.
24. Graham, J. *In the company of others.* New York: Harcourt, Brace & Jovanovich, 1982.
25. Garfield, C. *Psychosocial care of the dying patient.* New York: McGraw-Hill, 1979.
26. Kubler-Ross, E. What is it like to be dying? *American Journal of Nursing,* 1971, 71, 54–62.
27. Weisman, A. The psychiatrist and the inexorable. In H. Fiefel (Ed.). *New meanings of death.* New York: McGraw-Hill, 1977.
28. Corr, C. Hospices, dying persons, and hope. In R. Pacholski & C. Corr (Eds.). *New directions in death education and counseling.* Arlington, VA: Forum for Death Education and Counseling, 1981.
29. Gibran, K. *The prophet.* New York: Alfred A. Knopf, 1966.
30. Parkes, C. & Weiss, R. *Recovery from bereavement.* New York: Basic Books, 1983.
31. Aldrich, E. The dying patient's grief. *Journal of the American Medical Association,* 1963, 185⁵, 329–31.
32. Shneidman, E. *Voices of death.* New York: Bantam, 1982.
33. Scott, S. On the spot: Death education and counseling. In R. Pacholski & C. Corr (Eds.). *New directions in death education and counseling.* Arlington, VA: Forum for Death Education and Counseling, 1981.
34. Calkins, K. Shouldering a burden. *Omega,* 1972, 3, 23–36.
35. Albertson, S. *Endings and beginnings.* New York: Ballantine Books, 1980.
36. Weisman, A. & Worden, J. Psychosocial analysis of cancer deaths. *Omega,* 1975, 6, 61–75.
37. Pattison, E. *The experience of dying.* Englewood Cliffs, NJ: Prentice-Hall, 1977.
38. Stephenson, J. *Death, grief, and mourning.* New York: Free Press, 1985.
39. Charmaz, K. *The social reality of death.* Reading, MA: Addison-Wesley, 1980.
40. Feifel, H. (Ed.). *The meaning of death.* New York: McGraw-Hill, 1959.
41. Simonton, O., Simonton, S. & Creighton, J. *Getting well again.* New York: Bantam 1980.
42. Siegel, B. & Siegel, B. Holistic medicine. *Connecticut Medicine,* 1981, 45, 441–42.
43. Sudnow, D. *Passing on: The social organization of dying.* Englewood Cliffs, NJ: Prentice-Hall, 1967.
44. Kavanaugh, R. *Facing death.* Baltimore: Penguin, 1974.
45. Fiefel, H. (Ed.). *New meanings of death.* New York: McGraw-Hill, 1977.
46. Ufema, J. Do you have what it takes to be a nurse-thanatologist? *Nursing,* 1977, 77, 96–99.
47. Kubler-Ross, E. *On death and Dying.* New York: Macmillan, 1969.
48. Shneidman, E. *Deaths of man.* Baltimore: Penguin, 1973.
49. Weisman, A. *On dying and denying.* New York: Behavioral Publications, 1972.
50. Kellogg, B. *Relating to the Terminally Ill.* 1982, Videotape produced by Learning Resources, Potsdam College, Potsdam, NY
51. Kastenbaum, R. *Death, society and human experiences.* (3rd ed.). Columbus: Merrill, 1986.

52. Hinton, J. *Dying.* Baltimore: Penguin, 1967.
53. Evans, E. *A psychological study of cancer.* New York: Dodd, Mead, 1926.

Chapter Six

SELF-ESTEEM AND COPING

No significant aspect of our thinking, motivation, feelings, or behavior is unaffected by our self-evaluation.

Nathaniel Branden in *Honoring The Self*

A cheerful heart is a good medicine, but a downcast spirit dries up the bones.

Proverbs 17:22

Of course, how you see yourself is often related to what you do with yourself.

Hans Selye

I believe my grief would not have lasted as long or have taken so much out of me if I had developed a better self-image and some self-esteem. Rejection seemed to be twice as bad because I didn't like myself enough to bounce back.

Joy, a college junior

In his collection of essays entitled, *The Ordeal of Change*, Eric Hoffer[1] writes:

We can never be really prepared for that which is wholly new. We have to adjust ourselves, and every radical adjustment is a crisis in self-esteem: we undergo a test, we have to prove ourselves. It needs inordinate self-confidence to face drastic change without inner trembling (p. 1–2).

Although these words were written over three decades ago in relation to a whole population undergoing drastic changes, this is a statement incisively supporting the central argument to be made concerning the resolution of a major loss: what we believe about ourselves before and after a loss occurs is vital to how quickly and how completely healing occurs.

Our value-judgement of ourselves affects *everything* we do in life. Self-esteem is an absolute necessity in order to exist; there is no meaning-

135

ful life without it. As self-esteem changes so does the nature of our behavior. After all, when we think of ourselves as confident, ready, strong, or prepared, we meet a problem-solving situation with a set of skills and a frame of mind which help us deal with the unexpected.

We must possess self-esteem, or end up playing games to get people to like us. This is what happens when someone becomes addicted to another person as often happens with romantic relationships. Personal power is given to the other in a vain attempt to have needs met. We are forced to become people-pleasers out of fear of being rejected. Infatuation is mistaken for love; the former causes a narrowing of our focus, the latter is energizing and expanding in nature.

Of course, it is important that people feel good about themselves for the right reasons: they are inherently good (our primary identity) and not because they possess fame and fortune or specific talents (our secondary identity). Not infrequently, those who reject us become disillusioned with our secondary identity.

ORIGINS OF SELF-ESTEEM

Where does self-esteem originate? At bottom, it is the product of all social interaction beginning at birth, having our basic needs met, using our talents, and achieving personal goals. All human relationships leave an indelible mark, for better or for worse. Parental and other adult relationships are especially influential.

Everyone has their highs and lows in the fluctuations of self-esteem. We feel terrible after we say or do something that results in hurting another. Or if the boss reprimands, if a colleague makes fun of something held dear, or if we receive a low grade on an examination, we experience a temporary reduction in self-esteem. Usually, most people get over these common cases of negative feelings toward the self, especially if they have previously experienced much more success than failure.

It is *consistent* failure in a variety of forms—interpersonal, economic, or skill—that makes major inroads on self-esteem. We come to view ourselves as inadequate, as being unable to cope and without ability to adapt. Consequently, self-esteem drops further when separation occurs. As self-esteem plummets problems multiply, since the most devastating belief of all is that we are inferior to others. Psychotherapists commonly state the obvious: those with acute mental-health problems are notorious for having low opinions of themselves and find it hard to make the tough decisions in life. Interestingly, our beliefs about ourselves are often not consciously sensed.

On the other hand, *successes* are the building blocks of a positive self-image. People are products of thousands of successes and failures. If the successes predominate, particularly those perceived as most important, feelings about the self will be strong and positive. Being able to fall back on a positive identity in time of loss is a definite advantage. The realization that one still has much available—people to lean on, skills to engage, abilities to use, life itself—acts as a beacon to direct energies and give new direction in times of radical change.

Perhaps the biggest "success" of all is when we discover strengths we never new existed and we receive the respect and attention of others. In particular, when we discover that the unconscious mind delivers answers to our problems and is the source of a storehouse of wisdom and energy self-esteem increases. Sometimes, it is referred to as intuition, a sixth sense. Despite the label given, this inner resource can be conditioned in such a way as to bring about the most profound changes imaginable. Becoming aware of this innate source of help should become a primary goal of people of all ages especially when in need. More about this in the next chapter.

THE MOST IMPORTANT BELIEF

Self-belief is the prime mover of what we become. St. Augustine phrased it this way: "We become what we love." The nature of our self-belief is an index to emotional health. Strikingly, it is the essential element in dealing with life's problems. The most important belief we possess is that concerning ourselves. Our self-image and the way we view our capabilities are the basic tools that allow us to manage the aftermath of separation. "As a man thinketh in his heart, so is he." Whatever we do to rebuild self-esteem or to help others regain feelings of self-worth if we are caregivers, provides a sound start for resolving grief and establishing continuity in life. Most important in this regard is *the manner in which we relate to people,* whether before a loss occurs or after it for human interaction has a profound effect on self-belief. We literally contribute to the rise and fall of the levels of esteem of others. Social interaction is the flywheel of self-belief or as Frank[2] observes " . . . every person is influenced by the behavior of others toward him."

This is especially significant in helping the bereaved or coping with our own losses. It has long been recognized that significant others shape the way we feel about ourselves. Mental health specialists agree: everyone has a need for attention. It comes through acceptance by others and their recognition of our goodness, as well as their undivided concern when we need encouragement and reassurance. Therefore, accumulated interpersonal experiences heavily influence how we react to the problems of the present and the future.

A young woman whose boyfriend ended their two-year relationship tells us much about the importance of feeling good about the self in adapting to relationship losses: "My own coping mechanism, or rather my best antidote for pain, is staying useful and important. I want people to see me as a strong person and I want their respect and acceptance. In a way, I guess this is a stage which means I have finally accepted what has happened." The key phrase, "staying useful and important" is the basis of "working through" the various adjustments to life after a major loss. If we realize we still have much to offer others—that we still possess talents and skills and can utilize them—our recovery is assured. Often it takes time and the assistance of caregivers to come to that conclusion, because we need to discover that we still have an important social role to fill. Unfortunately, separation anxiety, fostered by the sense of loss of self in the relationship, appears to demand much of our efforts[3]. The rediscovery of social importance helps minimize feelings of inadequacy, inferiority, and weakness. More about this shortly.

Our sense of importance is best restored by the *interest shown* from those perceived as significant persons in our lives. "It seemed that everyone cared that I had a problem," said Marty, "and was there to talk about it." Marty's "problem" was the death of a loved one, and the care and attention shown by those around him enhanced his sense of worth; it also was a prime motivator in his coping behavior. Therefore, how others interact with survivors in crisis builds or destroys self-esteem. ("It helped when I was praised and told how good a person I was and how I didn't deserve to have bad things happen to me.") Self-healing is always more likely when griever and caregivers deeply respect and trust each other.

THE LOSS OF SELF-ESTEEM

In the experience of loss, what erodes self-esteem? There are many answers to this question: rejection, pain, failure, depression, fear, guilt, anger. However, the drop in self-esteem is especially regulated by our perception of the particular loss and our present self-worth. *Loss is in the eye of the beholder.* It is essentially a blow to our feelings of power and control over life. More important, it signals the destruction of the default assumption of uninterrupted continuity. We further deplete self-esteem when we compare ourselves with others who have not suffered the same type of loss and ask: Why me?

Since our successes in life usually outweigh our failures, major loss becomes a wound to the ego for many, with temporary feelings of devalued self-worth. Although everyone does not lose self-esteem when loss occurs, there is little doubt that the way people feel about themselves is integrally tied to their adaptation processes. "The way in which one copes with a loss," said Jackie, "has a lot to do with one's self-image — one's self-confidence. A person who is happy with herself and is confident of her value is much more able to cope with the type of loss I experienced." Jackie's loss was the end of a love relationship which she was able to resolve only after a long struggle. A key phrase in her remarks, "is confident of her value," is of special significance. It speaks to the gentle way support persons must approach the task of helping friends realize their inherent goodness. Maintaining and elevating self-worth is integrally related to progress in grief work. When in the throes of tragic loss evidence of continued value to others is essential. This is especially significant in the broken *dependent* relationship which results in a radical change in self-image[4].

When loss erodes self-worth, the tendency is to think negatively, to create impossibilities and distort our outlook on the future. We increase our pain.

The breakup of a love relationship seems to be especially demeaning to feelings of being valued. During one of my classes on the topic of grief, a young woman who was surrounded by her peers courageously offered: "After I was divorced, I felt like I was a failure." Her remark is constantly replicated in many relationship losses, especially those involving the breakup of long-term love relationships. The pain of having been rejected, coupled with the knowledge that the other person is dating someone the former lover has found to be of greater value, destroys self-confidence and spawns a destructive assumption. Because one person dumps on us we need to come to terms with the fact that we are still good, important, and loveable, that there are others who care about us, and that there is nothing "wrong" with us. We *are* special, regardless of what another person may think. When a relationship ends our value as a person always remains. It's irrational to think otherwise whether the loss is through death or a breakup.

AVOIDING THE BEREAVED

We digress for a moment to consider a common problem which accentuates feelings of loneliness and low self-esteem. It is the avoidance behaviors of others who normally would stop to talk to a survivor on the street, campus, or in the market, but who hesitate to do so when they first see the newly-bereaved. Others who meet the bereaved and speak often avoid talking about the loss for fear of causing more pain. This is regretable, since, in most instances, grievers would like to talk about their losses. They interpret avoidance of the topic as a lack of sincere interest in their plight. A further sense of loss is perceived; this time a loss of friends who truly care. This is clearly illustrated in Dawn's remarks after the death of her grandmother, when friends took her out and talked about topics other than the death. "Sometimes I wished that they had wanted to talk about it a little more; they avoided the subject and so I didn't feel they really understood how much the person meant to me. It seemed as though they didn't really care sometimes."

There are few experiences which are more crushing to the ego than to sense increasing insecurity and isolation as our support system is perceived as unwilling to remain involved and firm. Feelings of powerlessness are a source of deep frustration and chaos in this regard. The assault on self-identity seriously hinders the ability to persevere. Grievers often assume that others want them to return to "normal" as soon as possible. Breaking the barrier of public silence in order to continue care for the bereaved is an obligation not to be taken lightly.

RESTORING SELF-ESTEEM

What can be done to shore up the self-beliefs of those who have been devastated by loss? Or how can we regain self-esteem? There are many answers. Early on, being *consistent* with how care is given sends the message that the griever is still a significant person who is loved. To know that we are still *lovable and important to others*, allows hope to blossom so that we endure the transition. Hope is the stabilizing force in grief[5]. Sheryl vividly recalls the consistent care she received on the breakup of her love relationship:

> I still was depressed but eventually I opened up to my sister, my best friend, and my mom. For once they understood what I was going through and were able to offer a helping hand. My sister was very helpful because for weeks on end she would listen to me talk about anything and everything that I needed to say. For so long this had been kept inside me, only making my heart hurt worse.
>
> My best friend from home wrote special letters every so often relating to me some of her experiences and her philosophy concerning life. By this time I was realizing that there were people who cared about me and who were offering the support I needed. Of course, I still had my daily cry, but I was coming to terms with reality and this seemed to be most effective for me.

Permissive listening by her sister and letters from her friend at home were critical reminders to Sheryl that people still cared and that she was still very important to them. This type of long-term caring is at the heart of assisting someone in the reorganization of life, a life without the estranged person. Talking about loss is the most common coping response utilized in the process of adaptation[6-7].

The same need is applicable to the individual grieving the death of a loved one. In either situation, believing as Sheryl did that "they understood what I was going through" is a turning point in recovery. Tanner[8] reminds us that: *"To feel understood is to feel loved"* (p. 52). It follows that *to feel loved is at the heart of self-belief.*

Marianne, after suffering a breakup sums it up with, "My family was especially supportive and helped me feel I still had someone who cared and loved me, and that I wasn't alone." *The critical message from Sheryl and Marianne for caregivers is the importance of conveying "I care" to the bereaved.* Although this is normally shown by the *quality* of support given, it should also be verbally expressed. It may be appropriate to say: "You must be feeling such deep pain. I want you to know I love you very much and will help in any way I can." Regardless of the nature of the loss, the awareness that someone cares is often the critical factor in recovery—the force which compels us to go on. "Love is the chief restorative power in the remaking of psychic health and wholeness"[9.] (p.247). So maintains psychiatrist, James A. Knight.

In the final analysis, we must be our own best motivators to heal by what we say to ourselves and what we do. We have to reverse the unconsciously held belief that we cannot cope. Regardless of previous negative attitudes about ourselves—we can change them by changing our beliefs about our unused potential. Thus, how we "talk to ourselves" has much to do with raising or lowering self-esteem.

As caregivers, on the other hand, we plant the seeds of hope so that survivors replace negative messages with positive ones about themselves. The ability to cope is primarily compromised when the support network withdraws too soon without completing this task. On the other hand, knowing we have a supportive community that will *always* be there is a reassuring base from which to tackle any of life's problems. Clearly, the community and the culture are continuously powerful formers of beliefs.

REESTABLISHING CONTINUITY IN LIFE

A major goal in adapting to traumatic loss is the reestablishment of continuity in life. In this regard, it is specially significant to help the griever get in touch with personal skills and interests once again. Gradually, when the person begins to reorganize his life, you, as caregiver, can suggest ways to bring old skills and interests back into play. For example, if the person possesses skill as a painter or plays a musical instrument, the use of these skills can assist in the transition of living a life which has changed. Through skills we experience our own power. Interest in art, museums or the theater should likewise be slowly rekindled. There are no limitations to the healing process if the griever can regain interest in hobbies, sports, or work. Such involvements enhance feelings toward the self as the individual again interacts with those in his immediate environment. Recognizing and praising strengths at the appropriate time has long been a way of reawakening a sense of importance.

When death occurs survivors are commonly overwhelmed with attention and concern by family and friends for the first few days. However, the real work of grieving begins when we are alone and attention diminished after the funeral or memorial service. This is when periodic and consistent contact with the bereaved is essential in the gradual restoration of continuity. Telephone calls, visits, and invitations to go shopping or share lunch time become the social building blocks to renewed interest in life and feelings of importance. Human contact of this sort is often the difference in prolonged or shortened grief work.

Avery Weisman[21] in *The Coping Capacity* asks: How can the demoralized rise above misfortunes like the Stoics of ancient times? His response is: "the best assurance of being able to cope with adversity is belief that one *can* cope, and the surest sign of despair is to be certain that one cannot." It is the *continuous contact* of caregivers which sends the message to the bereaved that they can cope, they will prevail. Through the acceptance of others self-acceptance is nurtured. What we *believe* about ourselves is, in the final analysis, what motivates and maintains coping ability. Dwelling on our strengths is the surest way to regain confidence and restore continuity in life. *Repeat what you do well.* Use and use again your superior skills. Every small success adds to feelings of worth. Here are some examples of beginning successes after major loss:

1. Visiting or having dinner with old friends.
2. Playing a musical instrument again.
3. Painting or drawing a picture.
4. Going to a lecture.
5. Cooking a good meal.
6. Writing a short poem.
7. Repairing a leaky faucet.
8. Buying a new piece of clothing.
9. Give a gift to a *special* friend.
10. Playing tennis, racquetball, or bridge again.

The important concept to consider is: whatever we do for ourselves maintains or elevates self-esteem. By completing positive tasks we create more positive feelings. Experiencing success in coping increases self-confidence and self-esteem. Most important, we send positive messages to the unconscious. But all of this depends on *our active participation* in recovery.

One other point. Whether fighting a life-threatening illness or grieving a major loss, a person needs to feel needed. Many people have been motivated by their friends, roommates, or significant others to go on with their lives. The motivation takes the form of helping the bereaved recognize that *others depend on them.* They eventually realize they still possess skill and wisdom that others share—they truly are prominent in their lives. On occasion, we all require a gentle reminder of how much we have to offer others. We forget when confronting personal crises because we become obsessed with loss.

OTHER APPROACHES

As caregivers, we need not be confined to encouraging the utilization of skills and interests which individuals possessed before the loss occurred in order to help them adjust to their new environment. It is entirely possible that a new project or skill evolving from the former interests of the deceased may be used by the survivor to reinvest emotional energy. Survivors often have to learn to develop skills and internal resources to cope well. Perhaps it could be an entirely new hobby, such as continuing a loved one's coin collection; supporting a favorite charity; writing a book; or beginning a class in painting, sculpture, cooking, small motor repair, or yoga. It could mean rekindling an interest the griever had in early childhood that was later abandoned, like quilting or playing the piano. Whatever activity is chosen, our continued *interest* and reassurance to the griever always fill an important role until that person is able to function again in a wholesome way.

There is always a need to know that someone is close in spirit, not merely physically present. We provide that closeness through being a lasting friend, *not* a temporary advisor in the search to find new goals. Frequently, survivors are abandoned by friends after several months because they are not responding to their friend's timetable for recovery. What were symbols of hope become reminders of isolation. The bereaved need to regain self-esteem in conjunction with finding new meaning in life. Finding meaning is a fundamental motivational force[22]. Helping others in this search takes much time and an awareness on the part of caregivers that grief is erratic, not serially progressive. Therefore, what seems to be complete recovery is often followed by a complete reversal of emotion and thoughts. Moreover, we may have to wait hours or days for the right opportunity to help. Strikingly, our patience will be a testimony of belief in the person's worth. Never forget that continued presence of caring friends and family is the basis for reaffirming the beliefs of importance of the self.

To this end interaction between the survivor and caregivers may include planned or unplanned activities, visits by very special people, or outward expressions of love. They also involve our knowing when *not* to force the issue. Sharon advises: "I think something that helped me the most was that people didn't force me to talk about it. They didn't avoid the subject and they didn't force it; they gave me time to sort it out for myself." As we seek to help others, it is useful to consider building their self-esteem as *the natural progression of interactions with friends and relatives of the deceased.*

If appropriate, suggest that the griever find a part-time job. Work is an excellent means of enhancing self-esteem just as taking on a new project at school would be. In *Lifelines,* Lynn Caine[23] wrote: "Work provides a link to the rest of the world, introduces you to new ideas, new people, helps define you, not by giving you a work-related identity but by forcing you to analyze your interests and abilities and then using them." The same can be said for volunteer work on campus or in the community.

One more thing. It is essential for any griever to recognize that there are many events we cannot control. This is an important belief to cultivate because it effects self-esteem. Most major losses are like the weather, the chain of command in the Army, or the boss's decision—clearly beyond our control. Accepting this belief and choosing to adjust accordingly, reduces the enormity of trauma we experience. The famous Serenity Prayer is based on the need to determine what we can and cannot control. By recognizing what is not controllable we will not ruin a day, a week—or a lifetime by irrational thoughts of omnipotence.

SELF-ESTEEM, UNCONDITIONAL LOVE, AND THE PERCEPTION OF DEATH

After forty years in the practice of psychiatry Smiley Blanton[10] wrote:

As I look back over the long, full years, one truth emerges clearly in my mind—the universal need for love. Whether they think they do or not people want love. Their spoken words may tell of other things, but the psychiatrist must listen to their unconscious voice as well. They cannot survive without love: They must have it or they will perish (p.11).

This penetrating statement illustrates a contemporary view about the impact of love which is shared by psychologists and sociologists the world over. It is nothing short of phenomenal that medicine is beginning to recognize the healing power of unconditional love in conjunction with conventional treatment modalities[11].

Unconditional love is giving oneself totally without expectation of return, giving without reservations or conditions. In other words, it is "doing someone else's thing." The presumptive views of giving in order to get, trying to change or control the other is not included in this definition. It recognizes that to love and grow we have to be vulnerable.

Unconditional love is a *commitment* not a feeling, an *offering* not a bargaining chip. Because this definition may be alien to long-held beliefs which equate feelings with love, it is important to reemphasize that loving unconditionally is a commitment not a feeling or an attraction. Since love is learned, there is no such thing as falling in love. That is a physical attraction. Psychiatrist M. Scott Peck[12] explains:

> However, by stating that it is when a couple falls out of love they may begin to really love, I am also implying that real love does not have its roots in a feeling of love. To the contrary, real love often occurs in a context in which the feeling of love is lacking, when we act lovingly despite the fact that we don't feel loving (p. 88).

In fact, unconditional love presupposes that one must love the self first. Self-love is an absolute prerequisite for self-esteem as well as perceiving death as a normal part of existence. This is the beginning of the answer to how unconditional love affects our perception of death, for self-love does much to minimize fears of living and dying. It should not be concluded, however, that all fears magically disappear. In truth, self-love provides the shield to combat the imaginary fears which spring from cultural conditioning.

The reader may scoff at this point: How can love conquer fears of death? Kalish[13] suggests that those who love life the most fear death the least. Kavanaugh[5] argues that fear of death is fear of life. Although fear is a normal emotion early in life, it becomes a major energy drain as we age.

Clearly, there are three factors which spring from unconditional love which auger well for transcending death fears and enhancing self-esteem. First, unconditional love creates a radically different mind-set, an alternate reality for the believer. As Fromm[14] points out, it is "an attitude, an orientation of character." Loving with no expectation of return culminates in a view of reality which accepts death as *one of a sequence of life events* filled with meaning. There is no room for fear since the quality of our involvements with others is meaningful. Theologian Robert Neale[15] insists that we fear death because of the lack of quality in relationships with others.

Most important in this regard is that two basic survival skills permeate reality: openness and honesty. These skills are absolutely essential in altering our perception of death because they eliminate the necessity to hide behind masks. At the same time they are catalysts for building trust and talking about any fear in life or death. Not only is love positively associated with physical and mental health, but in the well-known thirty-five year Grant Study of ninety-five healthy men Harvard psychiatrist, George Valliant[16], found a strong connection between fearfulness and the inability to love.

It should be noted that it is not easy to love unconditionally—especially when love is not returned. Like many other desirable parts of life, patience leads to personal fulfillment. In the long run, unconditional love possesses its own internal rewards. As an old Indian proverb has it: "All that is not given is lost." Love never fails. Eventually, it returns tenfold. Unconditional love is self-renewing. We never run out of it, only decide not to give it.

This brings us to the second major inroad that unconditional love makes on death fears, namely, the sharing of our deepest fears and feelings with another who is trusted. As Bowlby[17] observed, it is the capacity of the bereaved to form loving relationships and respond to stress which is a major variable affecting the course of mourning. At the same time, one of the salient factors which affects the overall adaptive maturation of the adult is "the effect of sustained relationships with loving people"[16]. Because unconditional love seeks to facilitate the growth of others, the bond of trust between individuals is strengthened allowing for an exchange which dissipates groundless fears and reduces the magnitude of most others. Those who love unconditionally participate in life in a manner which reduces stress levels because there is always someone to listen. Love is a motivator to change, to cope. Pressure on oneself is diminished when the emphasis is not on obtaining, seeking more, or keeping up with the Joneses. Notably, one focuses on the *needs* of those who are loved[18]. In this vein, it follows that *unconditional love is the most effective coping mechanism* for the problems of separation, since it allows us to transcend any tragedy, regardless of its dimensions. It culminates in the ability to risk being vulnerable—a characteristic of high self-esteem and a sign that we are completing our grief work. There is nothing that can better replace lost self-esteem than giving and receiving unconditional love. It is part of all healing.

If at this point the reader is rather uncomfortable with the thought that love has a rehabilitative function, that it can radically alter our perception of crises, reality, or recovery I suggest the study of the literature recommended by treatment centers for those with drug dependencies. To illustrate, the programs of the Hazeldon Foundation or the Parkside Medical Service Corporation provide examples of the importance of love in the recovery process. In addition, The Center for

Attitudinal Healing, a support network for children with catastrophic illnesses, has received critical acclaim for reducing pain and suffering through altrustic approaches. In their work love is the most important medication. Its founder, psychiatrist Gerald Jampolsky, has written that "love is the total absence of fear"[19]. There *are* unmeasurable, non-physical aspects to reality which radically affect human behavior in the recovery from separations and coping with stress which results.

As noted in the previous chapter, surgeon Bernie Siegel has suggested that love is the most powerful immune stimulant known to medicine[11]. Alcoholics Anonymous, the largest self-help group in the world, is based on a fellowship of love and concern for each other; this is what is part of the "spiritual experience" which has made the group highly successful. Love has a profound effect on the development and maintainence of self-esteem. There is increasing evidence of the power of love in over-coming all forms of physical and emotional illnesses—if one is open to looking at anecdotal evidence at the risk of being unscientific. Ironically, numerous professional services for people in crises emphasizes caring, love, and elevating self-esteem, nevertheless the scientific community refuses to recognize the power of love to change perceptions of fear and hopelessness.

The third factor evolving from loving without expectation of return, and a most powerful belief to cultivate, is that this type of love never dies, even though the body dies. It exists continually, spanning life and death. In this way, the love received from others stay with the recipient; it becomes a bridge between two worlds. This is why some religions encourage praying to the deceased and why some individuals believe that a part of the deceased loved one is present within the survivor. For love given never dies. Therefore, the unconditional love for another is a major link to eternity. This belief has a profound impact on the course of grief work as well as behavior before death occurs. It culminates in death being viewed as transition, an ancient belief of immense importance. Thornton Wilder said: "There is a land of the living and a land of the dead, and the bridge is love, the only survival; the only meaning." Unconditional love transcends any separation.

The eternal nature of love is often reflected in life by our willingness to listen. Suffering people need to be heard. Active listening is a commit-ment as well as a means of showing attention through love[12, 18]. True listening is hard work but it culminates in both an understanding of the self and the speaker, for what is *not* spoken is sometimes as important as what is said. We discover much about ourselves through the careful attention paid to others[20].

Significantly, in relation to the eternal nature of love, death is non-existent. Although the body dies, the spirit of love exists forever. In this way, although still very painful, it is easier to let go of unnecessary suffering; regrets are eliminated; there is *never* any unfinished business. One does not look back and say: "If only I had said this or did that or told her how much she had inspired me." Survivors are sad. They hurt, but they do not pay an unconscious price in pathological behavior. Fear is dissipated and self-esteem maintained.

Unconditional love allows us to face any fear. Overall, facing fear is actually less energy consuming and anxiety producing than the continuous struggle to suppress and run from it[5]. What is essential here is that the ability to deal with fear is always made easier when we discuss it and bring it into the open. This is the first step to coping with fear and is facilitated through loving relationships. Usually, a great discovery is made—one is not alone—others are dealing with fear of various kinds. Fear is *not* abnormal. Rather, it is part of being human, to be expected when non-judgemental relationships do not exist.

Finally, it is important to remember that traditional thinking imposes limits on our capacity to cope. Unconditional love currently does not fit into the traditional thinking mode and is therefore discarded. However, the mind and spirit have made things happen which traditional thinking has never attained. We need not be shackled by the past.

EMPATHY

At the heart of caring for those coping with a major loss is the degree of empathy we can generate. Empathy is the ability to create in oneself the awareness of what is occurring inside the griever; it is entering the world of the survivor. This empathic pursuit can never be totally accomplished, but whether we have experienced a similar loss or not, we can train ourselves to imagine what the griever is experiencing. What is essential in this regard, and in developing an effective relationship, is *desiring* to understand, for empathic understanding is at the heart of the helping relationship[24]. Through it we fashion an unbreakable bond needed during a crisis.

Each of us possess the inherent ability to empathize compassionately as part of our continuity of care. Be cautious, however, for this is much like walking a tightrope; if empathy is too strong, we may lose our effectiveness because of our emotional involvement. If empathy is too weak, we cannot fully appreciate the needs of the bereaved because we remain aloof, unable to visualize the range of support we are capable of providing. Too many professionals, especially physicians, tend to eliminate empathy from their work. Their results suffer from its absence. There is quite a difference between doing a job and a labor of love.

Developing a sensitivity to the hurt that others are experiencing is primarily a commitment of the heart—coupled with a remembrance of our own vulnerability to change. Later, our basic contribution is to articulate compassion as a quiet center of support. As Marsha tells us: "Being able to cry unrestrainedly in the presence of a non-family loved one, near a water fountain one night, was the turning point. To be able to talk in this person's presence without being interupted or pampered was very helpful. Acceptance and understanding were the keys to my recovery." Each of us can provide that needed presence, that empathy without words as Marsha's friend did.

Accepting behavior and understanding the frequent need "to get it all out," are characteristics of the expression of empathy. Warmth and affection are clearly visible to the griever. It should be pointed out that in coping with any loss, few things are more detrimental to the successful completion of grief work than misplaced trust. The bereaved must trust others to let them step out of character with their grief, to be free to protest, or to give their version of the experience. The empathic caregiver is aware of these needs.

Empathy needs vary among grievers simply because *personality differences exist which influence coping styles.* What is important to understand is that personality heavily influences coping patterns employed and the degree of empathy and sympathy needed. Psychologist Catherine Sanders[25] when investigating the issue of premorbid personalities in bereaved persons, found four distinct grief patterns associated with personality factors: (1) an "inadequate" or disturbed group, (2) a depressed group, (3) a "denial" group, and (4) a normal group.

The disturbed group included individuals with low self-esteem and feelings of inadequacy. They possessed little confidence in themselves and were very insecure, suggesting that they still suffered from severe, long-lasting, emotionally negative aftereffects of their major loss. In Sanders's words: "They need tremendous nurturance and empathy" (p. 3). Members of the depressed group included people characterized as having suffered multiple major losses, were highly emotional, inordinantly sensitive, and reported that they suffered much depression. People in the "denial" group used their physical symptoms as the focus of their grief. The loss itself was not denied, their emotional reactions were. They did not express emotional involvement in their grief work they suffered physical symptoms instead. Although some sorrow and sadness were expressed, they were more intensely involved in activities and distractions which fostered their flight from having to accept the loss and its consequences. The normal group contained people who possessed very high ego-strength, openly expressed their sorrow and sadness, and recognized such losses as a part of life. "The essence of their personality was not lost in a crisis situation"[25, p.2]. People in this group made the best adjustment of all persons studied.

The significance of Sanders's study lies in the evidence which strongly suggests that it is not loss *per se* which is responsible for complications in grieving, but rather factors having to do with the personality itself. This is why some individuals were better able to cope with a specific loss than others.

The importance of this study for support persons who hope to help the bereaved is to suggest that they should be aware of great differences in each person's capacity to express grief and the differences in empathy needs in relation to individual personality. Grieving styles vary as widely as do needs for empathy. And while most of our caregiving may be directed toward those who can eventually cope with the crisis, even within this group variations in needs will surface. These variations will challenge our ability to alter approaches to caregiving. Our attempt to see the griever's struggles, *through his eyes,* will guide our efforts in the important work of support, for the emphathetic person is first and foremost *a good listener.*

SELF-DISCIPLINE, LOSS, AND SELF-ESTEEM

> *You can't really be prepared for the death of a friend, especially at my age. It is unnatural for a young person's life to end so suddenly, so you can only try to accept it after the fact. Preparation would be impossible in such a situation. Mental firmness does help in dealing with it afterward.*
>
> Stephen

Self-discipline spans all human endeavor: success in space, education, skill development, love, technological advancement. In the final analysis, the way we accommodate loss experiences in life depends to a great extent on *how* we are willing to confront what seems to be insurmountable odds. This confrontation inevitably consists of carrying on with life when the temptation to run away from it is overpowering. In order to accomplish this critical task we are forced to do the undesirable. It follows that to bear pain is essentially a process of self-discipline when we reach the crossroads in deciding to accept loss or embrace grief indefinitely. For it is self-discipline which is the main catalyst for whether we grow through loss or permanently withdraw from life. And it is emotions allowed continuous free rein which lead to devalued self-worth and withdrawal.

Today, more than at any other time in history, the word *discipline* is equated with punishment. This obscures the significance of discipline as the essential ingredient in achieving happiness and meeting lifetime problems requiring the delay of immediate gratification for long-term benefits.

If there is a single, consistent need throughout life, one which holds the key to love, health and survival, it is self-discipline. I define it as doing the undesirable; doing what we dislike doing at the time it should be done. In order to endure, to meet the new demands of each year with its challenges and changes, it must prevail. Coping with change is an exercise in self-regulation. A breakdown in this area brings with it a flood of additional frustrations and aggravations, increasing problems and the fear of not being able to overcome them. The ability to respond healthfully to the stresses of life is related to an environment in which discipline abounds[26].

Because each day is filled with decision-making (problem-solving), and much of the process depends on "mental firmness," as Stephen suggested, the process of coping with loss demands critical decisions. Now it is not easy to choose between chocolate sundaes, rich brown gravy, or a favorite pie, and cutting down on calories. Nor is it easy putting the self second and others first. Obviously, it is equally demanding to put aside what we desire at the moment in favor of what is actually needed. However, these are all instances in which self-discipline is essential and must continue for life. Decisions induced by change necessarily entail similar personal sacrifice and doing what we dislike doing. The more we habitually do the distasteful (within reason), the better we are able to meet adversity.

There is no escaping this issue of decision-making. Parents, counselors and teachers, for example, all make difficult decisions heavily influencing other people's lives. The self-discipline needed to make the extra effort, to give time and energy, to bear the brunt of criticism (you're damned if you do and damned if you don't) never seems to stop. How well we discipline ourselves directly influences our self-esteem as well as how we confront problems of loss because there is a sense of triumph in having met tragedy and prevailed—added misery if we feel we are unable to stand-up to the task. Obviously, the capacity to accomplish this varies immensely from person to person, but we can build coping capacity. This increase is achieved by changing our self-evaluations and realizing that worthwhile goals are attained through commitment, hard work, and unwavering beliefs.

We cannot simply desire self-control—we need repetition in action to accomplish it. This is especially true in recovering from a major loss: we habitually have to face new unknowns in the reconstruction of continuity in living. This entails great courage and perseverence, without which no one survives. There is no other time in life when self-discipline is more in demand than when we have to pick up the pieces of our shattered existence and build a new identity without our loved one.

For one thing, managing the emotions associated with grieving is a most challenging and sometimes complex task. Emotions tend to overwhelm us, especially if we have not had prior experience which necessitated a commitment to doing the difficult. Most of us have not embraced that path with open arms. The discomfort that such regulation calls forth is hardly appealing. Consequently, many emotional reactions go unchecked, and they take advantage of us like a would-be friend who first borrows your comb, then an article of clothing, finally money, and then feels entitled to whatever you own. Without setting limits, without doing what we dislike doing, it is extremely difficult to undertake and complete any troublesome task. Sometimes it means following the advice of a therapist or trusted friend. (Many psychiatrists tell how a patient will agree on a course of action to be taken, only to abandon it when the time comes to carry it out.) We must manage our emotions, or they will manage us. Confronting emotions is a herculean task even for the practiced, but the job is even harder when major loss is involved. We at once have to cope with conditioning from early childhood, the expectations of friends and loved ones, and our own desires, fears and attitudes. Though painful and energy consuming, it is something that must be accepted and dealt with.

Does managing emotion mean denying feelings about what has

happened? Not at all. Self-control in loss management never implies inhibiting emotional expression. *It means limiting withdrawal from life, refusing to decline responsibility for recovery, and eliminating the belief that we have been singled out to endure tragedy.* These three factors are powerful forces inhibiting recovery if they are allowed to go unchecked and are accompanied by powerful emotions. Here is where self-discipline has to be employed, where we actively participate in recovery or suffer from our inappropriate response.

It is tempting to believe that grief must be passively endured when in fact we can and *must choose to participate in our own healing.* As Thomas Attig[27] suggests: "Active involvement in the work of relearning the world can restore self-confidence and a sense of purpose in the grieving process itself" (p.60). A deliberate conscious commitment to deal with grief and reacquire a sense of purpose is a fundamental exercise in self-discipline. It has been accomplished by those who have experienced the worst imaginable losses.

Perhaps it would help to consider that there are losses which can be much worse than the natural death of a loved one. I know a young woman whose brother was brutally murdered at a young age. Her health suffered terribly because of the related thoughts: he was so young and it was so senseless. I also remember a young woman whose mother was committed to a mental institution for the rest of her life. "I would keep reminding myself that I had nothing to be ashamed of," she said. "My mother was not a freak, she was just sick." This was her response to the unkind remarks of others when she was a very young girl. Seven years later she wrote: "I do believe, though, that I am still grieving in my own way. Even though she has not died, I think I grieve more when I look at her now. I feel it is very unfair. I sometimes still blame myself, my father and even God." Undoubtedly, this is a devastating, ongoing experience.

The stigma attached to suicide especially anguishes survivors because they are flooded with anger, guilt and self-doubt. For various reasons, most survivors believe they are partly to blame, and they should have prevented the suicide. Society still views survivors with suspicion and reinforces their neurotic guilt ("It's because of the way she was treated at home").

For the most part, it is the refusal to face the pain of loss (the reality of it, the changes, the uncertainty, the feelings toward the "object of loss," the fear of what will happen to us) which is a major source of complicated and prolonged grief. Fear is especially damaging to self-esteem in this instance. Obviously, if refusing to face the distasteful has not been a part of our lives, we must begin this task at a most unfortunate time. But begin it we must—with the help of others—and all the courage we can muster. *Everyone* possesses this innate courage which can be called forth if the task of readjustment is to begin. We will feel pain, we will feel defenseless, but we are built to endure it. *This is a critical belief to develop.*

In the early stages of grief, when we are fighting reality, trying to assimilate the catastrophic loss, the urge to panic and give up may surface. When panic hits, *ask for help* from God, family or friends. Persist in this search. Panic cannot last indefinitely; it will subside. This is a time when everyone needs that one person who is a link to security, the one who is a symbol of strength.

Of course, at that moment of anguish we do not feel it will ever be possible to climb out of the eternal blackness and free ourselves from a meaningless existence. Early on, one simply cannot be expected to make weighty decisions, to immediately reach out to someone else when in such a state of disorganization. But once the time comes—and it will—when we realize that it *has* happened, that our life *has* changed, that "I am different than before," then also comes the constant flood of negative versus positive thoughts, and the onslaught of damning self-doubt. Now is the time we must begin to do what we dislike doing, to continue a life without the physical presence of our loved one, without the companionship of our ex-boyfriend or girlfriend, or without the material goods we have lost. This reality may not occur for weeks or even months. Eventually, when we find ourselves at the crossroads, then come the hard choices as to how to go on with life and respond to a different world. Have we all not had to perform this ritual many times in the past during lesser losses? Of course we have! Ours is a life history of loss which each of us owns, a history shaped by unique personal experiences, one hurriedly dismissed from our thoughts because of the painful memories.

Here we must guard against the seduction of grief. We can be lured into holding on to misery and sadness far too long because of the attention it brings from others. It feels good to know that others care, are sympathetic and show a very special kindness. The attention often is much more than we have previously experienced, more than is reasonably expected. We become too comfortable with it, tending to put off facing routine burdens and frustrations. In time, we must break the bonds of the past. This is a most difficult choice to make.

What has been discussed up to this point is in no way an attempt to minimize the "pain beyond comprehension" which is associated with loss experiences. The event leaves an indelible mark on our psyche. But what the foregoing does imply is that we are accountable not only for the responsibilities associated with bringing up a family, holding a job, fulfilling marriage vows, or obtaining an education but we are also *accountable for our losses* and particularly the way we regroup, recover, and face the unexpected again and again. It is a difficult road to travel, but one *we are capable* of managing. At various points in the recovery process survivors are called upon again and again to carry on, to do what they dislike doing. This experience, often avoided, is at the core of all of life's turning points.

Clearly, loss experiences demand the self-discipline that is always a *choice* during the process of coping. Our willingness to do the distasteful is directly related to the progression of the grief process and the restoration of self-esteem. Without it, we regress. Not surprisingly, each person alone makes the decision to endure. There is always a reason to continue on if we persist in the search to recognize it.

REFERENCES

1. Hoffer, E. *The Ordeal of change.* New York: Harper & Row, 1952.
2. Frank, J. *Persuasion and healing.* Baltimore: Johns Hopkins Press, 1961.
3. May, R. *The meaning of anxiety.* New York: Ronald, 1950.
4. Horowitz, M., et al. Pathological grief and the activation of latent self-images. *American Journal of Psychiatry,* 1980, 137, 1157–62.
5. Kavanaugh, R. *Facing death.* Baltimore: Penguin, 1974.
6. LaGrand, L. *Coping with separation and loss as a young adult.* Springfield, IL: Charles C Thomas, 1986.
7. Parkes, C. & Weiss, R. *Recovery from bereavement.* New York: Basic Books, 1983.
8. Tanner, I. *Loneliness: The fear of love.* New York: Harper & Row, 1973.
9. Knight, J. Spiritual psychotherapy and self-regulation. In E. Goldwag (Ed.). *Inner balance: The power of holistic healing.* Englewood Cliffs, NJ: Prentice-Hall, 1979.
10. Blanton, S. *Love or perish.* Greenwich, CT: Fawcett, 1955.
11. Siegel, B. *Love, medicine, and miracles.* New York: Harper & Row, 1986.
12. Peck, M. *The road less traveled.* New York: Simon & Schuster, 1978.
13. Kalish, R. *Death, grief, and caring relationships.* Belmont, CA: Wadsworth, 1985.
14. Fromm, E. *The art of loving.* New York: Bantam, 1963.
15. Neale, R. *The art of dying.* New York: Harper & Row, 1973.
16. Valliant, G. *Adaptation to life.* Boston: Little, Brown, 1977.
17. Bowlby, J. *Loss: Sadness and depression.* New York: Basic Books, 1980.
18. Powell, J. *Unconditional love.* Allen, TX: Argus, 1978.

19. Jampolsky, G. *Love is letting go of fear.* New York: Bantam, 1981.
20. Jackson, E. *The role of faith in the process of healing.* Minneapolis, MN: Winston Press, 1981.
21. Weisman, A. *The copying capacity.* New York: Human Sciences, 1984.
22. Frankl, V. *Man's search for meaning.* Boston: Beacon, 1962.
23. Caine, L. *Lifelines.* New York: Dell, 1977.
24. Rogers, C. *On becoming a person.* Boston: Houghton Mifflin, 1961.
25. Sanders, C. Bereavement typologies and implications for therapy. *Forum Newsletter,* Forum for Death Education & Counseling, 7[1], January, 1984.
26. Jackson, E. *Understanding grief.* Nashville: Abingdon, 1957.
27. Attig, T. Death education and life-enhancing grief. In R. Pacholski & C. Corr (Eds.). *New directions in death education & counseling.* Arlington, VA: Forum for Death Education & Counseling, 1981, 57–66.

Chapter Seven

THEORY INTO PRACTICE: ALTERING ASSUMPTIONS AND BELIEFS

We are often simply too unaware of how our minds work and what we really believe.

Douglas Hofstadter in
Default Assumptions

New assumptions about the world, a world without the deceased, must be developed.

Therese A. Rando in *Grief, Dying and Death*

Every idea which enters the conscious mind, if it is accepted by the unconscious, is transformed by it into a reality and forms henceforth a permanent element in our life.

C. Harry Brooks in *Better and Better Every Day*

The noted historian Arnold Toynbee[1] wrote: "There are two parties to the suffering that death inflicts and in the apportionment of this suffering, the survivor takes the brunt" (p. 221). This is not only applicable to the event of death but I believe it is equally true of separations other than death, whenever a person believes he has been rejected by another. In this chapter we will explore ways to ease the suffering survivors of death or a breakup face by actively involving them in the troublesome matter of recovery.

Since major separation experiences result in profound emotional upheaval, several needs arise: A thorough review of the relationship, determining how and why the death or breakup occurred, managing physical and emotional reactions, and building a life without the other. To accommodate the rebuilding phase three significant factors need to be addressed: belief in the methods used to facilitate adjustment, positive expectancy in adapting to transition, and implicit trust in those who may be involved as caregivers.

159

Believing in the method means learning as much as possible about how a particular approach is useful and how it is best employed. Gathering the necessary information to make this judgment is critical in forming the mental commitment necessary for success. Without strong faith in the attempt, there is little hope for a smooth transition.

Since the conscious mind is a gateway to the unconscious this faith in the process *must* be strong and unswerving. Establishing such a strong conviction may involve discussions with professionals, extensive reading, comparing alternatives, attending professional meetings, or utilizing informal sources of information. The strength of belief in an approach is an index to positive outcome.

In fact, positive expectancy is an integral part of confronting adversity by challenging fallacies in thinking and replacing them with new assumptions. Expecting success forms an outlook which is essential in dealing with any form of adversity. If we are unconvinced that we can cope with tragedy, recovery will be arduous and never-ending. Expectancy anticipates desirable results and is at the heart of what is commonly called a positive attitude.

It is a shame that the biochemical factors that accompany a positive attitude are not fully understood by the general public, that is, that the neural and hormonal changes which accompany a positive frame of reference auger well for physical health, the reduction of bodily stress, and for recovery from loss. On the other hand, since we learn in childhood to repress anger and develop irrational thinking about loss, we cause an excessive flow of adrenalin, put the body into overdrive, and pay the price of a full blown stress response when we are confronted with loss.

However, we *can* intervene in this automatic process, and satisfactorily cope with the most tragic loss imaginable if we generate this positive expectancy. Again, this depends heavily on the realization that we *do possess the inherent capacity to cope*. But this expectancy can only prevail if hope is kept alive, for we cannot exist without it[2]. There is *always* a way if we continue to look for it.

CHANGING THOUGHTS TO ADAPT TO LOSS

Most major losses challenge root beliefs. Among the most telling assaults on beliefs occurs when the fantasy of unending continuity in relationships crumbles. Death in particular, causes intensive evaluation of long held beliefs about mortality and the meaning of existence. Breakups challenge our beliefs about ourselves and relationships. Assumptions and beliefs about life fly in the face of the steady stream of separations everyone faces. On the other hand, altering thoughts and/or beliefs about the self, loss experiences, and the future is often at the core of successful coping. The ability to make this transition demands utilizing the available support network of people and our individual resources. It further involves a lamentable but unescapable truth: my personal world has changed and so must the way I relate to it.

Since the strongest source of beliefs is experience, it is imperative that we change our experiences, if we are to alter our beliefs about our ability to cope with devastating losses. This means we must reach out for help as difficult as that may seem when we are grieving. Dwelling on the past, on what has happened, is useless. The question everyone must answer when death or any separation occurs is: What should I do now? Shaping the future is our only positive alternative.

To facilitate this active reaching out let us examine three proven methods for altering assumptions and beliefs available to everyone in the quest to adapt: friends and family, self-help groups, and autosuggestion. All three methods have a single factor in common: they are the springboard for replacing default assumptions about loss and our ability to cope with it. These methods augment what Schneider[3] refers to as holding on strategies whose purposes are to help limit the dimensions of change imposed by loss. These strategies are optimistic and used by individuals who "believe that: 1) they have the capacity to overcome any crisis; 2) they can outlast any intruder; 3) their hard work will overcome anything; 4) they can find and maintain meaningful and supportive relationships; or 5) they can usually unquestionably believe in the inherent good and trustworthiness of all people" (p. 130–131).

1. THE SEARCH FOR SOCIAL SUPPORT

My roommates at college allowed me to talk about the losses of both my brother and mother without making it seem morbid. Remembering is a good way to cope. I also have developed a close relationship to my father because he and I are the only ones left of our nuclear family. We turned to each other for support. Things I couldn't tell people, I wrote down (I'm a writer) and then shared it with them. If you love someone, let them know it now. They may not be here tomorrow.

Barbara, age 21

The first base of outside support in altering thoughts to cope with massive change is a caring, trusting colleague, family member, or friend willing to spend the hours necessary to comfort, listen, and advise. There is no more pressing need when personal tragedy strikes than the presence of someone who represents stability amidst the shattering turmoil. It is not only legitimate, it is essential to lean on others, using their strength in time of our weakness. *Interdependence must become a shared belief.*

I once asked a man with colo-rectal cancer how he was able to maintain his positive attitude for so long. He replied: "I can't say enough about friends. I think you have to use your friends. I don't mean use in a negative way. My friends know my treatments, my operations and my reactions to them. I've made them share some of the burden. I don't know how people can survive without sharing. Just having someone to talk to—there's a fear. It's such a relief for a person. You can't keep it bottled up or you would explode. That's why I think I'm still here."

The same comments apply to survivors: They need to "use" their friends and family and share the burden through emotional expression. Peer therapy is both practical and highly effective.

MUST WE BE STRONG?

The myth of "being strong" is just that, a product of storytelling, or false assumptions born of circumstances in which strict independence was considered the ideal. As psychiatrist Colin Parkes[4] tells us, the early stage of bereavement "is a time when family, friends and others should rally round and relieve the newly bereaved person of some of his roles and obligations." Indeed, the bereaved should allow this assistance to occur for it helps both the griever and caregivers alike.

At first glance, this appears to be a simple, readily acceptable practice. In reality, finding an acceptable support network or even a single support person may be a difficult task. Nevertheless, it is quite clear that this support will mitigate the effects of tragic loss by enhancing our self-esteem and assisting in the transition to a life without the significant other[5-6].

Giving in to loss must include alterations in the basic way a person thinks about loss. Within limits, everyone is capable of changing "reality" to include separation as a normal, not a punishing, event. This has been accomplished by millions of people, sometimes through dramatic experiences of a paranormal nature. It also occurs through child-like trusting relationships which are more likely to be formed in the course of managing loss. Accordingly, it is highly significant to note that such relationships heavily influence how we reorganize "reality" after a major loss experience.

Perhaps the most difficult time to find a support person who is consistent in caring is a month or two *after* the loss occurs. Early in the grief process there is usually much attention and concern. Later, when everyone expects the bereaved to be resuming a normal life, needed support is absent. Not uncommonly, grievers have many would-be support persons around them immediately after a death occurs. After the funeral, the number begins to dwindle. Once relatives have returned to their homes, when the griever is alone for the first time, then the real work of grief begins—and support is minimal. Sarah, whose boyfriend died as the result of an automobile accident, wrote me the following: "You are so right about people not wanting to be around grieving people. I got so many phone calls and cards for about two weeks. Now there is just one of my friends who still calls. Just one."

It is "just one" such person who assists in the three major tasks of grieving suggested by Erich Lindemann[7]: emancipation from the bondage of the deceased, formation of new relationships, and readjustment to an external environment without the deceased. These tasks demand changes in thought life. However, the abandonment of survivors by support persons occurs for two reasons: most people believe that one should be "getting better" within a few weeks and they often are not aware that support, especially someone to talk openly with, is needed for many months, sometimes years, after a traumatic loss. Nevertheless, completing the tasks of grief is impossible without changes in assumptions about a world without the loved one.

Consequently, it is important for the bereaved to find others who can be trusted with their deepest feelings and, at the same time, assist in taking the first faltering steps toward helping them establish a new identity. Making those outward motions, coupled with the conviction that we can endure, is a major advance in resolving life problems. As William James said: " . . . if we wish to conquer undesirable emotional tendencies in ourselves, we must assiduously and in the first instance coldbloodly, go through the outward motions of those contrary dispositions we prefer to cultivate"[8]. To put it another way, we must act as we wish to be not as we are.

Of course, in choosing our support persons, we must *avoid* those who add to our sadness. Sometimes a professional counselor fills this need. However, there is nothing that can match the understanding of another person who has suffered a similar loss or has had much experience as a caregiver and is willing to listen unconditionally. This is true for major losses other than death as we are reminded by Celeste.

> People mostly gave me standard replies when they found out my parents were divorced. The best thing is just having someone around who understood and was willing to listen when I wanted to talk about it. They did not pry or say those stupid things.

Listening is at the heart of resolving life's problems. Lisa points this out in explaining what she does when there is nobody to listen.

> I think it is of the ultimate importance to always have someone to listen to you when you are depressed about anything. I have what I call my "Nothing Book" and it is full of blank pages. When I am upset and have no one to talk to I write everything I am feeling in the book, sometimes in the form of a letter to the person I am upset with. This makes me feel like I got it off my chest.

Expressing what is within is essential for progress in completing our adaptation to change. Also, the listener is a critical factor in reestablishing self-esteem[9]. Fortunately, such a person plants the seeds of hope by his/her mere presence or by responding to expressions of fear and disorganization.

There is little doubt that it is helpful for the griever to find someone who has had a similar loss. Those who have experienced a similar tragedy frequently emerge from it with new sensitivities to the needs of others as well as information which disarms some fears and worries. The relationship often focuses on how they coped, how they have gone on with their lives, and in particular how they have achieved happiness again. They will have answers to all of these questions, answers which are to be considered as options not final solutions.

People need to take advantage of people who have been there and overcome adversity. A cancer patient once told me that talking to another person with the same type of cancer "made me feel less fearful." Though we should avoid the overanxious helper who acts as though he/she has all the answers, in the vast majority of instances the experience of others provides a sense of security, hope and affirmation of life.

Strong relationships are catalysts for behavioral change and are often the origin for altering assumptions about present conditions and prospects for the future. Trust in another individual opens the door to alternatives in restructuring a world which has collapsed. Not only do people with such meaningful relationships cope well and live longer, but these relationships mitigate the invasive effects of stress[10]. The nature of a relationship therefore is critical in managing loss.

People we trust often hold great suggestive power over us just as doctors, lawyers, and therapists heavily influence clients if their clients believe in their expertise. Frequently, trusted friends and loved ones by their presence, provide a similar suggestion to the unconscious—that we are not alone, are still loved, and important and will cope with the tragedy. The survivor's belief that another person deeply cares keeps the flame of hope in the future alive. As Martha tells us after the death of her father: "I would have to say that talking with my family about my father was what helped most. Sometimes we would just sit and talk and cry. My mother was the person who helped me the most. The summer after he died, I was in shock. Christmas time was the worst, but we got through it as a family."

On the separation from her friend, Susan put it this way. "I do feel that good friends who you trust, are the greatest help of all. They help you sort out your irrational ideas about the situation and better understand what is real. You definitely need contact. Loneliness is one of the worst feelings."

Friends and family also present ideas which are the basis for new assumptions and beliefs about how to cope: draw, paint, or keep a diary about your feelings if you are unable to talk about them; help others and you help yourself; happy memories of the deceased are important grieving tools; plan your free time so you are not always alone and dwelling on your loss; it is all right to be good to yourself and enjoy yourself again. You will not be demeaning the memory of the deceased.

The false assumption that a person cannot cope with the conditions of massive change, a common experience in the early days of grief, is replaced through the persistent presence of those who care. The realization that others care becomes a link to forming thoughts of being able to endure without the loved one, of shedding our shackles of despair. Strength is renewed, motivation to affirm life found, and techniques for adapting tried.

Shedding the Illusions of Immunity

Social support then, is an integral force in changing assumptions and beliefs about separation and our ability to integrate these events into life.

According to Weisman's[11] astute assessment, everyone has to deal with the illusions of immunity they harbor about loss. These default assumptions only add to the intensity of pain experienced when separations occur. In changing these assumptions, significant others help survivors normalize what is being experienced and arrive at the more rational belief that separation is a normal aspect of life.

This can counter another instance of irrational thinking that frequently surfaces in grievers. It is the assumption that they have somehow been "cheated" in their loss experience, as if they were somehow entitled to or deserving of the continued presence of persons now dead[4]. Not surprisingly, it is not easy to break through such a perspective on separation. It is the interchange between griever and caregiver over time which commonly leads to giving up this assessment. It is noteworthy that through the work of grief we create a new identity, withdraw emotional energy from the deceased, and establish a different relationship with the loved one.[12]. All of these processes demand changes in erroneous assumptions and premises as suggested in the following.

EXAMPLES

A. *Before my husband left our relationship had deteriorated so much I actually hated him and wanted him to leave, yet when he did I was hysterical for awhile. I had many friends who listened, let me cry with them and one special friend who was always there, who shared her marital problems and gave me hope that mine would be resolved the way I wanted them to be.*

B. *I spoke to a friend who had a similar occurrence. She helped me by telling me how she handled the situation. It helped me to know I wasn't the only one who had gone through this. By talking it out with her, I could better organize my feelings and what had to be done to move on to bigger and better things. It was also nice to know the two of us could sit and pray about the entire situation. It helped to know God would listen and help heal the pain.*

C. *A close friend who just went through the same situation two weeks earlier has helped me by talking to me, telling me how everything eventually fell into place for her, and keeping me busy with new things to do.*

Accompanied by a trusted friend, the burden of the journey through loss is lightened and the survivor becomes more open to accepting the new. Finally, whether griever or caregiver, it is important to recall Bowlby's[13] observation that the absence of interchange with someone who cares diminishes hope and often precipitates depression. Friends can reduce the intensity of depression. Furthermore, in an earlier paper he states that as "long as there is active interchange between ourselves and the external world, either in thought or action, our subjective experience is not one of depression"[14]. While depression is a very normal part of the giving up process, and to be expected at times, severe depression can be thwarted when we revise assumptions with the help of others. In particular, trust in the self and others reinforces the will to risk and alter perceptions about present conditions.

2. CHANGING ASSUMPTIONS AND BELIEFS THROUGH SELF-HELP GROUPS

My governing value after Tony's death was pure survival — my own and that of the family I had remaining. . . . I had to talk about it and if others had trouble with that, it was their problem. I had to survive. Family as family was important, not just the individual members, but the relationships and the cohesiveness. Value today, make it count, don't pass up any opportunity to be together, to make this moment worth remembering, in case it's all we ever have. Going to TCF (The Compassionate Friends) and being active, got me in touch with others who were thinking the same way. I was okay and so were they. That was comforting, when I reached the stage of caring again.

Ronnie Petersen

If we are unable to find the right person who is willing to share the path to healing, then it becomes essential to look for a self-help group who will provide nurturance and ideas for enduring the difficult transitions which lie ahead. Ideally, friends and a self-help group make an effective support network for coping with change and shedding old beliefs and assumptions.

Self-help groups have been part of the American way of life from the founding fathers to the present. In various forms and for numerous purposes they have been used world-wide for centuries. For example, China exists on the concept of mutual assistance. On closer examination we find that there are hundreds of thousands of self-help groups throughout most countries for people who share common problems or goals. To illustrate, Alcoholics Anonymous, the largest self-help organization in the world, has an estimated one million members in 58,000 groups in 114 countries[15]. In the United States there are a variety of support groups for widows, bereaved parents, and children. Organizations such as the Widow to Widow Program, The Candelighters, The Compassionate Friends,

Parents of Murdered Children, and THEOS (They Help Each Other Spiritually) are found in most states.

In practice, self-help groups for the bereaved are essentially mutual assistance groups, people helping each other and who themselves are at different stages of adjusting to loss. There is an imitative process occurring which spawns new ideas and knowledge about present circumstances. One thing emerges clearly here, the most recently bereaved draw nurturance from those who are near the end or have passed the most critical periods of their grief, and eventually are able to help others.

Those who help others reap benefits from their willingness to be around pain. Arthur Petersen, former executive director of The Compassionate Friends, a self-help group for parents of deceased children, decided to turn to this group to reach out to others and share what he had learned from the death of his seventeen-year old son in an automobile accident. In a recent letter to me he wrote:

> Helping bereaved parents has turned out to be far more satisfying than I could have anticipated. For those who believe as I do and who approach life as I do, one very important characteristic of self-help group activity is to get to "make friends with your shadow." I know that I've moved from introvert toward extrovert and from thinker toward feeler during the past eight years. I have become a more considerate, more sensitive, more compassionate human being as the result of association with so many loving, caring, suffering, bereaved parents.

This poignant expression of change through group interaction illustrates the range of possibilities for growth and change within the context of group work. For many people, their group participation becomes the most important growth experience of their lives.

Among the major functions of self-help therapy are:

1. The social bonding which takes place among members becomes a source of hope that we can meet the challenge of coping with massive change. As individuals observe others who have made it through tragedy, there is a glimmer of hope that they too might make it.
2. A source of information is provided on the normalcy of emotions which seem out of control. Also, information on a wide variety of coping techniques is exchanged among members.
3. A sense of unconditional acceptance is inherent in the self-help movement. Regardless of the type of loss, one is free to express outrage, sorrow, and fears in an atmosphere free of judgments. Such non-judgemental acceptance is important to restoring self-esteem

while allowing for the expression of anger and other suppressed feelings.

Changes in Behavior: The Fundamental Goal

Although seldom voiced in meetings, the fundamental goal of self-help support groups is behavioral change, which is never accomplished without cognitive change. Specifically, the ideology of the group may function as a "cognitive antidote" to the negative thoughts which permeate loss experience[16]. Self-help groups provide an environment of freedom and openness in which assumptions and beliefs about dilemmas to be faced are dramatically altered over time. Motivation for change is facilitated by observing the living proof that others are healing.

Most importantly, the interaction with those who are living examples of successful copers becomes the springboard to confronting three common emotions: anger, guilt, and depression. The relevancy of ideas and suggestions of group members are meaningful because of the many pitfalls they have overcome on their own road to healing. Strikingly, *all* healing is based on positive expectancy. Since adjustment to separation always involves resistance—a refusal to accept change—any attention given to the emotions of resistance keeps alive opposition to adjustment.

For example, anger, justified or not, is incompatible with peace of mind. Writing in *Love Is Letting Go Of Fear*, psychiatrist Gerald Jampolsky[17] observed: "To have inner peace as our single goal we need to correct the erroneous belief that justified anger or grievances brings peace" (pp. 101–2). Justification of continuous anger is a trap. At the same time, there is nothing like unexpressed anger to increase stress and prolong grief. This type of learning occurs in self-help groups.

Furthermore, self-help groups not only defuse much of the normal anger which accompanies loss, but at the same time assists in what has been called the "search for meaning"[18]. During this search, feelings are validated, that is, they are recognized as real not abnormal. Nor are they minimized, which so often occurs with friends, because group members have shared and overcome similar feelings. They have deep insight into why it hurts so much. Intuitively, they know that suppressed emotions are forms of self-punishment.

It is noteworthy that suggestion is the most potent force for change within self-help groups just as it is in one-to-one therapy or in individual attempts to cope without assistance from the group. In particular, the non-verbal suggestions that we possess the capacity to cope, that peace of mind will be reached, and that various emotional reactions are normal given the circumstances, culminates in the gradual reduction and eventual elimination of bitterness, exhaustion, self-pity, and feelings of isolation and loneliness. There is a restoration of self-confidence generated by acceptance and freedom to share in a nonjudgmental environment, further conveyed through compassion and genuine love. Not infrequently, a sense of caring and loving becomes the source of developing coping techniques by changing how we think. Lynn, whose son died eight days after birth, put it this way:

> I have the deepest respect for bereaved parents who have survived and remained strong enough to live again. I need their example and special understanding for support. This is why I believe an organization such as Compassionate Friends has a very important purpose. It helps me to share with people who really understand and it gives me a chance to help others by understanding.

Through such understanding many changes occur. Some of the most frequently reported are changes in belief systems concerning religion, life, death, what is important in life, altruism, and increased empathy for others[19]. Whether or not one reaches such levels of reintegration and understanding depends to a large extent on willingness to accept new conditions and alter assumptions about the past. Commonly, group participation results in massive changes in basic premises because one is supported by trusting others.

One other point: if you attend a meeting or two and do not like the experience, try a different group and location. Each group possesses unique characteristics, its own personality. Try others until you find one you are comfortable with. Refuse to give up on group assistance because of an initial negative experience. We turn now to facilitating change through autosuggestion.

3. ADAPTING TO ENDINGS THROUGH AUTOSUGGESTION

In Chapter 1, I emphasized that suggestion is a potent learning tool as well as a creative force in shaping how we choose to meet adversity. As defined earlier, autosuggestion is the placing of an idea, concept, or plan in the unconscious mind through visualization and self-talk. We cope successfully with any separation or loss when we decide to alter assumptions about the self, our loss, and the world which now confronts us. As history attests, this is the essence of coping. Positive changes have occurred in millions of people from primitive man to the present through either direct or indirect forms of autosuggestion. Its use is not affected by your level of education, occupation, or socioeconomic status. Autosuggestion has been referred to rightly or wrongly by a variety of names: conscious self-suggestion, self-talk, imaginative thinking, creative visualization, self-hypnosis, and autogenic training. William James labeled it the mind-cure technique[20]. In any case, the technique utilizes an unadulterated creative force, a resource of immense value — the unconscious or subconscious mind.

Religion and science agree on the importance of beliefs (which are grounded in continuous self-suggestion) in coping with life's problems. Science insists that how stress is perceived is crucial to how it is dealt with, while the world's religions have long held that if we believe, if we have faith, any confrontation can be met with assurance of success. The basis for this agreement is the truism that whatever individuals believe or imagine to be true about themselves and an event determines in large measure how they respond to it[21]. It follows that anyone can decide what to believe and change their assumptions accordingly. This is exactly what occurs in self-help groups, therapy, or in one-to-one conversations. At various times, particularly when in need, everyone is highly suggestible.

Consider the power of a single thought when we perceive a person or an event in a very positive way. Have you ever been tired after a long day, or mildly depressed, and you receive great news? Perhaps you receive a surprise visit from someone you love very much. In either case your energy level rises, fatigue disappears. What happens is the brain sends messages to the adrenal glands and we immediately receive a surge of energy. This happens internally without fanfare. And we can initiate it *without* an outside stimulus — it can come from within.

The success of autosuggestion is based on the fact that people continuously influence how and what they believe both consciously and unconsciously. The long-term goal being to coordinate the conscious and unconscious minds toward the desired outcome. In other words, we need to develop the capacity of the right-brain intuitive mind so that the left-brain logical mind does not dominate our lives. Furthermore, centuries of observational and correlational evidence makes it clear that what we think influences our every action and feeling. An old saw is appropriate here: "The attitude is the father of the action." In this respect, it is important to realize that negative thinking is the forerunner for the tired, hopeless assumption that "all is lost." Or, as Burns[22] states: "Intense negative thinking *always* accompanies a depressive episode, or any painful emotion for that matter" (p. 28). In short, negative thinking prolongs and intensifies emotional pain.

When the full implications of what conscious and unconscious autosuggestion creates is realized, we will never allow negative thoughts to take root in the mind. (How often have you said to yourself "I *know* if such and such happens I will get a headache"—and it happens.) To reach that point of self-awareness takes time. Nonetheless, it is significant to understand that everyone has reserves of untapped energy in the unconscious which are liberated through conscious autosuggestion. This resource ultimately changes behavior and facilitates adaptation to loss.

Autosuggestion has a wide variety of uses from inducing the relaxation response and treating physical ailments to controlling emotions, problem-solving, and coping with massive life-change. For example, some therapists use a verbal aversion therapy with alcoholics in which they ask the client to imagine going through the usual drinking sequence. Then the therapist instructs the alcoholic to vividly imagine an aversive stimulus, like vomiting, pairing a very nauseous scene with the consumption of alcohol.

However, some survivors may not be ready to fully utilize conscious autosuggestion because they are not ready to let go of grief. We hold on to grief for many reasons: fear of demeaning the memory of the deceased, fear of losing the attention we are receiving, fear that others will forget the deceased, believing that one is unable to enjoy life without the deceased, or refusing to give up anger and resentment. Sometimes the bereaved continually open old wounds by repeatedly visiting places or doing things which bring back memories that foster increased sadness. Nevertheless, at some point when the decision is made that "I must cope, I must adjust, I must go on with my life," then commitment to a course of action follows. This may include joining a self-help group and talking to others about how they have coped as well as employing autosuggestion.

It should be pointed out that autosuggestion is not the training of the will, but the creative utilization of the imagination[23]. As Napoleon said: "Imagination rules the world." For what we imagine to be true and acceptable is acted upon by the unconscious and culminates in desired or undesired behavior. The central nervous system does not know the difference between reality and imagination, truth or irrational beliefs. It will simply act on what it is sent from the senses and the conscious mind.

This further implies that the conscious mind acts at times as a filter preventing certain suggestions from impacting on the unconscious.

I should also call your attention to the normalcy (given the condition that science has us in its thrall) of becoming suspect and skeptical of the benefits of a process which cannot be fully explained by formulas, equations, and unequivocal experimental evidence. Ideas which challenge the concept of scientific objectivity are subject to immediate rejection. To the scientific mind, anything not quantifiable is a pseudoscience and considered the child of the charlatan. Autosuggestion falls into this category for some.

Early in the present century the medical establishment dismissed it as fantasy, but later recanted when the impact of belief, suggestion, and imagination was demonstrated as quite capable of influencing behavior, both medical and non-medical. Today many psychiatrists and psychologists use autosuggestion as an adjunct to therapy with their patients and to induce relaxation in the course of dealing with specific treatment modalities. If the reader is suspect, there is one course of action to settle your misgivings. Try it. The use of autosuggestion is disarmingly simple: relaxation, visualization, repetitive self-talk, and belief. It works this way.

A. Commitment

The initial prerequisite for consciously changing assumptions and beliefs about separation and programming the unconscious to do so is the strong *decision* to willingly accept and take responsibility for coping with change. This is the same decision that thousands of people who have cured themselves of cancer have made; they chose to be fighters. This means that in coping with separation, we seek support but recognize that the ultimate force for adaptation comes from within. This should be accompanied by an understanding that the process of self-suggestion is not a training of the will or developing willpower. On the contrary, it is a passive communication approach to the unconscious in which expectation and imagination become the bedrock to change and self-mastery. Through relaxed repetition of specific thoughts, conscious visualizations, and images the unconscious brings about dramatic change.

History is replete with instances where actors, writers, poets, inventors, and great orators received ideas or solutions to problems directly from their unconscious minds during sleep or when in the drowsy state. Everyone has experienced the birth of ideas and found new approaches to a problem during these time periods although they often are forgotten if not immediately written down.

Full commitment to the process of consciously changing thoughts accompanied by a strong belief in our ability to execute these changes is a prerequisite to recovery. If you want to cope, if you *really* want to go on with your life, you can. Jim, at twenty-three, the victim of a motorcycle accident which cost him the use of one arm and numerous other injuries said:

> Superiority is often felt by being "knocked down" then being able to rebound and get better every day. Recovery following loss is an ongoing process which depends on your inner self and what you can do for yourself. Others may help, but whatever happens results from *you*.

The relevance of the desire to change the present conditions of unhappiness and despair, to break out of the pattern of hopelessness, must not be underestimated. Desire recognizes and overcomes the fact that recovery from separation is never a straight-line uphill journey; it is filled with setbacks, flashes of success, as well as pitfalls. Grief revisits often. Put another way, adapting to massive change brought on by separation is hard work, with many uneasy moments. The road is difficult and uphill, yet it can always be traveled when one is determined and committed. Since we have all been programmed to expect instant results, it is necessary to patiently persist. It takes time to change thought patterns. However, the vehicle for coping with change is your *attitude* and a *plan* to adapt to your new environment.

B. Relaxation

Being open to and desiring to employ autosuggestion is followed by the need to set the stage for increasing suggestibility. This is best achieved through putting the body in a relaxed state as muscular tension is a distraction to the mind. Any technique can be used such as the relaxation response, meditation, or yoga practices[24-25].

If you are unfamiliar with these practices, the following technique is easily employed. Sit relaxed in a chair, both feet on the floor, or lie down and first take several slow breaths, counting to five when inhaling and when exhaling. Open your mouth when exhaling. Be sure the breaths are deep enough to cause the diaphragm to expand and contract (the stomach will rise and fall). Increase your count as you practice. Work to the point where you are taking between 4–5 breaths per minute. Spend at least 10 minutes on breathing exercises every day. The increased oxygen to your body will be welcomed, but the real benefits come in the form of tension and anxiety reduction. Deep abdominal breathing has always been the number one anti-anxiety agent, better than any drug. Use it at any time to reduce tension. Breathe slowly and deeply when fear or guilt surfaces. Breathe out guilt and fear, breathe in peace and tranquility.

Now beginning with the toes, visualize the relaxation of muscles in the feet. See your muscles relaxing as a rubber band which has been stretched. Feel the tension draining out onto the floor. Silently repeat "release," "let go," or "give it up" when focusing on a particular muscle group. Next, focus attention on the lower legs and knees, repeating the process of visualizing tension draining from the legs onto the chair or floor. Now move slowly up the body to the hips, then chest, arms and head. Continue this procedure in conjunction with slow breathing until the entire body is relaxed. Picture you are breathing out all your worries and breathing in relaxing energy. Feel the release.

Pay special attention to the muscles of the forehead, around the eyes, lips, and jaws. At all times picture tension melting into the chair, bed, or floor. Now focus on your eyelids—and make them become lighter. Feel them become weightless. This relaxation approach will put you in a mental state that researchers classify as Alpha—where you can most effectively influence the unconscious. You can teach yourself to reach the alpha state—which is simply a measure of electrical activity in the brain—any time you choose. Explore other forms of meditation and relaxation which best suit your needs as you practice. Be receptive to images provided by your unconscious mind in the process.

The same procedure may be followed in the evening before going to sleep. Although the unconscious can be influenced at any time, the most fertile occasions are often just before we drop off to sleep and just before fully awake in the morning. These are times when we are actually in a hypnotic state most open to suggestion. At these times, with muscles relaxed and tension all but vanished, we effortlessly introduce new concepts or repeat meaningful aphorisms. This is a daily practice. Having reached a state of relaxation we have actually already experienced our first success with autosuggestion; relaxation was achieved through self-talk and visualization.

C. Visualization

One of the most effective techniques for changing inward and outward conditions is to imagine in detail the desired outcome. Visualization often referred to as movies-of-the-mind, is unquestionably the most underused, yet potent technique for coping with change and influencing life. The process pre-dates written and spoken language. For centuries it has been used to enhance relationships, practice social roles, increase creativity, induce healing, strengthen spiritual life, and as the catalyst in the effective use of hypnosis. All civilizations have practiced it in some form.

In essence, visualization *is* the way we think[26]. We use our imagination in creative and meditative ways. Space and time are bridged through this process because every detail is controlled by the conscious mind. Without realizing, everyone uses it daily, often in a detrimental way. Here is where a vivid imagination is a strong ally or a destructive enemy. The Renaissance physician Paracelsus taught that the imagination is a tool in our invisible workshop, a creative power of infinite value[27]. Einstein said: "Imagination is more important than knowledge." Physical objects—buildings, bridges, automobiles—would not exist unless they were first visualized by their creators. The same is true of human behavior whether good or bad. It is first visualized by the conscious mind. What is continuously imagined is often received.

Act As You Wish To Be

By clearly painting a mental picture of the way we want to cope or feel, seeing ourselves going through actual scenes where desired behavior is exhibited, we establish new patterns of thought. We influence the unconscious mind to externalize what we created within. If the suggestion has to do with increased energy, strength and endurance, then we flash on our mental screen pictures of the movements, time, place, sounds, and feelings associated with those traits. It is useful to include as much detail as possible: see the self walking, smelling the freshness of the air, hearing the sounds of the birds, the train, or a barking dog—all as part of the scene in which you are filled with boundless energy and endurance. Negative thoughts are never allowed to compete with these efforts. If the mind begins to wander, which is quite normal, we simply refocus on the objective of visualizing the original scene. The emphasis here is on a *passive* refocusing. Gently bring the mind back to the previous scene.

The same procedure is used any time during the day when negative thoughts compete for our attention. We prepare for any future event we think might be stressful, like being alone at a gathering without our loved one, by way of our mental movies. We practice the way we want to deal with the situation.

Making the correct appeal to the unconscious is the backbone of autosuggestion and the process of change. In fact, mental practice is a form of direct communication with the unconscious. What eventually happens "out there" must happen first in the mind. Mental images eventually turn into behaviors. Any griever has already experienced this fact of life as demonstrated by thoughts of despair, anger, hopelessness and frustration which cause fatigue, sleeplessness, and loss of appetite. These are the forerunners of listlessness, immobility, weariness, and eventual depression. Therefore, we must visualize the end products to be achieved: successful coping, a return of physical strength, an acceptance of our new state in life. We act as though the goal is being reached. *Act as you visualize and it* will *come to pass.*

Ways to Influence the Unconscious

While there are many ways the unconscious is influenced without our awareness, we can consciously program it with new messages as well. In addition to visualization, all of the following feed positive messages to the unconscious: self-talk (internal dialogue), pictures, aphorisms, subliminal messages, talking out loud to oneself, writing in a diary, and listening to audio tapes. Audio tapes made commercially or tapes made using your own voice are highly effective. Choose one or a combination of these approaches. The central nervous system always reacts to what it is fed—and the unconscious mind is *always* listening.

Physical education specialists are well aware of the effectiveness of the role of the unconscious and mental practice on skill development. The power of visualization has been used in the training of Olympic athletes weight lifters, and in professional sports[28-30]. If individuals persistently visualize the way they want to perform they achieve better performance. Through seeing oneself execute the exact movements for a particular sequence of skills *those skills are honed to perfection.* So too can our ability to manage emotions, avert unnecessary suffering, and cope with a new state in life. Always picturing the end product, the way we want to be able to function and believing that we are reacting in that way alters the original state. As I have written earlier, however, this takes hard work and repetitive practice.

In one of the most inspirational books ever written, *The Magic of Believing*, Claude Bristol[31] observed: "When we realize that the subconscious mind is sensitized to the point that it works accurately to externalize the suggestion which is most greatly impressed upon it, we then get a better understanding of the necessity for concentration and for constant repetition of the one suggestion" (p. 85).

Visualization "allows people to gain an element of control over their world and to shape their daily life into something more beautiful and enjoyable"[26]. By "seeing" ourselves refusing to believe our condition is hopeless, that life is unfair, or that reactive depression will not lift, a deadly thought process is reversed. In fact, we visualize the self accepting, getting stronger, feeling less self-conscious, less fearful, and better prepared to meet the new circumstances which life presents. We rehearse a successful outcome. It has been shown repeatedly that the mind influences the autonomic nervous system and all of the involuntary processes of the body. There is undeniable evidence that the thoughts we entertain play a significant role in preventing disease or reversing its progress once it has gained a foothold.

One more consideration. Sometimes in trying to visualize a particular sequence of events we may find some discordant elements. What I mean here is that we may be auditory, visual, or tactile learners and need to emphasize in our visualizations what seem to come easiest to us. We may not be able to visualize a *feeling* of strength, but we can *see* ourselves completing tasks during the day which demand strength and endurance. Therefore, we emphasize what comes most naturally to the mind's eye, images which utilize that particular sense. However, it can be very useful to recall what it *feels like inside* when you have been in a happy state. Try to duplicate those feelings in your visualization.

Daily, we reinforce a strong mental picture of a particular goal by using reminders that are placed in our rooms, offices, or automobiles. For example, I keep a 3" by 5" card on my desk with three "trigger" words written on it: Happiness, Endurance and Strength. During the day when I am at the desk I may look up and see this reminder which causes me to pause and slowly read and create a picture in my mind based on these words. The same may be accomplished by hanging meaningful photographs in a location that will catch your eye. Some people place a motto or Bible verse on their bathroom mirrors. The point is, these techniques keep our focus on a goal and continually influence the unconscious.

Many self-help organizations utilize the same technique as part of their attempts to help members change behavior through constant reminders of healthy thinking and reacting.

An important question clearly emerges: How do we know that the repetitive use of aphorisms, slogans, or sayings will help alter beliefs and assumptions permitting us to cope with adversity? The process sounds too simple and unscientific. The process is simple, though only one part of the mosaic for change. Conclusive evidence of success comes from the most influential self-help group in the world, Alcoholics Anonymous. This organization has helped hundreds of thousands of people cope with traumatic change.

Part of dealing with those changes came through the imprinting of indelible messages in the unconscious such as: One Day At A Time, First Things First, Live And Let Live, Let Go And Let God, and Easy Does It. Each saying is placed in a conspicuous spot; they may appear in a picture frame placed on the mantle or on a bumper sticker for an automobile.

These slogans give specific messages in picture form to the unconscious helping initiate behavioral adjustment. Similar to the goals of most self-help groups these reminders favor altering our view of the world and *how* to adopt a more promising perspective. They work because the messages are believed as true, the unconscious becomes gradually programmed to a different set of beliefs, and positive expectancy permeates the transaction. What you visualize, over time, you will become.

Since the unconscious mind is *always* open to suggestion it is appropriate to consistently accentuate positive messages especially when confronted with discouraging circumstances or at opportune times when waiting for a friend, a bus or train, or in the waiting room of a professional. Enter your inner world and keep the mind filled with the expected goal to be reached, condition to be mastered, or feelings desired. This means expect to cope well, regain strength, overcome guilt, anger or depression.

Recall that so much suggestion occurs influencing the unconscious of which the individual is not aware. Every thought is a potent form of suggestion. Now since no one can think two thoughts simultaneously, choosing to fill the mind with positive expectations clearly assures that negative thought life will never predominate. We must be ready to immediately replace negative thoughts which occur with a verse, slogan, picture or action. This presupposes we have these at our disposal ready for use. Here is where preparation is essential for success. Use the materials suggested in this chapter or write out your own suggestions to the unconscious mind. Consider yourself a map maker. You are plotting the way to your goal—and reaching it each time.

Energy Drains

Negative thinking not only immobilizes, it also drains energy needed in the recovery process. Here is a list of common energy drains which are important to eliminate from grief work. These catastrophic thoughts and beliefs generate feelings of hopelessness and despair, encourage resentment, and fuel fears of continuous unhappiness.

- The hurt will never end.
- Nothing can be done.
- I should have been there when he/she died.
- I can't help the way I feel.
- My position is hopeless.
- I've tried everything and nothing works.

When such thoughts occur we counter immediately with some of the following. These positive affirmations will completely transform our negative attitudes and the nature of our grief.

- I AM a fighter. I AM persisting.
- I AM adapting to my new surroundings.
- If God is with me who can be against me.
- There are others who love me and are helping me.
- My grief is leading to healing.
- It was *not* my fault; I AM human not superhuman.
- There are other options and solutions and I AM finding them.

Always employ phrasing which suggests being in the *process of doing* such and such a thing or having reached a goal. An effective technique used by many people is to focus on the opposite of the negative thought being entertained. If you think "I can't cope," it should be changed to "I know I AM coping," or if you say "This shouldn't happen to me," that sentence should be replaced with "This does happen to everyone not just me and I AM managing it." This is not self-deception. Rather, it is an acknowledgement that what eventually comes to pass in our behavior must first occur in our mental processes.

The French pharmacist, Emil Coúe, achieved enviable success with autosuggestion helping thousands of people by encouraging them to repeat: "Every day, in all respects, I get better and better"[23]. You may wish to use the following. "I AM fully capable of dealing with my loss. I AM prevailing and adjusting to my new environment. I believe I AM doing better every day. I believe. I believe. I believe." Do not attempt to "will power" your way out of negative self-talk. Use your imagination. Let it happen. In your imagination you can *always* cope. That fact can be turned into positive behavior.

Since emotional pain is always greater when the conscious mind is inactive, you must do something to counter despair. Occupying the mind with positive visualization, becoming actively involved in healing, has been successfully practiced throughout the world. We must never consciously allow destructive visualization to exist when the very same forces can be adapted to stimulate recovery. The imagination creatively produces images to correspond with thought processes. Accordingly, we create mental pictures of helping others in distress, using skills and abilities, and carrying on with responsibilities and interests in life. Furthermore, the unconscious is a mecca of creativity. We need only to continuously utilize this source of wisdom to build new assumptions and beliefs about the world and how life can continue again despite major loss. The emphasis here is on the word continuous. Every day repeat and repeat the suggestions which reinforce the mental pictures leading to adaptation. *Expect to cope well.*

D. Meaningful Repetition and Self-Talk

We are constantly talking to ourselves—judging, criticizing, comparing. This endless commentary occurs so automatically we are hardly aware it is happening. But our unconscious mind is taking it all in, every piece of information. The self-dialogues are normal responses to the world around us and are the methodology of attitude formation. Since attitudes are born from beliefs, changing habitual attitudes means planned repetition. The repetition of meaningful coping skills and the thoughts which accompany them is at the heart of accommodating new behaviors and routines. For it is our thoughts, the way we talk to ourselves, which are the basis for the emotions experienced and ultimately the way responses to separation are structured. A fundamental concept clearly emerges here: If what we think is at the root of what we feel, then repetition of thoughts (our self-talk) and behaviors which facilitate *acceptance* (the only alternative), will strengthen beliefs in our ability to cope, and spawn hope for the future. This must be carefully planned for.

Repetition by itself, void of meaning, is an exercise in futility. Meaningful repetition breaks old habits of thinking. It means slowly dwelling on ideas or thoughts over and over again (as if chanting) especially when we find our attention distracted, which normally happens.

Grievers can minimize distractions by deciding on the most opportune times to practice. Location need not be a limitation in this choice. While it has been often said that repetition is the mother of learning, it is most importantly the foundation of autosuggestion shaping how we influence the unconscious mind. People everywhere are constantly bombarded with repetition in song, advertisements and catchy campaign slogans from the media which eventually effect behavior: they whistle the tune, buy the product, or vote for the candidate. Just as prayers or mantras are repeated so too should personal suggestions—twenty to twenty-five times on each occasion. When possible, say the words out loud. Of course, this can be embarassing if others are nearby. Since others will think you are crazy, a good place to practice is alone in your car on the way to work. Still, there is nothing wrong with talking to ourselves out loud—it is good programming for the unconscious. Stay with it even though you feel uncomfortable. The results of believing what you say will be astonishing. Remember: The process is never forced, always executed without tension. Repetition occurs as a gentle incantation, not as a forceful exhortation. In order to reach the unconscious, the repetitive process must be effortless[23].

Many people incorporate their belief in God with the use of autosuggestion. They preface their repetitive self-talk with an expression of faith in the creator[32]. This is very important if we believe that by putting all of our faith in the unconscious mind we are demeaning the Lord. Since many believe we are made in the image and likeness of God and that "The Kingdom of God is within you," the unconscious mind *is* God within. "But we have the mind of Christ" (1 Corinthians 2:16) is another reminder.

Finally, mental practice in conjunction with visualizing the desired goal must become an integral part of everyday life until the goal has been reached. We should be especially vigilant to repeat desired thoughts whenever feelings of emptiness or fatigue start early in the day, or if we lapse into deep self-pity. The habit of refusing to allow those moods to predominate is gradually formed. Finding children to talk to, people to greet and seeking other forms of human contact help the transition. Our frame of reference will change from negative to positive. This is the result of the fact that mental rehearsal of behavioral alternatives plays a leading role in reducing the intensity and repetition of emotional and physical pain associated with change.

E. Belief As Power

All of the preceding will be of no avail without the belief that we possess the inherent ability to change internal conditions by changing the way we perceive ourselves and our problems. It follows that most negative thinking is filled with gross distortions[22]. We exercise our power of belief in the wrong way. In this instance, distortions center on thoughts of an unfair world, that loss is punishment for past transgressions, that "I don't deserve this," or that we do not have the strength to persevere and cope with the turmoil of separation.

There is no stronger example of the negative power of beliefs than the endless number of psychosomatic complaints which are brought to physicians' offices by their patients. Reversing such negative thinking demands input from others who gently provide a sense of normalcy in the face of disruption, but who also provide information to counter distortion: loss is *not* punishment but occurs randomly, people do possess the inherent courage and strength to overcome hardship, self-pity is to be expected but it becomes self-destructive if it is allowed to continue unchecked. Among the most striking realizations to be acknowledged is the fact that thoughts directly affect feelings and it is absolutely essential to change thinking if emotions causing pain are to be managed. In other words, it's *not* the separation which brings unmanageable pain but belief systems about separation which *can be changed* [33].

Wisdom of the Ages

In this vein, the following belief is of paramount importance in adapting to change: "I can and will alter the way I view separation." The opportunity is always present. This truth has been rediscovered down through the ages, for what is believed about a present condition determines what the condition will be. This venerable belief is reflected in centuries of statements.

Epictetus: "Men are disturbed not by things, but by the views which they take of them."

Buddha: "All that we are is the result of what we have thought."

Marcus Aurelius: "A man's life is what his thoughts make of it."

Julius Caesar: "People readily believe what they wish to be true."

Mark 9: 23: "If you believe, all things are possible."

St. Augustine: "Faith is to believe what we do not see; and the reward of this faith is to see what we believe."

Shakespeare: "There's nothing either good or bad but thinking makes it so."

Goethe: "Whatever you can do, or dream you can, begin it."

Emerson: "A man is what he thinks all day long."

Lincoln: "Most people are as happy as they make up their minds to be."

These and other writers, poets, and leaders are saying simply that belief is clearly the most powerful weapon for coping with all of life's changes (separations). Strong belief accomplishes *everything*. It is absolutely fundamental to success in anything we do.

In *The Will To Live,* William James, the father of modern psychology, said: "Believe that life is worth living and your belief will create the fact." This idea that belief creates fact is of untold importance in dealing with loss. Survivors can decide to believe that their tragedies will pass and they will grow in wisdom because of them. In short, the implication is that what is believed *causes* what is observed.

That is, beliefs change external conditions as they relate to us. We are the cause of what happens on the outside because we *create* our *experience* of what occurs on the outside. This is not at all far-fetched as it may appear. The proof is seen in the lives of hundreds of millions of people whose beliefs have changed their personal worlds. Strong beliefs have been the reason why the moon has been explored, why William Harvey convinced the medical profession that blood flowed through a closed circulatory system, and why thousands of terminally ill people prolong their lives to the amazement of their physicians.

What is especially intriguing is that many cancer patients have been cured by altering assumptions and beliefs about cancer and their power over it[34]. Voodoo deaths and unexplained sudden deaths of apparently healthy people are due to strong beliefs of powerlessness, helplessness, and hopelessness. Nothing shuts down the functioning of the immune system like hopelessness. Thoughts, convictions, beliefs all drastically change emotion, behavior, and physiological conditions. The powers of the mind to deal with the problems of separation have hardly been tapped. In short, belief is electrifying. When the state of mind is characterized by faith in internal resources dramatic change occurs.

Know Thyself—Wisdom Unheeded

Over the Temple of Apollo at Delphi stood the simple yet profound wisdom of Socrates which has been unheeded by millions: Know Thyself. It is as relevant today as it was over 2,000 years ago. It has gone unheeded because most of us are completely unaware of how the unconscious is influenced by the conscious mind. At any rate, choosing to believe—the core of coping with any problem—sets in motion the power of the unconscious.

What does all this have to do with the practice of autosuggestion? Simply this: strong belief in this proven approach to managing emotions and physical stressors depends on our knowledge of the unconscious mind and the *realization that the best way to utilize this storehouse of wisdom is through our conscious mind.* Since the greater part of mental activity occurs outside of conscious awareness, it is critical for survival to tap into that fund of knowledge. Listen to that inner voice. What the hydraulic controls are to a supersonic jetliner, so the unconscious is to our behavior—sending us on our computed course. How we program that course is vital to coping and to life in general. Our goal: train the conscious to follow the unconscious. Refuse to allow the intellect to get in the way of healing.

Convince yourself by experiencing changes in skin temperature through biofeedback. Read *Superlearning* by Sheila Ostrander and Lynn Schroeder[35], Emil Coué's *Self mastery Through Conscious Autosuggestion* or Barbara Brown's[36] *New Mind, New Body.* Reread this chapter and chapter one. Come to grips with the understanding that *for every thought there is a corresponding physical manifestation,* just as there is a corresponding physical state for every emotion experienced. It means becoming aware of the *evidence* of the power of our inner resources.

Dr. Herbert Benson[24] has shown in his research that by changing thought patterns high blood pressure is lowered. It is abundantly clear from studies conducted by medical researchers that our thoughts have a great deal to do with speeding the healing process. Athletic coaches throughout the country know that the attitudes their players bring with them to a contest will effect their performance in many ways, both positive and negative. Cardiologists insist that getting rid of old belief systems is essential in order to eliminate free-floating hostility and reduce possibilities of heart attack[37]. The results of using our unconscious minds borders on the miraculous. And remember: We change beliefs by changing what we *TELL* the unconscious. Convince yourself that the unconscious mind is a treasure trove of strength, energy, and problem solving abilities.

The point to be emphasized is that no individual has to be locked into a belief system dictated by a culture which says unless we can see, hear, or touch, an approach to deal with separation it should be discarded. The most powerful forces on earth are invisible. Regardless of age, whether young or old, the habit of believing in a particular way can be changed. Meaningful repetition and motivation will replace any habit. Thinking is a habit and changing it takes time. This is part of our grief work. However, choosing to believe that each person possesses in the unconscious the wisdom to accomplish whatever is needed to cope is the first task. *Knowing* we can succeed must be followed by a plan to incorporate new habits into our lifestyle.

Now comes a very important step. Banishing discouragement is a habit to be developed. Since old habits take time to replace there will be regressions to negative ways of thinking. Here is where self-discipline must prevail. When these relapses occur, refuse to allow discouragement a permanent entry into thought life. No one copes flawlessly. Initiate positive self-talk: "I AM going on with my life. I AM accepting the new conditions of my life. I AM using my strengths to give and reinvest in life." Your unconscious will do the rest.

In summary, changing beliefs about separation involves becoming aware that everybody is constantly the "victim" of self-suggestion whether they want to be or not. There is no choice here. People and events which occur in life are sources of suggestion which have positive or negative effects depending on how we decide to interpret them. Therefore, it becomes essential to analyze and reverse automatic thoughts like "I can't deal with this" or "There is nothing to look forward to." Among the most fundamental techniques to accomplish this is to picture oneself coping with change, meeting new people and the challenges of a different world, all while planting in the unconscious ideas such as "I AM doing better and becoming stronger again; I believe I AM finding new meaning in life," or "I AM coping better, my fear is diminishing, I AM growing through this experience." The conscious repetition of these and similar thoughts throughout the day will turn the ideas on which they are based into firm convictions at the unconscious level—but we must *constantly* keep in mind the end result desired. The use of visualization and imagery processes is "a basic human capacity that is inevitably part of the brain's storage process and one that has enormous potential for adaptive utility"[38]. There is little conscious use of visualization as a coping mechanism and yet this inherent tool of adaptation brings surprising relief from distress. This is the same visualization which causes excessive pain when we refuse to intervene in the replay of past hurts and transgressions.

Although it takes time, the all-knowing unconscious mind will restore meaning to recovery and energy in place of the fatigue induced by the stress of separation. Everyone carries within the means to cope with any separation. Autosuggestion then becomes complementary to, but not as a substitute for, a strong social support network. *In combination,* these approaches allow for a substantially healthy transition in adaptation to traumatic change.

ASSUMPTIONS AND BELIEFS ASSOCIATED WITH SUCCESSFUL COPING

It might appear at first glance to be outrageously presumptuous to suggest that specific assumptions or beliefs are commonly associated with meeting the transitions associated with separation. However, evidence to support such a contention has always existed.

In my own research on the topic a wide variety of assumptions and beliefs emerge depending to a great extent on our perception of the separation event and what is considered to be successful management of grief work. Here, with appropriate examples, are seven of the most frequently reported convictions from subjects in the Young Adult Study, students in my classes, and my work with survivors. In essence, they are examples of subjective realities, convictions which have worked for others. Perhaps they will work for you.

1. *Problems represented by death and other life changes are universal.*
   a. "I realized that others experienced the same or worse loss than I had."
   b. "The more I talked about it, the more I found out that I am not alone—that other people feel the same way I do too, and have had similar experiences."
2. *Love for survivors and helping others transcends inevitable change.*

a. "I coped by knowing my parents loved me and gave me their love and support."

b. "Two months after my father died a close friend went through the same thing. Talking with and helping her actually allowed me to help myself."

c. "The love one holds for another never dies, it lives on in those he has loved."

3. *Everything that is needed to cope with change ultimately comes from within.*

a. "My advice in a situation of loss—nurture and develop the strength within."

b. "When you realize you are at the end of your rope, turn around, you are actually at the beginning."

c. "I believe that nothing happens to us in life that we can't handle. Sometimes its difficult, but not impossible."

4. *Interdependence is life-affirming.*

a. "A friend who cried with me, even though she did not know my cousin, was very helpful."

b. "Many friends came to visit and even if the talk was sparse their nonverbal messages were super-hugs, a lot of physical contact, smiles, and sympathy cards; a lot of love was sent."

5. *Communication and expression of feelings is essential.*

a. "After the wake, each night we all got together, all of our friends, and we talked about losing our buddy."

b. "By being encouraged to expose and face all my inner feelings I did not face the danger of denial of the death and a prolonged acceptance."

6. *It's natural to feel certain emotional and physical sensations.*

a. "Seeing other people who were experiencing similar grief helped me."

b. "They told me of feelings they felt which were very similar to my problem. This made me feel that I wasn't the only person going through it."

7. *A faith in something outside the self integrates loss into life.*

a. "Out of everything that happens something good always comes forth." (This is an example of the Principle of Complimentarity discussed in Chapter 1.)

b. "Just know that God was and is always there. He will never let us get into a situation which through Him, we cannot cope with."

c. "When a person dies there are three things which are good to know in learning to live with the knowledge of death: (1) Remember, you will see them again some day (if you believe in heaven); (2) Remember all the good things and good times you had with the person; and (3) Remember, how they would want you to act if they saw you grieving."

There are probably as many beliefs and assumptions about coping as there are grievers. These seven are among the most prominent which have come to my attention. The strength of belief is in direct proportion to the degree that an individual can integrate loss into his life and go on.

REFERENCES

1. Toynbee, A. The relation between life and death, living and dying. In E. Shneidman (Ed.). *Death: Current perspectives,* (2nd ed.) Palo Alto, CA: Mayfield, 1980.
2. Fromm, E. *The revolution of hope.* New York: Harper & Row, 1968.
3. Schneider, J. *Stress, loss, and grief: Understanding their origins and growth potential.* Baltimore: University Park Press, 1984.
4. Parkes, C. *Bereavement: Studies of grief in adult life.* New York: International Universities Press, 1972.
5. Dean, A. & Lin, N. The stress-buffering role of social support. *Journal of Nervous and Mental Disease.* 1977, 165, 403–417.
6. Kaplan, B., Cassell, J., & Gare, S. Social support and health. *Medical Care,* 1977, 15, 47–57.
7. Lindemann, E. Symptomatology and management of acute grief. *American Journal of Psychiatry,* 1944, 101, 141–148.
8. James, W. *Collected essays and reviews.* New York: Russell & Russell, 1969.
9. Osteriweis, M., Soloman, F. & Green, M. (Eds.). *Bereavement: Reactions, consequences and care.* Washington, D.C.: National Academy Press, 1984.
10. Totman, R. *Social causes of disease.* New York: Pantheon, 1979.
11. Weisman, A. *The coping capacity.* New York: Human Sciences Press, 1984.
12. Rando, T. *Grief, dying and death.* Champaign, IL: Research Press, 1984.
13. Bowlby, J. *Attachment and loss* (vol. III). New York: Basic Books, 1980.
14. Bowlby, J. Processes of mourning. *International Journal of Psychoanalysis.* 1961, 42, 317–40.
15. *A. A. at a glance.* A. A. General Service Office, Box 459, Grand Central Station, New York, NY 10163
16. Antze, P. The role of ideologies in peer psychotherapy groups. In M. Lieberman & and L. Beaman (Eds.). *Self-help groups for coping with crisis.* San Francisco: Jossey-Bass, 1979.
17. Jampolsky, G. *Love is letting go of fear.* New York: Bantam, 1981.
18. Miles, M. & Brown Crandall, E. The search for meaning and its potential for affecting growth in bereaved parents. In C. Corr, J. Stillion & M. Ribar (Eds.).

Creativity in Death Education & Counseling. Lakewood, Ohio: Forum for Death Education & Counseling, 1983.

19. Videka-Sherman, L. Coping with the death of a child: A study over time. *American Journal of Orthopsychiatry,* 1982, 52⁴, 688–698.
20. James, W. *The varieties of religious experience.* New York: Modern Library, 1936.
21. Maltz, M. *Psycho-cybernetics.* New York: Pocket Books, 1977.
22. Burns, D. *Feeling good.* New York: New American Library, 1980.
23. Coué E. *Self-mastery through conscious autosuggestion.* London: Allen & Unwin, 1922.
24. Benson, H. *The relaxation response.* New York: William Morrow, 1975.
25. Le Shan, L. *How to meditate.* New York: Bantam, 1975.
26. Samuels, M. & Samuels, N. *Seeing with the mind's eye.* New York: Random House, 1975.
27. Hartman, F. *Paracelsus: Life and prophecies.* Blauvelt, N.Y.: Steiner Publications, 1973.
28. Swinn, R. Body thinking: Psychology for Olympic champs. *Psychology Today.* July, 1976, 38–43.
29. Louck, D. Winning through imagination. *Mainlines.* March, 1978, 48.
30. Schwarzenegger, A. The powers of the mind: An interview with Arnold Schwarzenegger. *New Age.* March, 1978, 38–43.
31. Bristol, C. *The magic of believing.* New York: Pocket Books, 1969.
32. Brooks, C & Charles, E. *Christianity and autosuggestions.* London: George Allen and Unwin Ltd., 1923.
33. Pelletier, K. *Mind as a healer, mind as a slayer.* New York: Dell, 1977.
34. Simonton, O., Simonton, S. & Creighton, I. *Getting well again.* Los Angeles: J. P. Tarchow, 1978.
35. Ostrander, S. & Schroeder, L. *Superlearning.* New York: Dell, 1982.
36. Brown, B. *New mind, new body.* New York: Harper & Row, 1974.
37. Friedman, M. & Ulmer, D. *Treating type A behavior and your heart.* New York: Alfred Knopf, 1984.
38. Singer, J. & Pope, K. (Eds.). *The power of human imagination.* New York: Plenum, 1978.

EPILOGUE

LOBSTERING

S hedding our shells of security and habit by risking is paradoxically the only way to survive, to continue to learn about coping, and enjoy living. Lobstering is just that: becoming temporarily vulnerable, facing new challenges, dealing with the constancy of change. Above all, it means checking on the orientation and direction we are moving in life. For it is goals and dreams which give meaning to existence.

Have we been caught up in the race of obtaining more and more of everything? Or have we found the key to coping with change? Have we realized that being of service to others as a life orientation brings peace regardless of change? To paraphrase John Kennedy, we should ask not what others can do for us but what we can do for others.

Now we do not have to be in a helping profession to create the ethic: *What can I give to the world?* There is not an occupation in existence that cannot be performed with this in mind. The bottom line is clear. Working towards a service orientation in life is a mental state that brings health, happiness, and peace of mind. Of course, in shedding our shells, occasionally we need the help of others to stand guard because of our temporary vulnerability.

The service orientation in life applies to family as well as occupation. This ethic could reduce so much daily stress if we would only embrace it. We can become caretakers instead of possessors for each of us have a talent and a purpose in life. We need only be open to discover it.

With this frame of reference I would suggest to the reader to reread the quotes which appear beneath the titles of each chapter. These twenty-six statements bring wisdom to lobstering: they are twenty-six ways to shed your shell, to enlarge your personal reality. Consider them carefully. Lobstering as a way of life prepares us for all of the shifting scenes of existence—even the last one.

In fact, lobstering is a condition of existence: We either go through life dragging our old shells with us or shed the old one and take on the new with acceptance and determination.

INDEX